MODERN CONSUMER THEORY

Modern Consumer Theory

Kelvin Lancaster

John Bates Clark Professor of Economics
Columbia University, New York

Edward Elgar

Published by
Edward Elgar Publishing Limited
Gower House
Croft Road
Aldershot
Hants GU11 3HR
England

Edward Elgar Publishing Company
Old Post Road
Brookfield
Vermont 05036
USA

British Library Cataloguing in Publication Data
Lancaster, Kelvin
  Modern consumer society.
  1. Consumer behaviour. Economics aspects
  I. Title
  339.47

ISBN 1 85278 384 2

Printed in Great Britain by
Billing & Sons Ltd, Worcester

Contents

PART I

THE BASIC MODEL

Introduction

This book contains a selection from those of the author's shorter works which relate to the introduction, development and application of the 'new approach' to demand theory with which the author's name has become associated. The nine previously published papers and two hitherto unpublished studies have been divided by topic into four groups. Part I contains the two 1966 papers in which the approach was first introduced. All but one of the remaining nine studies which constitute Parts II–IV are from the period 1975 to 1984. Most of the previously published papers are reprinted as they appeared originally (except that references in individual papers have been consolidated into a single reference list), but some have been revised to eliminate redundant presentations of the basic model or egregiously outdated comments.

BACKGROUND

The motivation for the development of a new way of approaching the relationship between goods and consumers came from the author's interest in welfare economics, where great conceptual difficulties arose from the introduction of new goods, or even from changes in existing ones. As the traditional theory stood, individual preferences were taken to be fully defined over points in a space of goods bundles. Following the introduction of a new good, the consumer was assumed to reorganize his preferences in the new goods space, but there was absolutely no guidance as to how the new ordering related to the old. This was true even if one took the extended view of the consumer[1] as having pre-organized preferences over all bundles of all *potential* goods as well as actual ones. The most that might be said with certainty is that, if the old goods were all still available on their original terms, the introduction and acceptance of new goods was welfare increasing.[2]

While it is true that it can be possible to have totally new goods, in the sense of goods that do something which could not previously be done at all (perhaps not even imagined), most new goods can be related to what previous goods did. The railroad, then the automobile, conveyed people from one destination to another, just as the horse had done – but with difficulties.

The potential functions of goods are determined by their properties, given the context. Bread is food and stones are not because, among other things, stones possess no complex organic chemicals that the body can process. A cupboard cannot function as a dining room because it is too small, and a basketball cannot be used to play baseball because it is too large and too soft. Not only are these properties objective and exogeneous to the individual consumer, but they represent relevant data that were given no place in the traditional model of consumer decision-making. The traditional model might be likened to the medieval physics argument that stones fell because they had a tendency to do so.

From these considerations, it seemed desirable to construct a model of consumer behaviour that could handle relationships between goods by taking account of data that would be known by consumers and was obviously relevant to their choice. Consumer decision-making would involve two stages, one in which the desired mix of properties was chosen, another in which the mix of goods that would give those properties at the least cost was determined. The second stage would be analogous to a production decision.[3] In such a model, the demand for goods would be a *derived* demand, derived from the demand for the properties they possessed. Knowing the properties of a new or varied good would then enable the demand for it to be related to the demand for bundles of properties and thus to the demand for existing goods.

THE BASIC MODEL

The essential features of the approach which was introduced in the two papers (Chapters 2 and 3) constituting Part I are as follows:

1. Consumers are not interested in goods as such, but in their properties or *characteristics*. It was decided to use the latter term as being more amenable to employment in a quasi-technical sense than 'properties'.
2. The relationship between goods and the characteristics they contain is objective (at least to an important extent) and determined by the *consumption technology*.
3. Whereas preferences are over characteristics, budget constraints are over goods. Thus the individual's constrained choice involves both the space of characteristics and the space of goods, linked through the consumption technology.
4. Individual preferences determine the relative weights given to the various characteristics in making choices, and thus different individuals may choose different goods or collections of goods even though they face a common consumption technology.

The model of consumer decision-making which is central to this approach is set out in the paper entitled 'A New Approach to Consumer Theory', reprinted as Chapter 2. This model emphasized what would later be described as the 'combinable' linear consumption technology, in which fully divisible goods could be combined in any proportions to give characteristics bundles that were the appropriately weighted sums of the characteristics of the component goods – in the same way a meal contains the nutrients and calories of its ingredients. Whereas this paper concentrated on the properties of decision-making within the framework of a given consumption technology, the simultaneously published paper 'Change and Innovation in the Technology of Consumption', reproduced here[4] as Chapter 3, emphasized the effects of changes in the consumption technology, primarily due to the introduction of new goods. Both papers discussed applications in the labour – leisure choice, as well as in choices over bundles of goods.

These two initial papers emphasized the following points, which highlight differences with traditional approaches:

- Part of the consumer's optimal choice involves an objective efficiency choice – the least cost combination of goods that would give the consumer his preferred combination of characteristics.[5] This introduces the possibility that consumers, like firms, might be *inefficient* in a clearly defined way. It thus highlights the potential social value of adequate consumer information.
- The presumption that, in general, the number of characteristics that enters the consumer's decision-making is small relative to the number of available goods leads to a natural explanation of why individual consumers purchase only small subsets of all the goods available. Thus aggregate demand cannot be explained in terms of a *representative consumer* who buys all goods, but must be explained by diversity of preferences. Consumers with differing preferences choose different subsets of goods as optimal ways of achieving different preferred bundles of characteristics.
- Objective and universal relationships between goods are determined by the structure of the consumption technology. Intuitive concepts such as degrees of similarity between goods, the difference between a totally new good and a differentiated version of an existing one, and essential complementarity, previously lacking an objective foundation, can be defined in terms of the possession or absence of common characteristics and in differences in the proportions of those characteristics.

- In particular, the goods *group* which is an essential element in the analysis of market structures involving product differentiation, could be defined objectively as a subset of goods possessing the same characteristics, but in different proportions, most of which were not shared by goods outside the group. Furthermore, degrees of product differentiation become in principle *quantifiable* in terms of some measure of the difference in characteristics proportions over goods in the group.

EXTENSIONS OF THE BASIC ANALYSIS

The three studies which constitute Part II of the volume take up some of the methodological issues of the basic model and some of the extensions which help in practical implementation. These come nowhere near to exhausting the topics, on which much has been written by other authors.[6]

The potential usefulness of the analysis of consumer choice in terms of characteristics and a consumption technology depends on the existence of objective characteristics that can be objectively related to goods, at least to a very substantial extent. Now goods may have very many objective properties – colour, weight, size, shape, smell, sound, all both overall and specifically for different parts and components, plus such data as load capacity, speed of operation, number of controls, efficiency, date of production. Many of these properties have no relevance for consumer choice (how many would choose a car by the colour of the paint on its engine?), while others are critical decision variables. By confining the analysis to the appropriate relevant characteristics, a group consisting of a large number of products can be analysed in terms of a relatively small number of parameters.

Thus an important problem is how a small set of *relevant characteristics* is related to the long list of objective properties. This is the problem which is tackled in Chapter 4, 'Operationally Relevant Characteristics in the Theory of Consumer Behaviour', the first study in Part II. This investigates what makes many properties irrelevant as characteristics in the decision set, including 'trivial' irrelevance, invariance over goods, technically fixed proportions, dominance and hierarchical effects, and different kinds of satiation, as ways in which the many technical properties are reduced to a few characteristics relevant to choice. Chapter 5, 'Hierarchies in Goods-Characteristics Analysis', expands on some of the ideas in Chapter 4 and considers multi-stage decision processes in more detail.

The content of Chapter 6, the last paper in Part II, is well described by its title, 'The Measurement of Changes in Quality'. The approach taken is that of considering the changes in the mix of relevant characteristics. This linked the characteristics analysis to work, both concurrent and earlier, on hedonic price indexes, which also sought to decompose changes in specific goods into changes in underlying properties.[7]

STUDIES IN COLLECTIVE CONSUMPTION

The three papers in Part III are studies in the application of the characteristics approach to problems in collective consumption – one on the family as a consumption group, the others on societies or communities. The common thread is that the concept of public or collective consumption *goods* is replaced by that of public or collective consumption *characteristics*. If all characteristics possessed by a good are public, then the good conforms to the traditional idea of a pure public good. The more interesting applications of the analysis are to cases in which only some of the characteristics are public.

Chapter 7, 'The Theory of Household Behaviour: Some Foundations', is the first and earliest paper in Part III. It commences with an investigation of a problem that occurs both in traditional consumer analysis and in the use of characteristics – the extent to which the observed behaviour of a household could be expected to possess the same properties as those of the individual, particular symmetry and quasiconcavity of the 'revealed' household utility function. It is shown that a pure aggregate household (members having their own budgets and preferences) may appear inefficient in the choice of goods to achieve the aggregated characteristics bundle, if viewed as a single entity. The study then goes on to consider the more realistic households and externalities and other interconnections. The existence of 'mixed' goods which possess some characteristics that are consumed jointly with other members as well as private characteristics tends to make the household behaviour approximate more closely that of the individual.

The second study, 'The Pure Theory of Impure Goods' (Chapter 8), expands the idea of the mixed good introduced in Chapter 7. This good, possessing both private and potentially public characteristics, is moved out from the context of the household to that of the community. The 'impure' public good of the title is a good (like education) with both private and public characteristics; public characteristics being defined in a manner analogous to the definition of pure public goods. Most goods conventionally described as public goods appear to be closer to impure public goods in this sense than to the classical pure public good. The optimal solution for the mix of the impure public good and a generalized aggregate private good is calculated and compared with two alternative solutions:

1. In which both goods are treated as private goods and provided through the market without intervention of any kind.
2. In which the impure public good is treated as a *pure* public good.

It is shown that not only will the first alternative oversupply the private good (not surprising), but that treating an impure public good as though it were pure public good will undersupply the public characteristic.

The title of Chapter 9, the third study of Part III (and previously unpublished), is 'Optimal Variety in the Provision of Public Services', which defines its contents clearly. If we have consumer diversity, that diversity is applicable to preferences over different types of publicly-provided goods and to different mixtures of public and private characteristics, which is the situation considered in this study. It commences with a typical problem of balancing diverse consumer interests against efficiency gains from scale economies – that of determining the optimal distance between firehouses in a linear city, balancing longer average response times for larger spacings against lower costs of operation. It then considers a variety of problems in the optimal provision of public services, public goods, and goods with both public and private characteristics. The analysis includes discussion of the appropriate size of the relevant supplying authority, including decentralization and federalism.

THE ANALYSIS OF PRODUCT VARIETY

In the realm of economic theory, perhaps the most important contribution of the characteristics approach has been its provision of the link between spatial analysis and the analysis of product differentiation. Much work in the revived Hotelling tradition of spatial oligopoly relies on this approach[8] to make the analysis relevant to the product differentiation case, which is of more importance than pure locational analysis. Similar considerations apply to the analysis of multi-product firms.[9] This link is apparent in the three chapters of Part IV.

Ever since the concept of product differentiation was developed, there has been debate over the welfare effects of product variety. Does the competitive market generate too much variety? Monopoly too little? How are the gains or losses from variety to be measured, anyway? Chapter 10,

'Socially Optimal Product Differentiation', the first paper in Part IV, sets out to answer these and related questions in terms of the characteristics analysis.

Although there may be some gain for each individual in having a degree of variety in his own consumption (a 'taste for variety'), it is clear that the enormous number of product variants available in a modern industrial society, only a few of which are consumed by any one individual, cannot be explained in these terms. Thus the emphasis in the paper is on variety in consumer preferences as the basic motive for variety in products. The proportions of characteristics vary over the many models within a product group, and different consumers prefer different combinations. Each consumer is considered to have an 'ideal' combination which he would most prefer if all combinations are available on equal terms.

If there were no scale economies in production or distribution, then it would be optimal to have everyone supplied with his ideal, custom-tailored good. Scale economies, however, permit resources to be saved when fewer varieties are supplied in larger quantities. Thus optimal product variety is determined as a balance between gains from greater variety and losses from smaller scale production.

A comparison is made in the paper between the optimal degree of variety, determined as above, and the degree of variety generated by competitive[10] and monopoly structures. In general, the former will give more than optimal variety, the latter less than optimal.

Chapter 11, 'Competition and Product Variety', is a later and more general analysis of the problem of product variety than that given in the previous chapter. It introduces 'outside goods' (goods other than those in the group) with variable elasticity of substitution between the group as a whole and the outside aggregate good. The more general model shows that there can be exceptions to the general rule that monopolistic competition leads to more than optimal product variety. The analysis of product variety in relation to monopoly is considerably expanded, and there is some consideration of market structures consisting of a few large multi-product firms.

Chapter 12, 'Sustainable Defensive Monopoly', the last study in the volume, has not previously been published. It explores the possibility that a firm having an initial monopoly position in a market, but unprotected by any formal barriers to entry, might so distribute its array of products over the potential product spectrum as to make it unprofitable for any other firm to enter while generating positive profit for itself. Using the characteristics approach in a locational analogue analysis, the existence of such a strategy is shown, provided the firm moves before *any* entry by other firms occurs. It is, in general, too late once there is even one rival product on the market. The analysis also clarifies the concept of the 'natural' monopoly.

NOTES

1. As in Debreu (1959).
2. See Lancaster (1959), a paper not included here.
3. Other production-oriented approaches to the consumer were being explored independently and contemporaneously, notably by Becker (1965) and Muth (1966), with a primary emphasis on consumption inputs other than goods, such as time.
4. But stripped of material already presented in Chapter 2.
5. Stigler (1945) had foreshadowed the recognition of such choices with his analysis of the diet problem.
6. For a sample of the methodological debate, see Ratchford (1975), Ladd and Zober (1977) and Blaug (1980). Examples of practical implementation include Shaw (1982) and Swann (1985).
7. See Griliches (1961, 1971). The hedonic approach was empirically oriented and not generalized into a decision model.
8. For example, Salop (1979), Friedman (1983) and Economides (1984).
9. Such as in Itoh (1983).
10. The most competitive structure, given the scale economies and diversity of preferences, will be monopolistic competition.

2   A new approach to consumer theory[1]

THE CURRENT STATUS OF CONSUMER THEORY

The theory of consumer behaviour in deterministic situations as set out by, say, Debreu (1959, 1960) or Uzawa (1960) is a thing of great aesthetic beauty, a jewel set in a glass case. The product of a long process of refinement, it has been shorn of all irrelevant postulates so that it now stands as an example of how to extract the minimum of results from the minimum of assumptions.

To the process of slicing away with Occam's razor, the author made a small contribution (1957). This brought forth a reply by Johnson (1958) which suggested, somewhat tongue-in-cheek, that the determinateness of the sign of the substitution effect (the only substantive result of the theory of consumer behaviour) could be derived from the proposition that goods are goods.

Johnson's comment, on reflection, would seem to be almost the best summary that can be given of the current state of the theory of consumer behaviour. All *intrinsic* properties of particular goods, those properties that make a diamond quite obviously something different from a loaf of bread, have been omitted from the theory, so that a consumer who consumes diamonds alone is as rational as a consumer who consumes bread alone, but one who sometimes consumes bread, sometimes diamonds (*ceteris paribus*, of course), is irrational. Thus, the only property which the theory can build on is the property shared by all goods, which is simply that they are goods.

Indeed, we can continue the argument further, since goods are simply what consumers would like more of; and we must be neutral with respect to differences in consumer tastes (some consumers might like more of something that other consumers do not want), that the ultimate proposition is that *goods are what are thought of as goods*.

In spite of the denial of the relevance of intrinsic properties to the pure theory, there has always been a subversive undercurrent suggesting that economists continue to take account of these properties. Elementary textbooks bristle with substitution examples about butter and margarine, rather than about shoes and ships, as though the authors believed that there was something intrinsic to butter and margarine that made them good substitutes and about motor cars and petrol that made them somehow intrinsically complementary. Market researchers, advertisers, and manufacturers also act as though they believe that knowledge of (or belief in) the intrinsic properties of goods is relevant to the way consumers will react toward them.

The clearest case of conflict between a belief that goods do have intrinsic properties relevant to consumer theory but that they are not taken into account has been the long search for a definition of 'intrinsic complementarity'. The search was successful only where Morishima (1959) turned from traditional theory to an approach somewhat similar to that of this chapter.

Perhaps the most important aspects of consumer behaviour relevant to an economy as complex as that of the United States are those of consumer reactions to new commodities and to quality variations. Traditional theory has nothing to say on these. In the case of new commodities, the theory is particularly helpless. We have to expand from a commodity space of dimension n to one of dimension $n + 1$, replacing the old utility function by a completely new one, and even a complete map of the consumer's preferences among the n goods provides absolutely no information about the new preference map. A theory which can make no use of so much information is a remarkably empty one. Even the technique of supposing the existence of a utility function for all possible goods, including those not yet invented, and regarding the prices of non-existent goods as infinite – an incredible stretching of the consumers' powers of imagination – has no predictive value.

Finally, we can note the unsuitability of traditional theory for dealing with many of the manifestly important aspects of actual relationships between goods and consumers in I.F. Pearce's (1964) recent heroic but rather unsuccessful attempts to deal with complementarity, substitution, independence, and neutral want associations within the conventional framework.

A NEW APPROACH

Like many new approaches, the one set out in this chapter draws upon several elements that have been utilized elsewhere. The chief technical novelty lies in breaking away from the traditional approach that goods are the direct objects of utility and, instead, supposing that it is the properties or characteristics of the goods from which utility is derived.

We assume that consumption is an activity in which goods, singly or in combination, are inputs and in which the output is a collection of characteristics. Utility or preference orderings are assumed to rank collections of characteristics and only to rank collections of goods indirectly through the characteristics that they possess. A meal (treated as a single good) possesses nutritional characteristics but it also possesses aesthetic characteristics, and different meals will possess these characteristics in different relative proportions. Furthermore, a dinner party, a combination of two goods, a meal and a social setting, may possess nutritional, aesthetic, and perhaps intellectual characteristics different from the combination obtainable from a meal and a social gathering consumed separately.

In general – and the richness of the approach springs more from this than from anything else – even a single good will possess more than one characteristic, so that the simplest consumption activity will be characterized by joint outputs. Furthermore, the same characteristic (for example, aesthetic properties) may be included among the joint outputs of many consumption activities so that goods which are apparently unrelated in certain of their characteristics may be related in others.

We shall assume that the structure we have interposed between the goods themselves and the consumer's preferences is, in principle, at least, of an objective kind. That is, the characteristics possessed by a good or a combination of goods are the same for all consumers and, given units of measurement, are in the same quantities,[2] so that the personal element in consumer choice arises in the choice between collections of characteristics only, not in the allocation of characteristics to the goods. The objective nature of the goods-characteristics relationship plays a crucial role in the analysis and enables us to distinguish between objective and private reactions to such things as changes in relative prices.

The essence of the new approach can be summarized as follows, each assumption representing a break with tradition:

1. The good, *per se*, does not give utility to the consumer; it possesses characteristics, and these characteristics give rise to utility.
2. In general, a good will possess more than one characteristic, and many characteristics will be shared by more than one good.
3. Goods in combination may possess characteristics different from those pertaining to the goods separately.

A move in the direction of the first assumption has already been made by various workers including Strotz (1957) and Gorman (1959), with the 'utility tree' and other ideas associating a particular good with a particular type of utility. The theory set out here goes much further than these ideas. Multiple characteristics, structurally similar to those of this chapter but confined to a particular problem and a point utility function, are implicit in the classical 'diet problem' of Stigler (1945), and multi-dimensioned utilities have been used by workers in other fields. The third assumption, of activities involving complementary collections of goods, has been made by Morishima (1959) but in the context of single-dimensioned utility.

A variety of other approaches with similarities to that of this chapter occur scattered through the literature, for example, in Quandt (1956), or in Becker (1965), or in various discussions of investment-portfolio problems. These are typically set out as *ad hoc* approaches to particular problems. Perhaps the most important aspect of this chapter is that the model is set out as a general replacement of the traditional analysis (which remains as a special case), rather than as a special solution to a special problem.

It is clear that only by moving to multiple characteristics can we incorporate many of the intrinsic qualities of individual goods. Consider the choice between a grey Ford Escort and a red Ford Escort. On ordinary theory these are either the same commodity (ignoring what may be a relevant aspect of the choice situation) or different commodities (in which case there is no a priori presumption that they are close substitutes). Here we regard them as goods associated with satisfaction vectors which differ in only one component, and we can proceed to look at the situation in much the same way as the consumer – or even the economist, in private life – would look at it.

Traditional theory is forever being forced to interpret quite common real-life happenings, such as the effects of advertising in terms of 'change of taste', an entirely non-operational concept since there is no way of predicting the relationship between preference before and after the change. The theory outlined here, although extremely rich in useful ways of thinking about consumer behaviour, may also be thought to run the danger of adding to the economist's extensive collection of non-operational concepts. If this were true, it need not, of course, inhibit the heuristic application of the theory. Even better, however, the theory implies predictions that differ from those of traditional theory, and the predictions of the new approach seem to fit better the realities of consumer behaviour.

A MODEL OF CONSUMER BEHAVIOUR

To obtain a working model from the ideas outlined above, we shall make some assumptions which are, on balance, neither more nor less heroic than those made elsewhere in our present economic theorizing and which are intended to be no more and no less permanent parts of the theory.

1. We shall regard an individual good or a collection of goods as a consumption activity and associate a scalar (the level of the activity) with it. We shall assume that the relationship between the level of

activity k, y_k, and the goods consumed in that activity to be both linear and objective, so that, if x_j is the jth commodity we have

$$x_j = \Sigma_k a_{jk} y_k \qquad (2.1)$$

and the vector of total goods required for a given activity vector is given by

$$x = Ay \qquad (2.2)$$

Since the relationships are assumed objective, the equations are assumed to hold for all individuals, the coefficients a_{jk} being determined by the intrinsic properties of the goods themselves and possibly the context of technological knowledge in the society.

2.   More heroically, we shall assume that each consumption activity produces a fixed vector of characteristics[3] and that the relationship is again linear, so that, if z_i is the amount of the ith characteristic

$$z_i = \Sigma_k b_{ik} y_k \qquad (2.3)$$

or

$$z = By \qquad (2.4)$$

Again, we shall assume that the coefficients b_{ik} are objectively determined – in principle, at least – for some arbitrary choice of the units of z_i.

3.   We shall assume that the individual possesses an ordinal utility function on characteristics $U(z)$ and that he will choose a situation which maximizes $U(z)$. $U(z)$ is provisionally assumed to possess the ordinary convexity properties of a standard utility function.

The chief purpose of making the assumption of linearity is to simplify the problem. A viable model could certainly be produced under the more general set of relationships

$$F_k(z,x) = 0, k = 1 \dots m \qquad (2.5)$$

The model could be analysed in a similar way to that used by Samuelson (1953b) and others in analysing production, although the existence of much jointness among outputs in the present model presents difficulties.

In this model, the relationship between the collections of characteristics available to the consumer – the vectors z – which are the direct ingredients of his preferences and his welfare, and the collections of goods available to him – the vectors x – which represent his relationship with the rest of the economy, is not direct and one-to-one, as in the traditional model, but indirect, through the activity vector y.

Consider the relationships which link z and x. These are the equation systems: $x = Ay$ (2.2) and $z = By$ (2.4). Suppose that there are r characteristics, m activities and n goods. Only if $r = m = n$ will there be a one-to-one relationship between z and x. In this case both the B and A matrixes are square (the number of variables equals the number of equations in both sets of equations) and we can solve for y in terms of x, $y = A^{-1}x$, giving $z = BA^{-1}x$. $U(z)$ can be written directly and unambiguously as a function $u(x)$. Otherwise the relations are between vectors in spaces of different dimensions. Consider some x^* in the case in which $m > n$: equation (2.2) places only n restrictions on the m-vector y, so that y can still be chosen with $m - n$ degrees of freedom. If $r < m$, then there are $m - r$ degrees of freedom in choosing y, given some z, but whether the ultimate relationship gives several choices of z for a given x, or several x for a given z, and whether all vectors z are attainable, depends on the relationships between r, m, and n and the structures of the matrixes A, B. In general, we will expect that the consumer may face a choice among many paths linking goods collections with characteristics collections. The simple question asked (in principle) in the traditional analysis – does a particular consumer prefer collection x_1 or collection x_2 – no longer has a direct answer, although the question, does he prefer characteristics collection z_1 or z_2, does have such an answer.

If we take the standard choice situation facing the consumer in a free market, with a linear budget constraint, this situation, in our model, becomes: maximize $U(z)$, subject to $px \leq k$, with $z = By$, $x = Ay$, and $x, y, z \geq 0$.

This is a non-linear programme of an intractable kind. The problem of solution need not worry us here, since we are interested only in the properties of the solution.

THE SIMPLIFIED MODEL

We shall simplify the model in the initial stages by supposing that there is a one-to-one correspondence between goods and activities so that we can write the consumer-choice programme in the simpler form: maximize $U(z)$, subject to $px \leq k$, with $z = Bx$ and $z, x \geq 0$.

This is still, of course, a non-linear programme, but we now have a single step between goods and characteristics.

The model consists of four parts. There is a maximand $U(z)$ operating on characteristics, that is, U is defined on characteristics-space (C-space). The budget constraint $px \leq k$ is defined on goods-space (G-space). The equation system $z = Bx$ represents a transformation between G-space and C-space. Finally, there are non-negativity constraints $z, x \geq 0$ which we shall assume to hold initially, although in some applications and with some sign conventions they may not always form part of the model.

In traditional consumer analysis, both the budget constraint and the utility function are defined on G-space, and we can immediately relate the two as in the ordinary textbook indifference-curve diagram. Here we can only relate the utility function to the budget constraint after both have been defined on the same space. We have two choices: (1) We can transform the utility function into G-space and relate it directly to the budget constraint; (2) we can transform the budget constraint into C-space and relate it directly to the utility function $U(z)$.

Each of these techniques is useful in different circumstances. In the case of the first, we can immediately write $U(z) = U(Bx) = u(x)$, so we have a new utility function directly in terms of goods, but the properties of the function $u(x)$ depend crucially on the structure of the matrix B and this, together with the constraints $x \geq 0$ and $z = Bx \geq 0$ give a situation much more complex than that of conventional utility maximization. The second technique again depends crucially on the structure of B and again will generally lead to a constraint of a more complex kind than in conventional analysis.

The central role in the model is, of course, played by the transformation equation $z = Bx$ and the structure and qualitative[4] properties of the matrix B. Most of the remainder of this chapter will be concerned with the relationship between the properties of B, which we can call the *consumption technology*[5] of the economy, and the behaviour of consumers.

Certain properties of the transformations between G- and C-space follow immediately from the fact that B is a matrix of constants, and the transformation $z = Bx$ is linear. These can be stated as follows, proof being obvious.

1. A convex set in G-space will transform into a convex set in C-space, so that the budget constraint $px \leq k$, $x \geq 0$ will become a convex constraint on the z's.
2. An inverse transformation will not necessarily exist, so that an arbitrary vector z in C-space may have no vector x in G-space corresponding to it.

3. Where an inverse transformation does exist from C-space into G-space, it will transform convex sets into convex sets so that, for any set of z's which do have images in G-space, the convexity of the U function on the z's will be preserved in relation to the x's.

The properties are sufficient to imply that utility maximization subject to constraint will lead to determinate solutions for consumer behaviour.

THE STRUCTURE OF CONSUMPTION TECHNOLOGY

The consumption technology, which is as important a determinant of consumer behaviour as the particular shape of the utility function, is described fully only by the A and B matrixes together, but certain types of behaviour can be related to more generalized descriptions of the technology. We shall distinguish broadly between structural properties of the technology, such as the relationship between the number of rows and columns of B and/or A and whether A, B are decomposable, and qualitative properties, such as the signs of the elements of A and B.

The leading structural property of the consumption technology is the relationship between the number of characteristics (r) and the number of activities (m), that is, between the number of rows and columns of B. It will be assumed that B contains no linear dependence, so that its rank is the number of rows or columns, whichever is less. We shall assume, unless otherwise stated, a one-to-one relationship between goods and activities.

1. The number of characteristics is equal to the number of goods. In this case, there is a one-to-one relationship between activities vectors and characteristics vectors. We have $z = Bx$, $x = B^{-1}z$. If B is a permutation of a diagonal matrix then there is a one-to-one relationship between each component of z and each component of y, and the model becomes, by suitable choice of units, exactly the same as the traditional model. If B is not a diagonal permutation, the objects of utility are composite goods rather than individual goods, and the model has some important differences from the conventional analysis. Note how specialized is the traditional case in relation to our general model.

If B is a diagonal permutation but there is not a one-to-one relationship between activities and goods so that A is not a diagonal permutation, we have a model similar to that of Morishima (1959).

2. The number of characteristics is greater than the number of goods. In this case, the relationships $Bx = z$ contain more equations than variables x_i so that we cannot, in general, find a goods vector x which gives rise to an arbitrarily specified characteristics vector z. We can take a basis of any arbitrarily chosen n characteristics and consider the reduced $n \times n$

system $\bar{B} = \bar{z}$, which gives a one-to-one relationship between n characteristics and the n goods, with the remaining $r - n$ characteristics being determined from the remaining $r - n$ equations and the goods vector x corresponding to $\bar{z}$. In this case, it is generally most useful to analyse consumer behaviour by transforming the utility function into G-space, rather than the budget constraint into C-space. What does the transformed utility function look like?

As shown in the Appendix, the utility function transformed into G-space retains its essential convexity. An intuitive way of looking at the situation is to note that all characteristics collections which are actually available are contained in an n-dimensional slice through the r-dimensional utility function, and that all slices through a convex function are themselves convex. The transformation of this n-dimensional slice into G-space preserves this convexity.

For investigation of most aspects of consumer behaviour, the case in which the number of characteristics exceeds the number of goods – a case we may often wish to associate with simple societies – can be treated along with the very special case (of which conventional analysis is a special subcase) in which the number of characteristics and goods is equal. In other words, given the consumption technology, we concern ourselves only with the particular n-dimensional slice of the r-dimensional utility function implied by that technology[6] and, since the slice of the utility function has the same general properties as any n-dimensional utility function, we can proceed as if the utility function was defined on only n characteristics.

3. In the third case, in which the number of goods exceeds the number of characteristics, a situation probably descriptive of a complex economy such as that of the United States, there are properties of the situation that are different from those of the two previous cases and from the conventional analysis.

Here, the consumption technology, $z = Bx$, has fewer equations than variables so that, for every characteristics vector there is more than one goods vector. For every point in his characteristics space, the consumer has a choice between different goods vectors. Given a price vector, this choice is a pure efficiency choice, so that for every characteristics vector the consumer will choose the most efficient combination of goods to achieve that collection of characteristics, and the efficiency criterion will be minimum cost.

The efficiency choice for a characteristics vector z^* will be the solution of the canonical linear programme: minimize px, subject to $Bx = z^*, x \geqq 0$.

Since this is a linear programme, once we have the solution x^* for some z^*, with value k^*, we can apply a scalar multiple to fit the solution to any budget value k and characteristics vector $(k/k^*)z^*$. By varying z^*, the consumer, given a budget constraint $px = k$, can determine a characteristics frontier consisting of all z such that the value of the above programme is just equal to k. There will be a determinate goods vector associated with each point of the characteristics frontier.

As in the previous case, it is easy to show that the set of characteristics vectors in C-space that are preferred or indifferent to z transforms into a convex set in G-space if it is a convex set in C-space; it is also easy to show that the set of z's that can be obtained from the set of x's satisfying the convex constraint $px \leq k$ is also a convex set. The characteristics frontier is, therefore, concave to the origin, like a transformation curve. For a consumption technology with four goods and two characteristics, the frontier could have any of the three shapes shown in Figure 2.1. Note that,

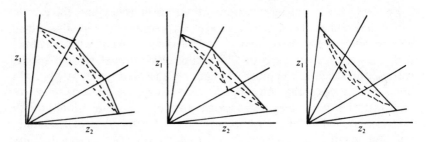

Figure 2.1

in general, if B is a positive matrix, the positive orthant in G-space transforms into a cone which lies in the interior of the positive orthant in C-space, a point illustrated in the diagrams.

A consumer's complete choice subject to a budget constraint $px \leq k$ can be considered as consisting of two parts:

(*a*)   An efficiency choice, determining the characteristics frontier and the associated efficient goods collections.
(*b*)   A private choice, determining which point on the characteristics frontier is preferred by him.

The efficiency choice is an objective not a subjective choice. On the assumption that the consumption technology is objective, the characteristics frontier is also objective, and it is the same for all consumers facing the same budget constraint. Furthermore, the characteristics frontier is expanded or contracted linearly and proportionally to an increase or decrease in income, so that the frontier has the same *shape* for all consumers facing the same prices, income differences simply being reflected in homogeneous expansion or contraction.

We should note that, if the consumption technology matrix has certain special structural properties, we may obtain a mixture of the above cases. For example, a matrix with the structure

$$\mathbf{B} \equiv \begin{bmatrix} B_1 & 0 \\ 0 & B_2 \end{bmatrix}$$

where B_1 is an $(s \times k)$ matrix and B_2 is an $(r-s) \times (n-k)$ matrix, partitions the technology into two disconnected parts, one relating s of the characteristics to k of the goods, the other separately relating $r-s$ of the characteristics to $n-k$ of the goods. We can have $s \geq k$ and $r-s < n-k$ giving a mixed case.

Dropping the assumption of a one-to-one relationship between goods and activities does not add greatly to the difficulties of the analysis. We have, as part of the technology, $x = Ay$, so that the budget constraint $px \leq k$ can be written immediately as $pAy \leq k$. The goods prices transform directly into implicit activity prices $q = pA$. Interesting cases arise, of course. If the number of goods is less than the number of activities, then not all q's are attainable from the set of p's; and if the number of goods exceeds the number of activities, different p vectors will correspond to the same q vector. This implies that certain changes in relative goods prices may leave activity prices, and the consumer's choice situation, unchanged.

In most of the succeeding analysis, we will be concerned with the B matrix and the relationship between activities and characteristics, since this represents the most distinctive part of the theory.

THE EFFICIENCY SUBSTITUTION EFFECT AND REVEALED PREFERENCE

At this stage, it is desirable to examine the nature of the efficiency choice so that we can appreciate the role it plays in the consumer behaviour implied by our model. Consider a case in which there are two characteristics, a case that can be illustrated diagrammatically, and, say, four activities.

The activities-characteristics portion of the consumption technology is defined by the two equations

$$\left. \begin{array}{l} z_1 = b_{11}y_1 + b_{12}y_2 + b_{13}y_3 + b_{14}y_4 \\ z_2 = b_{21}y_1 + b_{22}y_2 + b_{23}y_3 + b_{24}y_4 \end{array} \right\} \tag{2.6}$$

With activity 1 only, the characteristics will be obtained in proportion, b_{11}/b_{21} (the ray labelled 1 in Figure 2.2). Similarly with activities 2, 3, 4, one at a time, characteristics will be obtained in proportions b_{12}/b_{22}, b_{13}/b_{23}, b_{14}/b_{24}, respectively, corresponding to the rays 2, 3 and 4 in the diagram.

We are given a budget constraint in goods space of the form $\Sigma_i p_i x_i \leq k$. If there is a one-to-one correspondence between goods and activities, the prices of the activities are given by p_i. If there is not a one-to-one relationship, but a goods-activities portion of the consumption technology

$$x_i = a_{i1} y_1 + a_{i2} y_2 + a_{i3} y_3 + a_{i4} y_4 \qquad (2.7)$$
$$i = 1 \dots n$$

then the budget constraint can be transformed immediately into characteristics space

$$\left(\Sigma_i p_i a_{i1} \right) y_1 + \left(\Sigma_i p_i a_{i2} \right) y_2$$

$$+ \left(\Sigma_i p_i a_{i3} \right) y_3 + \left(\Sigma_i p_i a_{i4} \right) y_4 \leq k \qquad (2.8)$$

where the composite prices $q_j = \Sigma_i p_i a_{ij}$, $j = 1 \dots 4$ represent the prices of each activity. The number of goods in relation to the number of activities is irrelevant at this stage, since each activity has a unique and completely determined price q_j, given the prices of the goods.

Given q_1, q_2, q_3, q_4, and k, the maximum attainable level of each activity in isolation can be written down (corresponding to the points E_1, E_2, E_3, E_4 in Figure 2.2) and the lines joining these points represent combinations attainable subject to the budget constraint. In the diagram it has been assumed that prices are such that combinations of 1 and 2, 2 and 3, 3 and 4 are efficient, giving the characteristics frontier, while combinations 1 and 3, 2 and 4, or 1 and 4 are inefficient.

Suppose that the consumer chooses characteristics in the combination represented by the ray z^*, giving a point E^* on the frontier. Now suppose that relative prices change: in particular, that the price of activity 2 rises so that, with income still at k, the point E_2 moves inward on ray 2. If the movement is small enough, the characteristics frontier continues to have a corner at E_2, and the consumer will continue to obtain characteristics in proportion z^* by a combination of activities 1 and 2. If income is adjusted so that the new frontier goes through E^*, the consumer will use the same activities in the same proportions as before.

If the price of activity 2 rises sufficiently, however, the point E_2 will

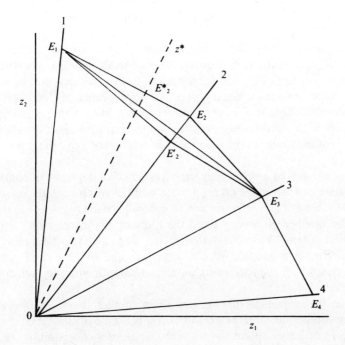

Figure 2.2

move inward past the line joining E_1 and E_3 to E_2'. Combinations of 1 and 2 and of 2 and 3 are now inefficient combinations of activities, their place on the efficiency frontier being taken by a combination of 1 and 3. The consumer will switch from a combination of activities 1 and 2 to a combination of 1 and 3.

Thus there is an efficiency substitution effect which is essentially a switching effect. If price changes are too small to cause a switch, there is no efficiency substitution effect: if they are large enough, the effect comes from a complete switch from one activity to another.

The manifestation of the efficiency substitution effect in goods-space depends on the structure of the A (goods-activities) matrix. There are two polar cases:

(*a*)   If there is a one-to-one relationship between goods and activities, the efficiency substitution effect will result in a complete switch from consumption of one good to consumption of another. This might be regarded as typical of situations involving similar but differentiated products, where a sufficiently large price change in one of the products will result in widespread switching to, or away from, the product.

(*b*)   If there is not a one-to-one relationship between goods and activities and, in particular, if all goods are used in all activities, the efficiency substitution effect will simply result in less consumption of a good whose price rises, not a complete disappearance of that good from consumption. If all cakes require eggs but in different proportions, a rise in the price of eggs will cause a switch from egg-intensive cakes to others, with a decline in the consumption of eggs, but not to zero.

The existence of an efficiency substitution effect depends, of course, on the number of activities exceeding the number of characteristics (otherwise switching of activities will not, in general, occur[7]) but does not require that the number of goods exceed the number of characteristics. In fact, with two goods, two characteristics, and three activities, the effect may occur. With two goods, two characteristics and one hundred activities (well spread over the spectrum), an almost smooth efficiency substitution effect would occur.

Since the efficiency substitution effect implies that consumers may change goods collections as a result of compensated relative price changes, simply in order to obtain the same characteristics collection in the most efficient manner, it is obvious that the existence of substitution does not of itself either require or imply convexity of the preference function on characteristics. In other words, the axiom of revealed preference may be satisfied even if the consumer always consumes characteristics in fixed proportions (and possibly even if the consumers had *concave* preferences), so that the 'revelation' may be simply of efficient choice rather than convexity. A formal proof is given in the Appendix.

OBJECTIVE AND SUBJECTIVE CHOICE AND DEMAND THEORY

In an economy or subeconomy with a complex consumption technology (many goods relative to characteristics), we have seen that there are two types of substitution effect:

1.   Changes in relative prices may result in goods bundle I becoming an *inefficient* method of attaining a given bundle of characteristics and being replaced by goods bundle II even when the characteristics bundle is unchanged.
2.   Changes in relative prices, with or without causing efficiency substitutions as in type 1, may alter the slope of the characteristics frontier in a

segment relevant to a consumer's characteristics choice. The change in the slope of the frontier is analogous to the change in the budget line slope in the traditional case and, with a convex preference function, will result in a substitution of one characteristics bundle for another and, hence, of one goods bundle for another. Note that, even with smoothly convex preferences, this effect may not occur, since the consumer may be on a corner of the polyhedral characteristics frontier, and thus his characteristics choice could be insensitive to a certain range of slope changes on the facets.

The first effect, the efficiency substitution effect, is universal and objective. Subject to consumer ignorance or inefficiency,[8] this substitution effect is independent of the shapes of individual consumers' preference functions and hence of the effects of income distribution.

The second effect, the private substitution effect, has the same properties, in general, as the substitution effect in traditional theory. In particular, an aggregately compensated relative price change combined with a redistribution of income may result in no substitution effect in the aggregate, or a perverse one.

These two substitution effects are independent – either may occur without the other in certain circumstances – but in general we will expect them both to take place and hence that their effects will be reinforcing, if we are concerned with a complex economy. Thus, the consumer model presented here, in the context of an advanced economy, has, in a sense, more substitution than the traditional model. Furthermore, since part of the total substitution effect arises from objective, predictable, and income-distribution-free efficiency considerations, our confidence in the downward slope of demand curves is increased even when income redistribution takes place.

Since it is well known that satisfaction of the revealed preference axioms *in the aggregate* (never guaranteed by traditional theory) leads to global stability in multi-market models (see, for example, Karlin 1959), the efficiency substitution effect increases confidence in this stability.

In a simple economy, with few goods or activities relative to characteristics, the efficiency substitution effect will be generally absent. Without this reinforcement of the private substitution effect, we would have some presumption that perverse consumer effects ('Giffen goods', backward-bending supply curves) and lower elasticities of demand would characterize simple economies as compared with complex economies. This seems to be in accord with at least the mythology of the subject, but it is certainly empirically verifiable. On this model, consumption technology as well as income levels differentiate consumers in different societies, and we would not necessarily expect a poor urban American to behave in his consumption like a person at the same real-income level in a simple economy.

COMMODITY GROUPS, SUBSTITUTES, COMPLEMENTS

In a complex economy, with a large number of activities and goods as well as characteristics, and with a two-matrix (A,B) consumption technology, it is obvious that taxonomy could be carried out almost without limit, an expression of the richness of the present approach. Although an elaborate taxonomy is not very useful, discussion of a few selected types of relationships between goods can be of use. One of the important features of this model is that we can discuss relationships between goods, as revealed in the structure of the technology. In the conventional approach, there are, of course, no relationships between goods as such, only properties of individual's preferences.

The simplest taxonomy is that based on the zero entries in the technology matrixes. It may be that both matrixes A, B are almost 'solid', in which case there is little to be gained from a taxonomic approach. If, however, the B matrix contains sufficient zeros to be decomposable as follows,

$$B \equiv \begin{bmatrix} B_1 0 \\ 0 B_2 \end{bmatrix} \tag{2.9}$$

so that there is some set of characteristics and some set of activities such that these characteristics are derived only from these activities and these activities give rise to no other characteristics, then we can separate that set of characteristics and activities from the remainder of the technology. If, further, the activities in question require a particular set of goods which are used in no other activities (implying a decomposition of the A matrix), then we can regard the goods as forming an *intrinsic commodity group*. Goods within the group have the property that efficiency substitution effects will occur only for relative price changes within the group and will be unaffected by changes in the prices of other goods. If the utility function on characteristics has the conventional properties, there may, of course, be *private* substitution effects for goods within the group when the prices of other goods changes. For an intrinsic commodity group, the whole of the objective analysis can be carried out without reference to goods outside the group.

Goods from different intrinsic commodity groups can be regarded as *intrinsically unrelated*, goods from the same group as *intrinsically related*.

If, within a group, there are two activities, each in a one-to-one relationship with a different good, and if the bundles of characteristics derived from the two goods differ only in a scalar (that is, have identical proportions), we can regard the two goods in question as *intrinsic perfect substitutes*. If the associated characteristics bundles are similar, the goods are *close substitutes*. We can give formal respectability to that traditional butter-margarine example of our texts by considering them as two goods giving very similar combinations of characteristics.

On the other hand, if a certain activity requires more than one good and if these goods are used in no other activity we can consider them as *intrinsic total complements* and they will always be consumed in fixed proportions, if at all.

Many goods within a commodity group will have relationships to each other which are partly complementary and partly substitution. This will be true if two goods, for example, are used in different combinations in each of several activities, each activity giving rise to a similar combination of characteristics. The goods are complements within each activity, but the activities are substitutes.

LABOUR, LEISURE, AND OCCUPATIONAL CHOICE

Within the structure of the present theory, we can regard labour as a reversed activity, using characteristics as inputs and producing commodities or a commodity as output. This is similar to the standard approach of generalized conventional theory, as in Debreu (1959).

We can add to this approach in an important way within the context of the present model by noting that a work activity may produce characteristics, as well as the commodity labour, as outputs. This is structurally equivalent to permitting some of the columns of the B matrix to have both negative and positive elements, corresponding to activities that 'use up' some characteristics (or produce them in negative quantities) and produce others. In a work activity, the corresponding column of the A matrix will contain a single negative coefficient for the commodity labour, or, more differentiated, for one or more types of labour. If a work activity corresponds to a column of mixed signs in the B matrix, it is a recognition of the obvious truth that some work activities give rise to valued characteristics directly from the work itself.

Consider a very simple model of two characteristics with two commodities, labour and consumption goods. Both labour and consumption goods correspond to separate activities giving rise to the two characteristics in different proportions – perhaps negative in the case of labour. With no income other than labour, and only one good available to exchange for labour, we can collapse work and consumption into a single work-consumption activity. Given the wage rate in terms of the consumption good, the characteristics resulting from the work-consumption activity are given by a linear combination of the characteristics from work and consumption separately, the weights in the combination being given by the wage rate.

Add another activity, leisure, which gives rise to the two characteristics, and the constraint that the weighted sum of the levels of activity labour and activity leisure is a constant.

The model is illustrated in Figure 2.3. w represents a work-consumption

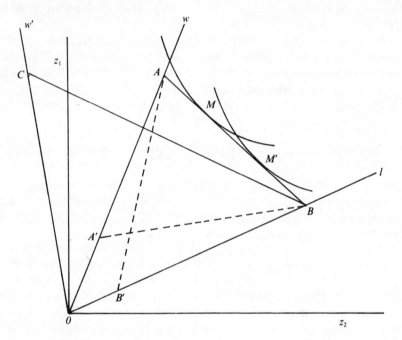

Figure 2.3

activity giving positive levels of both characteristics, l represents a leisure activity, also giving positive levels of both characteristics. The constraint on total time (so that a linear combination of w and l is a constant) is represented by some line joining w, l.

If the constraint line has, like AB in the diagram, a negative slope, then individual consumers' utility functions will be tangent to the constraint at different points (like m, m') and we will have a neo-classical type of labour-leisure choice in which the proportions depend on individual preferences. Some consumers' preferences may be such that they will choose A (maximum work) or B (maximum leisure), but it is a private choice.

In this model, however, for a certain level of the wage, given the coefficients of the technology, the constraint may have a positive slope as in $A'B$, or AB'. If the constraint is $A'B$ (corresponding, *ceteris paribus*, to a sufficiently low real wage), *all* individuals will choose B, the only efficient point on the constraint set $OA'B$. At a sufficiently high wage, giving constraint set OAB', A, the maximum labour choice, is the only efficient choice and will be chosen by *all* individuals.

The above effect, in which for some wage range there is a private labour-leisure choice between efficient points while outside the range all individuals will take maximum work or maximum leisure, can only occur if both the work-consumption and leisure activities give both characteristics in positive amounts. If the using up of characteristic 2 in labour exceeded the amount of that characteristic gained by consumption, then the work-consumption activity might lie outside the positive quadrant, like w'. In this case, a constraint like $A'B$ can exist, but not one like AB'. Furthermore, if the consumer will choose only positive characteristics vectors, no consumer will choose maximum work.

This model of the labour-leisure choice, which provides for objective and universal efficiency choices as well as private choices, may be the basis for a useful working model for an underdeveloped area. If the 'leisure' be defined as 'working one's own field', the work-consumption activity as entering the market economy, we see that there will be wages below which no peasant will offer himself as paid labour and that this is an *efficiency* choice and not a private choice.

We can use the same type of model also to analyse occupational choice. Suppose that we have two types of work (occupations) but otherwise the conditions are as above. If and only if the characteristics arising from the work itself are different in the two occupations, the two work-consumption activities will give rise to activities in different combinations. If the work characteristics are in the same proportion, the characteristics of the work-consumption activity will be in the same proportions and one or the other occupation will be the only efficient way to achieve this characteristics bundle.

Figure 2.4 illustrates one possible set of relationships for such a model. In the diagram, w_1, w_2 represent the characteristics combinations from work-consumption activities in occupations 1 and 2, l the characteristics combinations from leisure. The frontier consists of the lines AC (combinations of w_1 and leisure) and AB (combinations of w_2 and leisure). We shall impose the realistic restriction that an individual can have only a single occupation so that AB is not a possible combination of activities.

The choice of occupation, given the relationships in the figure, depends on personal preferences, being M_1 (combination of w_2 and leisure) for an

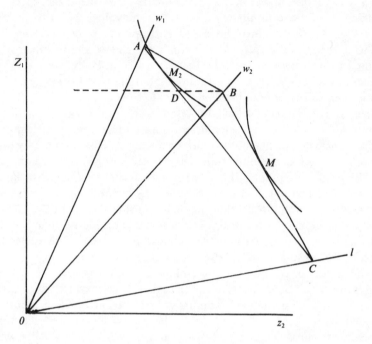

Figure 2.4

individual with preferences skewed towards z_2 and M_2 for an individual with preferences skewed towards z_1. But note a special effect. For some individuals whose indifference curves cannot touch BC but can touch AC, the efficient choice will be the corner solution M_3 ($=$ B). There is, in fact, a segment of AC to the left of w_2 (the part of AC to the right of w_2 is dominated by BC), lying below the horizontal through B which is inefficient relative to B and will never be chosen.

In a configuration like the above we have the very interesting effect, where those who choose occupation 1 will work very hard at it; leisure-lovers will choose private combinations of occupation 2 and leisure – surely a good description of effects actually observed.

The loss to certain individuals from confinement to a single occupation is obvious. Could he choose a combination of occupations 1 and 2, the individual at M_2 would do so and be better off than with a combination of occupation 1 and leisure. In a two-characteristic, three-activity model, of course, two activities will be chosen at most, so that leisure plus both occupations will not appear.

The configuration in the diagram (Figure 2.4) represents the situation for some set of technical coefficients and specific wages in the two occupations. A large number of other configurations is possible. In particular, if the wage rate in occupation 2 fell sufficiently, BC would lie inside AC and occupation 2 would cease to be chosen by any individual. All individuals, in this case, would choose their various personal combinations of occupation 1 and leisure.

Confinement to a single occupation need not result in a welfare loss, even when neither occupation dominates the other in an efficiency sense. If the technical coefficients were different, so that the characteristics vectors representing occupation 2 and leisure changed places, then the work-leisure combinations would be given by AB and BC, both efficient relative to any combination of occupations 1 and 2. In this case, all individuals would optimize by some combination of leisure and any one of the occupations.

Approaches similar to those outlined above seem to provide a better basis for analysis of occupational choice than the traditional, non-operational, catch-all 'non-monetary advantages'.

CONSUMER DURABLES, ASSETS, AND MONEY

Within the framework of the model, we have a scheme for dealing with durable goods and assets. A durable good can be regarded simply as giving rise to an activity in which the output consists of dated characteristics, the characteristics of different dates being regarded as different characteristics.

Given characteristics as joint outputs and two types of dimension in characteristics space – cross-section and time – any asset or durable good can be regarded as producing a combination of several characteristics at any one time, and that combination need not be regarded as continuing unchanged through time. In the decision to buy a new automobile, for example, the characteristic related to 'fashion' or 'style' may be present in relative strength in the first season, relatively less in later seasons, although the characteristics related to 'transportation' may remain with constant coefficients over several seasons.

Elementary textbooks stress the multi-dimensional characteristics of money and other assets. The present model enables this multi-dimensionality to be appropriately incorporated. 'Safety', 'liquidity', and so forth become workable concepts that can be related to characteristics. We can use analysis similar to that of the preceding sections to show why efficiency effects will cause the universal disappearance of some assets (as in Gresham's Law) while other assets will be held in combinations determined by personal preferences. It would seem that development along these lines, coupled with development of some of the recent approaches to consumer preferences over time as in Koopmans (1960), Lancaster (1963), or Koopmans, Diamond and Williamson (1964) might eventually lead to a full-blooded theory of consumer behaviour with respect to assets – saving and money – which we do not have at present.

In situations involving risk, we can use multiple characteristics better to analyse individual behaviour. For example, we might consider a gamble to be an activity giving rise to three characteristics – a mathematical expectation, a maximum gain, and a maximum loss. One consumer's utility function may be such that he gives more weight to the maximum gain than to the maximum loss or the expected value, another's utility function may be biased in the opposite direction. All kinds of models can be developed along these lines, and they are surely more realistic than the models (von Neumann and Morgenstern 1944; Friedman and Savage 1952) in which the expected value, alone, appears in the utility-maximizing decisions.

NEW COMMODITIES, DIFFERENTIATED GOODS, AND ADVERTISING

Perhaps the most difficult thing to do with traditional consumer theory is to introduce a new commodity – an event that occurs thousands of times in the US economy, even over a generation, without any real consumers being unduly disturbed. In the theory of production, where activity-analysis methods have become widely used, a new process or product can be fitted in well enough; but in consumer theory we have traditionally had to throw away our n-dimensional preference functions and replace them by totally new $(n+1)$ dimensional functions, with no predictable consequences.

In this model, the whole process is extraordinarily simple. A new product simply means addition of one or more activities to the consumption technology. Given the technology (or the relevant portion of it) and given the intrinsic characteristic of the activity associated with the new good, we simply insert it in the appropriate place in the technology, *and we can predict the consequences.*

If a new good possesses characteristics in the same proportions as some existing good, it will simply fail to sell to anyone if its price is too high, or will completely replace the old good if its price is sufficiently low.

More usually, we can expect a new good to possess characteristics in somewhat different proportions to an existing good. If its price is too high, it may be dominated by some *combination* of existing goods and will fail to sell. If its price is sufficiently low, it will result in adding a new point to the efficiency frontier. In Figure 2.5, ABC represents the old efficiency fron-

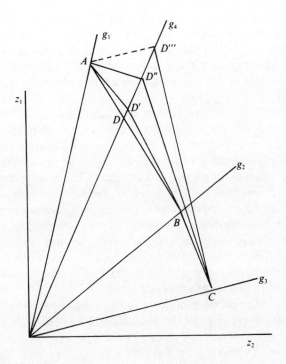

Figure 2.5

tier, on which some individuals will consume combinations of goods g_1 and g_2 in various proportions, some combinations of g_2 and g_3. If the price of the new good, g_4, is such that it represents a point, D, on the old efficiency frontier, some persons (those using combinations of g_1 and g_2) will be indifferent between their old combinations and combinations of either g_1 and g_4 or g_2 and g_4. If the price of g_4 is a little lower, it will push the efficiency frontier out to D'. Individuals will now replace combinations of g_1 and g_2 with combinations of g_1 and g_4 or g_2 and g_4, depending on their preferences. The new good will have taken away some of the sales from both g_1 and g_2, but completely replaced neither.

If the price of g_4 were lower, giving point D'', then combinations of g_4 and g_3 would dominate g_2, and g_2 would be replaced. At an even lower price, like D''', combinations of g_4 and g_3 would dominate g_2, and the corner solution g_4 only would dominate all combinations of g_1 and g_4 (since AD''' has a positive slope), so that g_4 would now replace both g_1 and g_2.

Differentiation of goods has presented almost as much of a problem to traditional theory as new commodities. In the present analysis, the difference is really one of degree only. We can regard a differentiated good typically as a new good within an existing intrinsic commodity group, and within that group analyse it as a new commodity. Sometimes there appear new commodities of a more fundamental kind whose characteristics cut across those of existing groups.

We may note that differentiation of goods, if successful (that is, if the differentiated goods are actually sold) represents a welfare improvement since it pushes the efficiency frontier outward and enables the consumer more efficiently to reach his preferred combination of characteristics.

Many economists take a puritanical view of commodity differentiation since their theory has induced them to believe that it is some single characteristic of a commodity that is relevant to consumer decisions (that is, cars are only for transportation), so that commodity variants are regarded as wicked tricks to trap the uninitiated into buying unwanted trimmings. This is not, of course, a correct deduction even from the conventional analysis, properly used, but is manifestly incorrect when account is taken of multiple characteristics.

A rather similar puritanism has also been apparent in the economist's approach to advertising. In the neo-classical analysis, advertising, if it does not represent simple information (and little information is called for in an analysis in which a good is simply a good), is an attempt to 'change tastes' in the consumer. Since 'tastes' are the ultimate datum in welfare judgements, the idea of changing them makes economists uncomfortable.

On the analysis presented here, there is much wider scope for informational advertising, especially as new goods appear constantly. Since the consumption technology of a modern economy is clearly very complex, consumers require a great deal of information concerning that technology. When a new version of a dishwashing detergent is produced which contains hand lotion, we have a product with characteristics different from those of the old. The consumption technology is changed, and consumers are willing to pay to be told of the change. Whether the new product pushes out the efficiency frontier (compared, say, with a combination of dishwasher and hand lotion consumed separately) is, of course, another matter.

In any case, advertising, product design, and marketing specialists, who have a heavy commitment to understanding how consumers actually do behave, themselves act as though consumers regard a commodity as having multiple characteristics and as though consumers weigh the various combinations of characteristics contained in different commodities in reaching their decisions. At this preliminary stage of presenting the model set out here, this is strong evidence in its favour.

GENERAL EQUILIBRIUM, WELFARE, AND OTHER MATTERS

Since the demand for goods depends on objective and universal efficiency effects as well as on private choices, we can draw some inferences relative to equilibrium in the economy.

A commodity, especially a commodity within an intrinsic commodity group, must have a price low enough relative to the prices of other commodities to be represented on the efficiency frontier, otherwise it will be purchased by no one and will not appear in the economy. This implies that if there are n viable commodities in a group, each in a one-to-one relation to an activity, the equilibrium prices will be such that the efficiency frontier has $n-1$ facets in the two-characteristic case. In Figure 2.6, for example, where the price of commodity 3 brings it to point A on

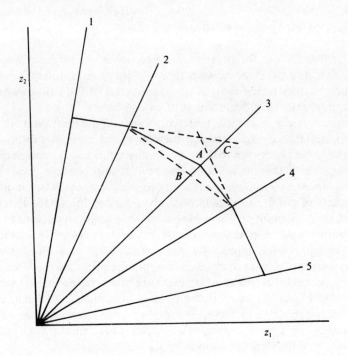

Figure 2.6

the efficiency frontier, that price could not be allowed to rise to a level bringing it inside point B, or it would disappear from the market; and if its price fell below a level corresponding to C, commodities 2 and 4 would disappear from the market. Thus the limits on prices necessary for the existence of all commodities within a group can be established (in principle) from objective data. Only the demand within that price range depends on consumer preferences.

With a large number of activities relative to characteristics, equilibrium prices would give a many-faceted efficiency frontier that would be approximated by a smooth curve having the general shape of a production possibility curve. For many purposes it may be mathematically simple to analyse the situation in terms of a smooth efficiency frontier. We can then draw on some of the analysis that exists, relating factor inputs to outputs of goods, as in Samuelson (1953b). Goods in our model correspond to factors in the production model, and characteristics in our model to commodities in the production model.

The welfare implications of the model set out here are quite complex and deserve a separate treatment. We might note several important aspects of the welfare problem, however, which arise directly from a many-faceted, many-cornered efficiency frontier:

1. Consumers whose choices represent a corner on the efficiency frontier are not, in general, *equating* marginal rates of substitution between characteristics to the ratio of any parameters of the situation or to marginal rates of substitution of other consumers.
2. Consumers whose choices represent points on different facets of the efficiency frontier are equating their marginal rates of substitution between characteristics to different implicit price ratios between characteristics. If there is a one-to-one relationship between goods and activities, the consumers are reacting to relative prices between different sets of goods. The traditional marginal conditions for Paretian exchange optimum do not hold because the price ratio relevant to one consumer's decisions differs from the price ratio relevant to another's. In common-sense terms, the price ratio between a Ford and a Granada is irrelevant to my decisions, but the price ratio between two compact cars is relevant, while there are other individuals for whom the Ford/Granada ratio is the relevant datum. If the A matrix is strongly connected, however, the implicit price ratios between different activities can correspond to price ratios between the same sets of goods, and the Paretian conditions may be relevant.

Finally, we may note that the shape of the equilibrium efficiency frontier and the existence of the efficiency substitution effect can result in demand conditions with the traditionally assumed properties, even if the traditional, smooth, convex utility function does not exist. In particular, a simple utility function in which characteristics are consumed in constant proportions – the proportions perhaps changing with income – can be substituted for the conventional utility function.

OPERATIONAL AND PREDICTIVE CHARACTERISTICS OF THE MODEL

In principle, the model set out here can be made operational (that is, empirical coefficients can be assigned to the technology). In practice, the task will be more difficult than the equivalent task of determining the actual production technology of an economy.

To emphasize that the model is not simply heuristic, we can examine a simple scheme for sketching out the efficiency frontier for some commodity group. We shall assume that there is a one-to-one relationship between activities and goods, that at least one characteristic shared by the commodities is capable of independent determination, and that a great quantity of suitable market data is available.

In practice, we will attempt to operate with the minimum number of characteristics that give sufficient explanatory power. These may be combinations of fundamental characteristics (a factor-analysis situation) or fundamental characteristics themselves.

Consider some commodity group such as household detergents. We have a primary objective characteristic, cleaning power, measured in some chosen way. We wish to test whether one or more other characteristics are necessary to describe the consumer-choice situation.

We take a two-dimensional diagram with characteristic 'cleaning power' along one axis. Along the axis we mark the cleaning power per £1 outlay of all detergents observed to be sold at the same time. If this is the same for all detergents, this single characteristic describes the situation, and we do not seek further. However, we shall assume this is not so. From our observed market data, we obtain cross-price elasticities between all detergents, taken two at a time. From the model, we know that cross-price elasticities will be highest between detergents with adjacent characteristics vectors, so that the order of the characteristics vectors as we rotate from one axis to the other in the positive quadrant can be established.

The ordering of 'cleaning power per £1' along one axis can be compared with the ordering of the characteristics vectors. If the orderings are the same, an equilibrium efficiency frontier can be built up with two characteristics as in Figure 2.7(a). The slopes of the facets can be determined within limits by the limiting prices at which the various detergents go off the market. If the ordering in terms of cleaning power does not agree with the ordering in terms of cross-elasticity, as in Figure 2.7(b), two characteristics do not describe the market appropriately, since detergent with clean-

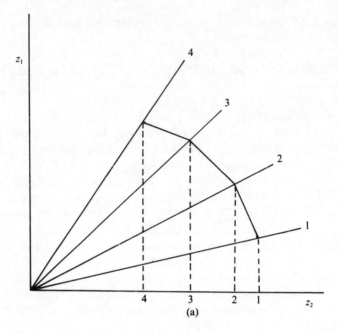

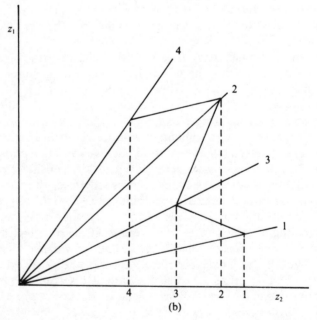

Figure 2.7

ing power 3 in the figure cannot be on the efficiency frontier. But with a third characteristic, detergent 3 could be adjacent to detergents 2 and 1 in an extra dimension, and we could build up an efficiency frontier in three characteristics.

Other evidence could, of course, be used to determine the efficiency frontier for a given market situation. Among this evidence is that arising from ordinary activity-analysis theory, that, with r characteristics we would expect to find some consumers who used r commodities at the same time, unless all consumers were on corners or edges of the efficiency frontier.

Last, but possibly not least, simply asking consumers about the characteristics associated with various commodities may be much more productive than attempts to extract information concerning preferences within the context of conventional theory.

In general, if consumers' preferences are well dispersed (so that all facets of the efficiency frontier are represented in some consumer's choice pattern), a combination of information concerning interpersonal variances in the collections of goods chosen and of the effects of price changes on both aggregate and individual choices can, in principle, be used to ferret out the nature of the consumption technology. Some of the problems that arise are similar to those met by psychologists in measuring intelligence, personality, and other multi-dimensional traits, so that techniques similar to those used in psychology, such as factor analysis, might prove useful.

Even without specification of the consumption technology, the present theory makes many predictions of a structural kind which may be contrasted with the predictions of conventional theory. Some of these are set out in Figure 2.8.

CONCLUSION

In this model we have extended into consumption theory activity analysis which has proved so penetrating in its application to production theory. The crucial assumption in making this application has been the assumption that goods possess, or give rise to, multiple characteristics in fixed proportions and that it is these characteristics, not goods themselves, on which the consumer's preferences are exercised.

The result, as this brief survey of the possibilities has shown, is a model very many times richer in heuristic explanatory and predictive power than the conventional model of consumer behaviour and one that deals easily with those many common-sense characteristics of actual behaviour that have found no place in traditional exposition.

This chapter is nothing more than a condensed presentation of some of

This theory

Wood will not be a close substitute for bread, since characteristics are dissimilar

A red car will be a close substitute for a grey car

Substitution (for example, butter and margarine) is frequently intrinsic and objective, will be observed in many societies under many market conditions

A good may be be displaced from the market by new goods or by price changes

The labour-leisure choice may have a marked occupational pattern

(Gresham's Law) A monetary asset may cease to be on the efficiency frontier, and will disappear from the economy

An individual is completely unaffected by price changes that leave unchanged the portion of the efficiency frontier on which his choice rests

Some commodity groups may be intrinsic, and universally so

Conventional theory

No reason except 'tastes' why they should not be close substitutes

No reason why they should be any closer substitutes than wood and bread

No reason why close substitutes in one context should be close substitutes in another

No presumption that goods will be completely displaced

Labour-leisure choice determined solely by individual preferences; no pattern, other than between individuals, would be predicted

No ex-ante presumption that any good or asset will disappear from the economy

An individual is affected by changes in all prices

No presumption that commodities forming a group (defined by a break in spectrum of cross-elasticities) in one context will form a group in another context

Figure 2.8   Comparison of this theory and conventional theory

the great number of possible ways in which the model can be used. It is hoped that a door has been opened to a new, rich treasure house of ideas for the future development of the most refined and least powerful branch of economic theory, the theory of the consumer himself.

APPENDIX

Transformation of the utility function into G-space

Consider some characteristics vector z^* which does have an image x^* in G-space, and consider the set P of all vectors z preferred or indifferent to z^*. If U has the traditional properties, the set P is convex with an inner boundary which is the indifference surface through z^*. Now $z \geq z^*$ implies z is in P so that every x such that $Bx \geq z^*$, a set S, is preferred or indifferent to x^*. If we take some other z' in P, every x in S' such that $Bx \geq z'$ is also preferred or indifferent to x'^*. Similarly for z'' in P and S'' such that $Bx \geq z''$, and so on. From the theory of inequalities, the sets $S, S', S'' \dots$ are all convex, and since P is convex, a linear combination of z', z'' is in P, so that a linear combination of x's in S', S'' is also preferred or indifferent to x^*. Hence the set $\bar{P}$ of all x preferred or indifferent to x^* is the linear combination of all the sets S, S', S'', ... and so is convex.

Thus the utility function transformed into G-space retains its essential convexity. A more intuitive way of looking at the situation is to note that all characteristics collections which are actually available are contained in an n-dimensional slice through the r-dimensional utility function and that all slices through a convex function are themselves convex. The transformation of this n-dimensional slice into G-space preserves this convexity.

'Revealed preference' in a complex economy

We shall use the structural properties of the consumption technology A,B (dropping the assumption of a one-to-one relationship between goods and activities) to show that in a complex economy with more activities than characteristics the efficiency choice always satisfies the weak axiom of revealed preference and will satisfy the strong axiom for sufficiently large price changes, so that satisfaction of even the strong axiom does not 'reveal' convexity of the preference function itself.

Consider an economy with a consumption technology defined by $z = By$, $x = Ay$, and a consumer subject to a budget constraint of the form $p^*x \leq k$ who has chosen goods x^* for activities y^*, giving characteristics z^*.

We know that if the consumer has made an efficient choice, y^* is the solution of the programme (the value of which is k).

$$\min p^*Ay \; (= p^*x) \tag{2.10}$$
$$By = z^*, y \geqq 0$$

which has a dual (solution v^*)

$$\max vz^* : vB \leqq p^*A \tag{2.11}$$

The dual variables v can be interpreted as the implicit prices of the characteristics themselves. From the Kuhn-Tucker Theorem, we can associate the vector v with the slope of the separating hyperplane between the set of attainable z's and the set of z's preferred or indifferent to z^*.

For the same satisfactions vector Z^* and a new price vector p^{**} the efficiency choice will be the solution y^{**} (giving x^{**}), v^{**}, of

$$\min p^{**}Ay : By = z^*, y \geqq 0 \tag{2.12}$$
$$\max vz^* : vb \leqq p^{**}A$$

Since z^* is the same in (2.10), (2.11) and (2.12), y^{**} is a feasible solution of (2.11) and y^* of (2.12). From the fundamental theorem of linear programming we have

$$p^{**}Ay^* \geqq v^{**}z^* = p^{**}Ay^{**} \qquad (2.13)$$
$$p^*Ay^{**} \geqq v^*z^* = p^*Ay^* \qquad (2.14)$$

A program identical with (2.12) except that z^* is replaced by hz^* will have a solution hy^{**}, v^{**}. Choose h so that $hp^{**}Ay^{**} = p^{**}Ay^*$. From (2.13) $h \geqq 1$. From (2.14),

$$hp^*Ay^{**} \geqq p^*Ay^{**} \geqq p^*Ay^* \qquad (2.15)$$

If we now write p for p^*, p' for p^{**}; $x = Ay^*$, $x' = hAy^{**}$, we have

$$p'x' = p'x \text{ implies } px' \geqq px \qquad (2.16)$$

satisfying the *weak axiom of revealed preference*.

The equality will occur on the right in (2.16) only if equalities hold in *both* (2.13) and (2.14), and these will hold only if y^{**} is optimal as well as feasible in (2.10) and (2.11), and y^* is optimal as well as feasible in (2.12). In general, if the number of activities exceeds the number of characteristics, we can always find two prices p^*, p^{**} so related that neither of the solutions y^{**}, y^* is optimal in the other's programme.

Hence, if the number of activities exceeds the number of characteristics (representing the number of primary constraints in the programme), we can find prices so related that the strong axiom of revealed preference is satisfied, even though the consumer has obtained characteristics in unchanged proportions (z^*, hz^*) and has revealed nothing of his preference map.

The above effect represents an *efficiency substitution effect* which would occur even if characteristics were consumed in absolutely fixed proportions. If the consumer substitutes between different satisfactions bundles when his budget constraint changes, this private substitution effect is additional to the efficiency substitution effect.

Just as the conceptual experiment implicit in revealed preference implies 'overcompensation' in the conventional analysis (see Samuelson 1948, 1953a), so the efficiency effect leads to 'external overcompensation' additional to private overcompensation.

NOTES

1.   Originally published in *Journal of Political Economy*, **74** (1966), 132–57.
2.   Since the units in which the characteristics are measured are arbitrary, the objectivity

criterion relating goods and characteristics reduces to the requirement that the *relative* quantities of a particular characteristic between unit quantities of any pair of goods should be the same for all consumers.

3. The assumption that the consumption technology A,B is fixed is a convenience for discussing those aspects of the model (primarily static) that are the chief concern of this chapter. The consequences of relaxing this particular assumption is only one of many possible extensions and expansions of the ideas presented and are discussed by the author elsewhere (Lancaster 1966).

4. 'Qualitative' is used here in a somewhat more general sense than in the author's work on the properties of qualitatively defined systems for which see Lancaster (1962, 1965).

5. If the relationship between goods and activities is not one-to-one, the consumption technology consists of the two matrixes B,A, as in the technology of the von Neumann growth model.

6. Assuming no decomposability or singularities in the consumption technology matrix B, then, if z_n is the vector of any n components of z and B_n, the corresponding square submatrix of B, the subspace of C-space to which the consumer is confined, is that defined by $z_{r-n} = B_{r-n}B_n^{-1}z_n$, where z_{r-n}, B_{r-n} are the vector and corresponding submatrix of B consisting of the components not included in z_n, B_n.

7. This is a somewhat imprecise statement in that, if the B matrix is partitionable into disconnected subtechnologies, for some of which the number of activities exceeds the number of characteristics and for others the reverse, an efficiency-substitution effect may exist over certain groups of activities, although the number of activities is less than the number of characteristics overall.

8. One of the properties of this model is that it gives scope for the consumer to be more or less efficient in achieving his desired characteristics bundle, although we will usually assume he is completely efficient. This adds a realistic dimension to consumer behaviour (traditional theory never permits him to be out of equilibrium) and gives a rationale for the consumers' union and similar institutions.

3   Change and innovation in the technology of consumption[1]

The general nature of the consumption technology has been set out in Chapter 2, and this chapter will be devoted to answering the question: Can we have change, innovation, and technical progress in consumption technology, just as we have in production?

In the case of production technology, considered in activity analysis form, changes in that technology can be regarded in one or more of the following ways:

1. 'Magic wand' effects, in which a particular input combination that gave a certain output in 1965 gives a greater output in 1966.
2. Shifts from actual capabilities, or the upgrading in efficiency of those firms whose productivity is below the known technological potential. Strictly speaking, this is not a change in technology but it will manifest itself in aggregate data in a similar way.
3. An identified technical change arising from the introduction of specified new activities.
4. A change in the nature of inputs such as the introduction of new capital goods, new labour or management skills.

In analysing production technology, output can be measured with relative ease, as can the input of broadly-defined factors. This places much emphasis on magic wand effects, such as unexplained residuals. On the other hand, information concerning the detailed nature of inputs is more difficult to discover, so that the effects of changes in the nature of inputs are less emphasized. In consumption technology the situation is reversed; we have information concerning the changes in the goods which form the inputs, but little information concerning the outputs. We have no interest, therefore, in magic wand effects, but the other three effects can be important.

Since our model of consumer behaviour provides scope for efficient choice and hence for the possibility that not all consumers are efficient, there is scope for technical progress in the special sense of increased consumption efficiency, even with no change in the nature of goods or consumption activities.

In consumption, as in production, the prime reasons for inefficient use of the existing technology are ignorance and lack of managerial skill. The consumer may not be aware that a certain good possesses certain characteristics or that certain goods may be used in a particular combination to give a specified bundle of characteristics. Producers or sellers may use advertising to ensure that no characteristics of their product regarded as particularly desirable should go unnoticed by consumers. They will go to less pains to ensure that consumers are aware of some other characteristics of their product.

Organizations, such as the Consumers Union, exist to provide more objective information on the characteristics of goods than is easily available elsewhere. Some consumers are willing to pay for information which assists in attaining efficient points on their characteristics possibility sets and, on the model presented here, are rational to do so. However, since efficient choices are the same for all consumers, there is a clear argument in favour of public information on these matters and in favour of legal requirements, such as composition and contents labelling, designed to increase knowledge of the available consumption technology.

We can use our model to demolish the old argument, favoured by sellers of established products, that, since consumers 'reveal' their preference for the product already, labelling laws are unnecessary. Traditional theory may seem to lend some weight to this argument, but the present theory does not, since actual choice by consumers can no longer be regarded as revealing their preferences for characteristics – they may merely be making an inefficient choice.

The consumption technology, in a society like that of the United States, is very complex. Efficient consumption, even in the presence of adequate information concerning the technology, involves some managerial skill. As any social worker will testify, many households are noticeably deficient in this skill. Conventional consumer theory leads to a presumption that the family which spends its income on an eccentric collection of goods is simply revealing its preferences for that collection. Of course, this might be true, but it may also be that the family is consuming inefficiently. If the consumer's desired characteristics collection could be ascertained even in a very general way, some type of advising might lead to more efficient consumption.

A crucial difference between the production and consumption sectors is that the market mechanism does not tend to guarantee efficiency in consumption in the same way it does in production. In a society at subsistence level, the inefficient consumer may not survive. In a more affluent society he will survive, but will remain at a lower welfare level than that potentially available to him. Again, this leads to the presumption that public consumer education would be socially valuable.

A relatively static technology, in consumption as in production, will, if coupled with stable relative prices, probably lead to a situation in which the efficient activities become generally known and traditional. Traditional consumption patterns will be efficient only within a relatively unchanging choice situation and only optimal for consumers whose preferences on characteristics approximate the society mode. Tradition will be less useful when the technology is changing rapidly, when relative prices are changing considerably, or when the consumer's preferences diverge from the mode. Furthermore, the typical consumer will inherit his traditions from his social background, and they may not serve him at a radically different income level. We are all aware that the *nouveau riche* may consume differently from persons already established in the higher income group. This analysis suggests that it is at least possible that the desired characteristics of the new and old rich need not be different: the newcomers may be less efficient in achieving their aims. The same considerations may work in reverse; so that a consumer suddenly thrust from a wage income to welfare payments may take some time to discover efficient methods at the new income level, although at this level efficiency may be crucial.

One suspects that there may be great scope for increasing consumption efficiency in the kind of changing situations outlined above. These include the transition from peasant to market economies and from rural to urban societies in developing countries and, within countries, among social groups migrating from one region to another or from one income level to another.

Because the market system does not place pressure on consumers to be efficient, this aspect of technical progress has been stressed more than it might be in discussing production. But innovation in the true sense occurs in the consumption technology, and this takes place primarily through the introduction of new goods or new variants and product differentiation.

Traditional consumer theory is at its most unenlightening when confronted by the problem of new goods. Introduction of a new good requires either that the preference function defined on n goods is thrown away, and with it all the knowledge of behaviour based on it, and replaced by a brand new function defined $n + 1$ goods, or the fiction that the consumer has a potential preference function for all goods present and future and that a new good can be treated as the fall in that good's price from infinity to its market level. Neither approach gets us very far.

In the present model, it may be that the good is so revolutionary that its characteristics are not possessed by any existing goods. We are no better off, in this case, than in the traditional one. But most new goods can be regarded as simply giving rise to existing characteristics in new proportions, and we have available an operationally meaningful way of approaching the problem. A new good of this kind – and this probably covers nearly all new goods and certainly all product variants – adds a new activity to the technology and is, in the proper sense of the word, an innovation in that technology. Whether the innovation is efficient depends entirely on the price of the new product. If the price is too high, its characteristics correspond to a point within the efficiency frontier and it will not be purchased by efficient consumers, except perhaps initial experimentation to discover whether it is efficient or not. If the price is sufficiently low, however, the new good will push part of the efficiency frontier forward and will enter the efficient technology. Unless that particular part of the frontier happens to contain no consumer's preferred characteristic collection, the new good will sell. Furthermore, the introduction of a successful new good will result in an increase in welfare, if other prices are unchanged.

It may not always be clear whether we should classify a new good as an innovation on the production or the consumption side, but it certainly seems most useful to regard a variant of an existing product, involving no fundamental change in the technical nature of the production process, as an innovation in consumption technology. In terms of our model of consumption, the difference between a new product and a product variant is only the degree to which the characteristics mix of the new product differs from that of existing products. We have, in this model, a satisfactory technique for analysing product differentiation.

If we consider the situation from the production end and look through the consumption technology, we see that a producer is ultimately selling characteristics collections rather than goods. The degree of product differentiation will depend on the possibilities, at the production end, of producing variants with characteristics, and at prices, that can compete with existing products.

A producer with some monopoly power (and we might note that the theory of product differentiation presented here does not require imperfect competition as a prerequisite) will seek the profit maximizing price and differentiation policy. A theory of imperfectly competitive behaviour can be built up by pursuing the above analysis, but it is not proposed to do this here.

If products cannot be utilized in combination, the analysis of product differentiation is somewhat different. Consider a highly simplified model of motor cars as consumption activities, expressed in terms of two characteristics, transportation per £1 of petrol and comfort. Let two variants, Fords and Volkswagens, be represented by A and B in the diagram. Now one cannot obtain a combination of these characteristics by taking half a Ford and half a Volkswagen, so that, although the points A and B are on the frontier, points on *AB* are not. Then a variant priced to give point *C"* might be preferred by some consumers to either *A* or *B*, and the convexity of the price-characteristics relationship is not a necessary condition for marketability in this case.

New goods and differentiated products may not simply add to the spectrum of consumption activities; they may replace previous goods. This replacement will occur when the characteristics and price properties of the new product push the frontier forward in such a way that some existing good is no longer part of the efficient set. This will, of course, happen if the new good, for the same outlay, gives more of all characteristics in approximately the same proportions as the old. Such a change seems to correspond to what is often meant by an 'overall improvement in quality'. In other cases a quality improvement may correspond rather to an increase in some characteristics, with the others unchanged.

Although the introduction of a new product or a new variant can be expected to increase welfare in the simple Paretian sense if the new product is actually purchased and if the existing product is still available at the old price, this may not be the case if the seller takes the old product off the market as he puts the new one on. If the new product, however much of some characteristics it may offer per £1 of outlay, offers less of some other characteristic than the old, then some consumer may be deprived of part of the efficient technology relevant to his particular tastes.

The distinction between the technology of production and that of consumption is a great convenience in analysis but is not based on an absolute criterion of any kind. The ultimate constraints on the system are resources; the ultimate products are characteristics. Some resources may be used to first produce goods which are intermediate goods in the final analysis, and these goods may then be used in the consumption technology to produce characteristics. But some resources may directly enter the consumption technology without the production of goods as intermediates. As the technologies of both production and consumption change, activities may move back and forth between the consumption and production sectors. This is particularly true of the service and distribution phases of production.

Ultimately the supply of resources, particularly labour, is determined by characteristics. A particular job will have associated with it several characteristics: some will be, in relation to characteristics derived from goods, of a negative kind, but some may well be of a positive kind. The traditional idea of 'non-monetary advantages' has been an attempt to face this obvious fact. We can expand the idea of the consumption technology to include the activities associated with the consumer's sale of labour or other resources. Since labour as an activity may have some characteristics associated with it that are shared by goods, the particular work a consumer performs may partly determine his choice of goods. A taxi driver may spend less of his budget on taking weekend drives than the social norm; yet traditional theory would find no connection between his consumption and his occupation.

New occupations and even new work conditions can be considered as changes in consumption technology. They may also lead to changes in production technology, but this is not necessarily the case.

It would be possible to follow through the kind of analysis we have been making here at very much greater length than is available, but I think the point has been made. There is a technology of consumption. It is the subject of continual change and innovation, just as is the production technology. This change does lead to increased welfare, but the direction from which change comes, the incentives for change, and the analysis and measurement of change differ considerably between production and consumption.

Note

1. Originally published in *American Economic Review* papers and proceedings, **56** (1966), 14–25. Since this was published simultaneously with the previous paper (Chapter 2), some material setting out the basic model was identical with that in the other paper and has been eliminated in this version.

PART II

EXTENSIONS

4 Operationally relevant characteristics in the theory of consumer behaviour[1]

The associated ideas of a hierarchy of wants and of want satiation figured prominently in the writings of the early marginalists, then fell into disuse. In this chapter, I shall develop related ideas for application in modern consumer theory. The emphasis here is on contemporary application, with only passing reference to the earlier literature. Ironically, the earlier forms of these ideas were discarded because they were considered non-operational, but it is because they are useful for the *operational* development of recent models of the consumer, that they are discussed here.

The context of the present discussion is a model of the consumer, the general structure of which has been set out in some detail elsewhere. The essential feature is that the consumer's relationship to goods is viewed as having two (at least) stages. Goods, singly or in combination, possess properties which I refer to as *characteristics*. These are typically viewed as joint outputs of a consumption activity, in which goods are the input. The consumer's preferences and choices are assumed to be concerned with the various collections of characteristics that are available to him, these being derived in turn from the available collection of goods. In the simplest case, the available goods are limited by a budget constraint. The goods collections give rise to characteristics collections, from which the consumer chooses his preferred collection, the choice being manifest by his choosing the *goods* collection which gives this particular collection of characteristics.

The version of the model which shows particular promise in operational and empirical approaches, at this early stage of its development, is that in which we confine our attention to cases in which we can work with characteristics which

1. are objectively observable and measurable;
2. have linear properties, so that twice as much of the good has twice as much of the characteristic;
3. are additive, so that if one pound of Good A has one unit of a characteristic and one litre of Good B has two units, the combination of one pound of A plus one litre of B contains three units.

For the purposes of this chapter, the essential features of the model can be illustrated by Figure 4.1, which shows a case in which there are two

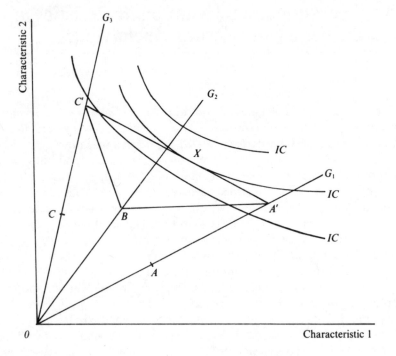

Figure 4.1

characteristics and three goods. Quantities of the two characteristics are
measured along the two axes. All three goods are assumed to possess both
characteristics, but in different proportions. The points A, B and C show
the quantities of both characteristics contained in goods *1*, *2* and *3*
respectively, taking a unit quantity of each good. Thus the ray OG_1
represents all the combinations of the two characteristics that can be
obtained from various quantities of good 1 only, with similar interpre-
tations for OG_2 and OG_3. By consuming goods in combination, characteristics in proportions which lie inside the cone G_3OG_2 can be obtained.

Suppose the budget constraint and prices were such that the consumer
could, by spending all his money on one good, purchase two units of G_3 or
G_1, or one unit of G_2. Then the budget would confine the consumer to
characteristics collections A', C' or B if he bought only one good. If the
goods are divisible, the consumer could attain characteristics combinations from combinations of goods – combinations of characteristics
along $A'C'$ – by spending the whole budget on combinations of G_1 and G_3,
along $A'B$ by spending it on combinations of G_1 and G_2, and along BC' for
combinations of G_2 and G_3.

In the particular case shown in Figure 4.1, more of both characteristics can be obtained by combinations of G_1 and G_3 than by any combination including G_2. At the current prices, it would be *inefficient* to purchase G_2, assuming that more of both characteristics is desired. The earlier discussions of the model were primarily concerned with the consequences of efficient and inefficient combinations of goods, a topic that does not concern us here.

Since the consumer's preferences are in terms of characteristics his preference map can be drawn directly on the diagram. Assuming regular preferences, the consumer whose indifference curves are drawn in the figure will choose characteristics collection X, a particular combination of G_1 and G_3 that can be determined from the characteristics content of the two goods.

We shall refer to a diagram, such as Figure 4.1, in which characteristics are measured on the axes, as drawn in *characteristics-space* or *C-space*. A diagram drawn with goods measured on the axes will be said to be drawn in *G-space*. Note that in this case, a diagram in G-space would be three-dimensional.

There is, of course, a relationship between points in C-space and points in G-space. This will not be a one-to-one relationship both ways if the number of goods is different from the number of characteristics. In Figure 4.1, for example, the point B does not correspond to a unique point in G-space since this collection of characteristics can be obtained from various combinations of G_1 and G_3, as well as from one unit of G_2.

Later, we shall need to consider relationships between C-space and G-space, for very simple cases. An intuitive feeling for the nature of the relationship can be obtained from Figure 4.1. Imagine the rays OG_1, OG_2, OG_3 to be loosely hinged together at O, and the lines $A'C'$, $C'B$, BA to be elastic. Then, if we swing OG_1 and OG_3 so that they are perpendicular, then swing up OG_2 so that it is perpendicular to the other rays, we have constructed G-space. $A'C'$, $C'B$ and BA' will all stretch, but remain straight, and will define a plane in three-dimensional G-space. This plane is, of course, the budget plane in terms of goods. The indifference curves will become indifference surfaces, but with curvature only in two dimensions – it will be possible to draw a straight line through every point on every indifference surface such that it lies everywhere on the surface.

In the linear version, with which we are concerned, the relationship between C-space and G-space is linear in the sense that a linear form (line or plane) in one space corresponds to a linear form in the other. Although (as in the example given) there may not be a unique point in G-space corresponding to a point in C-space, there will always be a unique point in C-space corresponding to a point (that is, a goods collection) in G-space.

The relationship is given by $z = Bx$, where z is the vector of characteristics, x the vector of goods. The matrix B consists of elements b_{ij}, giving the amount of the ith characteristic contained in unit quantity of the jth good. Since the relationships expressed by the b_{ij}'s are assumed both objective and universal, they depend on the *technical* properties of the goods and not on subjective considerations. We refer to the matrix B, therefore, as the *consumption technology*. It depends on the available goods and their exact specifications.

RELEVANT CHARACTERISTICS

The characteristics model of the consumer has important superiority in explanatory power over the traditional model in many cases, especially in the explanation of such 'intrinsic' substitutability as between butter and margarine and in the analysis of differentiated products. It also has great potentialities in empirically-oriented studies.

The application of the model is most useful in situations (such as the market for differentiated goods) in which the number of effective characteristics is smaller than the number of goods. The earlier discussions of the model, to which reference has already been made, assumed that the number of characteristics was less than the number of goods.

Now it is clear that, if we count as a characteristic every property of a good that is objectively observable and measurable, the number of such 'characteristics' might be almost limitless. In the use of the analysis, we are interested only in *relevant* characteristics. The idea of relevance was implicit in the earlier discussion of the model, but was not explicitly dealt with. To face this problem and to investigate criteria for deciding whether a characteristic is or is not relevant, is the purpose of this chapter.

We are interested in the problem of selecting the relevant characteristics for a given situation, where we mean, by *situation*, a relationship between some set of consumers (possibly containing only one member) and some set of goods. A characteristic possessed by one or more of the goods is relevant to the situation if ignoring its existence would change our conclusions about choice or ordering of the goods by the consumers.

A brief discussion how *ex post* relevance might be established from market data was given in an earlier paper,[2] and this idea has been developed further in unpublished work on the motor car market.[3] This technique requires, however, that one commences from a set of characteristics reasonably close to the ultimate relevant set, and so needs a preliminary screening.

Here we shall be concerned with a general discussion of some of the criteria that are useful in deciding *ex ante* whether a characteristic is likely to be relevant or not, in a specific situation.

Some characteristics might be ruled out as *ex ante* irrelevant in all situations simply on broad general considerations. One charactistic of motor cars, for examples, is their serial numbers. We would expect that ignoring this would leave our predictions of behaviour in the motor car market unchanged. We need not discuss such trivial cases further.

Characteristics bear a double relation to a given situation. On the one hand, characteristics have a *technical* relationship to the goods which possess them, and, on the other hand, characteristics have a *human* relationship to the consumers in question. Thus a characteristic may be ruled out as irrelevant for either technical or human reasons.

Technical irrelevance is not our prime concern here, but a brief discussion of some of the criteria is useful. Leaving aside such trivial bases as when a characteristic is simply not possessed by the goods under discussion, we can rule out some characteristics as *redundant* or *invariant* in the technical sense.

A characteristic is invariant over a situation if it is possessed to the same degree by all goods being considered. For a situation involving only choice between motor cars, the flying ability of cars is the same (zero) and thus not a relevant characteristic for choice. But if the choice situation involved both planes and cars, flying ability would be a relevant criterion – and it may one day be so between cars. On the other hand, 'startability', which once used to be a relevant criterion in the market for new cars, is no longer so, because it is possessed to the same degree (maximal) by all. Thus technological change may alter the set of technically relevant characteristics.

We have technical redundance when a group of characteristics is related to each other in some fixed technical way. In such a group it may be, for example, that all goods have the same shape and same density so there is a mathematically fixed relationship between length, width and height, and between any of these and volume or weight. Thus 'size' can be represented by a single parameter which acts as a proxy for all other size parameters,[4] the other 'characteristics' of size being redundant. More complex cases arise, as when the 'performance' of equipment may be expressed in a very large number of characteristics, all but one subset of which may be redundant, although difficult to choose.

In operational applications of the model, we can usually try to reduce the number of characteristics as much as possible by extending the above idea to 'almost redundant' characteristics and to use broad 'proxy characteristics' which stand for many characteristics bearing *approximately* fixed relationship to each other.

CHARACTERISTICS AND PEOPLE

As pointed out above, characteristics may be relevant or irrelevant because of their relationships to goods, or their relationships to people. It is this latter set of relationships which now concerns us.

In the earlier marginalists, goods were considered to be related to people because they satisfied 'wants'. I do not wish to enter into a discussion of what these writers really meant by 'wants'. It is sufficient that they were considered entirely human properties that were, in some way, matched with or 'satisfied' by certain goods, and that preferences depended on the relationship between wants and the properties of goods.

It was not supposed by these writers that there was a one-to-one correspondence between wants and goods. On the contrary, it was generally assumed that a particular good could satisfy a large number of wants, which were arranged in a hierarchy so that the first quantity of the goods satisfied the most urgent want, the next quantity the next most urgent, and so on. Thus Menger[5] describes the isolated farmer allocating corn first for his own, then his family's basic survival, then for above survival food, then for seed, then for beer (!), then for fattening livestock, and so on.

Characteristics, in our model, are observable properties of goods, but their relevance to *people* lies in their ability to generate some response (perhaps negative) in consumers. In this sense, we could refer to a characteristic as 'satisfying wants', in some fashion. Because of its conceptual redundance we shall avoid this way of stating the relationship, but there is an undoubted similarity to what the earlier writers had in mind. Since a characteristic is only a single property of a good, which may possess many, there is a closer matching of single characteristics with single psychological aims than there is of single goods.

A prominent feature of the 'wants' approach, which we wish to take up, is that of a *hierarchy*. One of Menger's examples has already been given and there are many others. Georgescu-Roegen[6] points to examples in Plato, Jevons, Wieser, Walras, Marshall, Pareto and Knight. At the behavioural level there are hierarchical implications in Engel's Law and other well-established relationships between income and the expenditure on a particular class of goods. Recently, Paroush[7] has found consistency in the order in which consumers acquire durables, again with hierarchical implications.

Hierarchy in goods does not necessarily represent an underlying hierarchy of wants, since technical relationships may also be involved, especially in the case of durable goods. A person may prefer sailing to driving, yet may buy a car before a boat because, without a car, he cannot transport the boat to water, but, without a boat, he can still use his car.

Characteristics, like goods, may be subject to technical complementarities that give hierarchical properties without any psychological implications. We can also have a hierarchy of characteristics (for psychological reasons) without any goods hierarchy being manifest, because the characteristics in question are not confined to an easily identifiable group of goods.

Closely associated with the idea of a hierarchy of wants is some kind of *satiation* effect. In the original arguments of Menger and other writers in the same vein, the hierarchy was relevant because the consumer satisfied his wants in order of importance. Obviously, unless the most important want was satiable, the next most important would be irrelevant. Jevons, for example, wrote, 'the satisfaction of a lower want ... merely permits the higher want to manifest itself.[8,9]

In contemporary economic analysis, satiation appears only negatively as the *nonsatiation* postulate built into formal versions of the traditional theory.[10]Nonsatiation is a convenient, rather than essential, assumption in formal traditional theory.[11] It is an easy assumption to live with in traditional consumer theory which is, in spirit, orientated to the description of consumer behaviour with respect to 'goods' conceived in rather broad terms. A typical good would be an aggregate – motor cars, rather than a specific model – and Hicks, appropriately, devoted considerable effort to his proof of the composite commodity theorem in *Value and Capital*.

Traditional consumer theory can be regarded as an adequate *coarse-structure* theory, concerned primarily with the analysis of consumer behaviour with respect to broadly-conceived goods such as 'food', 'clothing'. It is concerned with what I have elsewhere described as *macro-microeconomics*.

The characteristics model, on the other hand, is particularly adapted to *fine-structure* theory, such as the choice between differentiated products within a group. Inevitably, in moving from a broader coarse-structure model to a more detailed fine-structure analysis, we may expect to lose some smoothness and continuity. Thus we need to pay more attention to such phenomena as satiation.

SATIATION

A satiation relationship between a consumer and a characteristic implies that the consumer has no positive interest in further quantities of the characteristic. This may mean either of two things, leading to a classification of satiation into two types. The consumer may have had

1. zero interest in further quantities of the characteristic
2. a *negative* interest in further quantities.

We can illustrate the two types from a diet example. Consider a sophisticated consumer whose choice is restricted to choice of food only, who considers (among other things) the nutritive content of his food, and who needs (and knows he needs) a daily intake of 2500 calories and 5000 units of vitamin A. Thus, among the various characteristics of his food, he seeks to attain these particular levels of the nutrients.

Once he has obtained 5000 units of vitamin A, he has no further interest in this characteristic. Assuming that amounts of vitamin A above 5000 units have no effects, good or bad, we can assume the consumer has zero interest in further quantities. We shall refer to this type of satiation, where the consumer simply ceases to note the characteristic once the minimum level has been attained, as *open satiation*.

But once the consumer has attained 2500 calories, he may well be anxious to avoid gaining weight and so may have a negative interest in further calories. This does not imply that he will not, under any circumstances, consume further calories, merely that he will only do so if the excess food contains other characteristics (flavour, for example) in which he retains a positive interest. We shall refer to this type of satiation, in which a characteristic changes from being desirable to being undesirable, as *closed satiation*.

More formally, for a consumer's world of two characteristics,[12] z_1 and z_2, the consumer reaches

1. *open satiation* at level z_2 for characteristic z_2 if, for any characteristics collections Z, Z' such that

$$z_1 = z_1'$$
$$z_2, z_2' \geqq \bar{z}_2$$

we have $Z \, I \, Z'$, whatever the relationship of z_2, z_2'.

2. *Closed satiation* at level $\bar{z}_2$ for characteristic z_2 if,
    (a) for any collections Z, Z' such that

$$z_1 = z_1'$$
$$z_2 > z_2' \geqq \bar{z}_2$$

we have $Z' \, P \, Z$, and
    (b) for any collections Z, Z' such that

$$z_1 = z_1'$$
$$z_2 \geqslant z_2' \geqslant \bar{z}_2$$

we have $Z' \, \bar{R} \, Z$ (that is, Z' preferrred or indifferent to Z).[13]

Representative indifference maps illustrating the two types of satiation for the two-characteristic model are shown in Figure 4.2. In the open satiation case (Figure 4.2(a)), the indifference curves are vertical above the

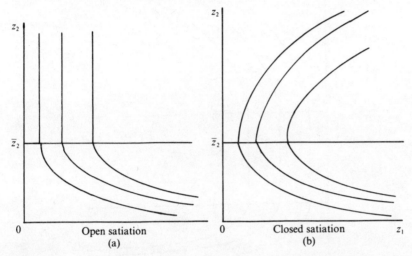

Figure 4.2

line $z_2 = \bar{z}_2$, while in the closed satiation case (Figure 4.2(b)), they have a positive slope in this region.

In some instances (including the calorie example already given) it may be more realistic to assume that open satiation is reached at one level, then closed satiation at a higher level. The consumer may, for example, decide he has approximately enough calories at 2000 and lose interest in them so long as he does not exceed 3000, at which level his negative reaction starts. This gives a region of open satiation or *neutral zone* with respect to the characteristic, as illustrated in Figure 4.3.

Satiation is generally assumed to be open satiation in the economics literature. Stigler's diet problem[14] (a precursor of the characteristics approach as well as of linear programming) assumed open satiation, permitting a linear programming solution for minimum cost subject to *minimum* nutrient content, without worrying about excess nutrients.

The 'want satiation' of the early marginalists was, of course, *open* satiation. Any characteristic of a good concerned only with supplying a more urgent want was assumed to have zero effect on the satisfaction of less urgent wants.

Satiation with respect to a characteristic may or may not appear as a satiation effect with respect to a good. To investigate the relationship, consider the simple case of a two-characteristic model, in which one

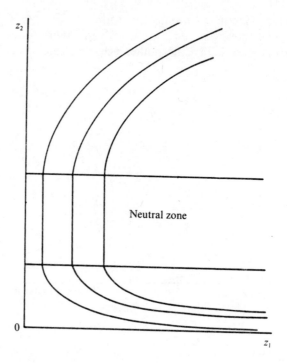

Figure 4.3

characteristic is subject to either open or closed satiation with respect to the consumer(s) in question. The other characteristic is assumed to be non-satiable. We shall consider a world of two goods, both of which possess both characteristics.

Figure 4.4 shows an illustration of the open satiation case. Figure 4.4(a) is drawn in C-space, with characteristics z_1 and z_2 measured along the axes. Characteristic z_2 is subject to open satiation at level $\bar{z}_2$. Rays OG_1, OG_2 represent the proportions in which the two characteristics are contained in goods G_1, G_2.

If we transform the diagram into G-space (hinging OG_1 and OG_2 about O until they are perpendicular), we obtain Figure 4.4(b). The sections of indifference curves (like FG) which are vertical in C-space have a negative slope in G-space, so that there is no satiation with respect to either of the goods. However, since the indifference curves for collections of goods which give amounts of z_2 above the satiation level are straight lines, choice subject to the typical budget constraint will give a *corner solution* in this region, either G_1 alone or G_2 alone, unless the budget line has exactly the same slope as FG.

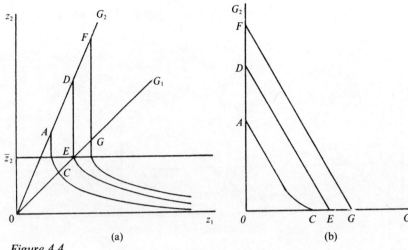

Figure 4.4

In the satiation region, we could predict which of the goods G_1 or G_2 would be chosen *without reference to* z_2. In the G-space diagram, point F (G_2 only) would be chosen if the budget line passed through F and some point on the G_1 axis to the left of G, such as E. Reference back to Figure 4.4(a) shows that F has more z_1 than does E. Similarly, if the budget line sloped from D to G in Figure 4.4(b), the consumer would choose point G, containing more z_1 than point D. Thus a characteristic becomes *irrelevant* in the region of open satiation with respect to it. In the example, all consumer behaviour in the region *beyond DE* in Figure 4.4(b) could be predicted from a knowledge of the content of z_1 in each of the goods and the relative prices.

Open satiation, therefore, does not necessarily lead to any satiation effects (even open satiation) on goods,[15] but it does make a characteristic *operationally irrelevant* in the region of satiation. The characteristic will not, of course, be irrelevant below the satiation level. Thus, assuming all consumers to have approximately the same satiation relation to the characteristic, it may be relevant in a poor society below satiation, but irrelevant in a rich society.

If there is closed satiation with respect to z_2, the situation with respect to goods is quite complex. Representative indifference curves showing three cases are given in Figure 4.5. In Figure 4.5(a), the indifference curve slopes positively above satiation, but with a slope steeper than that of OG_2 inside the attainable cone (defined by OG_2 and OG_1). Transformed into G-space, the portion AB of the indifference curve will have a negative slope, even though the slope is positive in C-space. There will be no satiation effect with respect to goods.

In Figure 4.5(b), the indifference curve is shown straight and parallel to

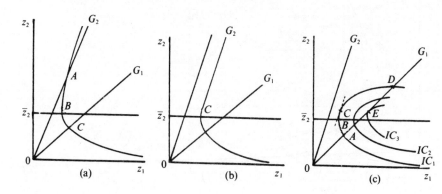

Figure 4.5

OG_2 from the point A. Transformed into G-space, this portion of the indifference curve will be vertical, giving *open satiation* on G_2, but no satiation effects on G_1.

In Figure 4.5(c), the indifference curves slope over enough to cut OG_1. Assuming both goods to have positive prices, any point to the north east of C along IC_1 would be an inefficient choice, since a preferred position (on IC_2) could be obtained with less of both goods. C is the point on IC_1 at which the slope is the same as that of OG_2. In this case, there is a most preferred goods collection (corresponding to the point E) giving satiation of *both* goods in the sense that with no budget constraint of any kind, the consumer would choose only G_1 and that only up to the amount corresponding to the point E. With no budget constraint, the consumer is subject to the *technical* constraint defined by the characteristics content of the two goods. If a new good was introduced with a higher proportion of z_1 to z_2 than G_1 (giving a ray OG_3 lying below OG_1 in Figure 4.5(c)), the consumer's attainable characteristics set would be expanded. Thus a new variant of a class of goods may result in expanded consumption of those goods, although there was satiation with respect to existing goods of that class.

DOMINANCE AND HIERARCHY

The simplest notion of a hierarchical kind that we can apply to characteristics is that of *dominance*. A characteristic is dominant within some group of characteristics, in some set of situations, if the consumer always prefers a collection with more of the dominant characteristic, whatever the amounts of the other characteristics.

Let us return to our diet example. For a starving man, all other characteristics of food may be dominated by calorie content, interest in other nutrients being subordinated to the need to obtain sufficient calories for survival in the short run. An alcoholic may rank wines by their alcohol content alone, irrespective of any other characteristics.

The alcoholic example is often used to illustrate lexicographical ordering. Dominance is a weaker assumption than lexicographical ordering, requiring, in effect, only that all words beginning with A come before all words beginning with B and not worrying about the ordering of words within the A-group. Operationally, dominance is observable, lexicographic ordering only so in rare instances.

Dominance, as in the diet example, may occur only over some region of choice. Consider the nutrition model, for we can illustrate many effects in it. Suppose that food has only two characteristics, calories and flavour.[16] A consumer is assumed to be given all non-food items in fixed quantities so that his choice context is confined to food.

We shall assume the following to be true of the characteristics-consumer relationship in this case:

1. at very low calorie levels, calories are dominant;
2. at medium calorie levels, flavour is relevant;
3. there is a neutral zone with respect to calories – open satiation at one level, followed by closed satiation at a higher level;
4. flavour is non-satiable.

An indifference map expressing the above properties would look like that in Figure 4.6. The lowest indifference curves would be horizontal (calories dominant), while higher ones would have a vertical segment (open satiation in the neutral zone) turning into a positive sloped segment (closed satiation).

If there were only two goods, G_2 having the higher ratio of calories to flavour, and the consumer faced a regular linear budget constraint, his choice would be determined in the following way:

1. At very low income levels, he would be interested only in obtaining the most calories for his money. This would be determined from the calorie content of the two goods and their relative prices. Note that he would *not* necessarily consume G_2, with the highest calorie/flavour ratio. He would consume the more flavoursome G_1 if that happened to have the highest calorie/outlay ratio at the market prices.[17]

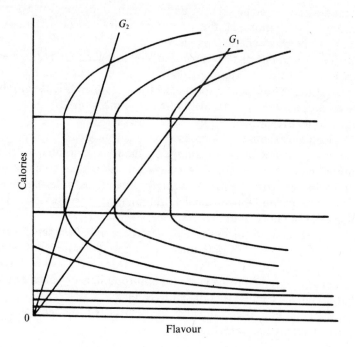

Figure 4.6

2. In the next income bracket, calories and flavour both count, and the content of both characteristics in both goods needs to be known.
3. The next income bracket covers the neutral zone, with calories subject to open satiation. In effect, flavour is a dominant characteristic[18] here and choice will be decided by the flavour/outlay ratio.
4. Finally, both characteristics count once more at high income levels, with calories regarded negatively.

Thus, in a single simple example, we see how the set of operationally relevant characteristics is reduced from two to one (a different one each time) at different income levels, while both characteristics are relevant (although one is first desirable then undesirable) at other income levels.

CONCLUSION

This chapter has given a brief glimpse of the kind of ways in which the very large number of potentially relevant characteristics in some situations involving consumer choice can be reduced to a much smaller number of *operationally relevant* characteristics. Part of the reduction can be made by considering *technical* (goods–characteristics) relationships, such as invariance and redundance. Further reduction is possible by using *human* (goods–people) relationships, such as dominance and satiation.

As far as technical relationships are concerned, the relevant set may change with the introduction of a new good, but does not depend on the group of consumers involved. Human criteria do, of course, depend on the consumer group. Thus the calorie content of food may be the dominant characteristic in a starving African society and, negatively, in a wealthy American society, while being irrelevant in a moderate-income European society.

The simple outline of ideas given here can be expanded very greatly. The idea of dominance can be extended to cover a *group* of characteristics which are the only relevant characteristics at low income levels. We could investigate social lag phenomena which occur as consumers move out of a region in which dominance by a group of 'basic' characteristics ceases, but awareness of other characteristics is not yet developed.

Like any economic model, however, the characteristics model of consumer behaviour is designed to simplify reality. Fitting it to any given situation ultimately involves some art as well as science. The aim of the essay has been to provide some guide to the artist, as well as analysis for the scientist.

NOTES

1. Originally published in Peston, M. and B. Corry, (eds) (1972), *Essays in Honour of Lord Robbins.*, London: Weidenfeld and Nicolson.
2. See Chapter 2.
3. Motor cars represent a group of differentiated products with a large number of observable characteristics which have been measured by various testing organizations and which can also be assumed to be known to consumers. Unfortunately, a motor car is a 'one-shot' capital purchase, to which the simple budget constraint is not applicable in defining the choice situation.
4. If we are concerned with the simple linear model, the chosen parameter must be one having the requisite linear property. For a diet choice, the appropriate parameter would be weight or volume, since nutrients will vary linearly with these. In this case, we would probably aggregate almost identical foods by weight and use a weight unit of measure. That is, instead of regarding 2in and 3in diameter apples as different goods, we would presumably just consider pounds of apples.
5. Menger (1950). Note that these and similar hypotheses by other writers are eminently testable!
6. See Georgescu-Roegen (1966).
7. See Paroush (1965).
8. Jevons (1924), p. 54.
9. The implied Victorian moral judgement, that wants satisfied at higher income levels after more basic needs have been met are (higher), is not essential to the argument.

10. See, for example, Debreu (1959), p. 55. Non-satiation in this context means the consumer always prefers more of at least one of the goods.
11. It is built in to the formal proofs of existence of equilibrium, but can be relaxed to require only that there be no satiation in an attainable state of the economy.
12. Easily extended to any number of characteristics.
13. Use of the weak relationship Z' RZ, rather than the strong relationship $Z'PZ'$ provides for the possibility of a change from open satiation to closed satiation at z_2. If we had $z_1 = z'_1$ and $z'_2 > \bar{z}_2 > z_2$, the preference ordering could not be predicted, of course, without an exact preference map.
14. See Stigler (1945).
15. Open satiation may occur, however, if a good contains no characteristic other than the one which is satiable. In such a case, the vertical portion of the indifference curve in C-space is also vertical in G-space.
16. Flavour is not easily measurable (although, in principle, it might be analysed into components and measured) and would not be suitable in a working model. We assume, for the sake of a simple two-characteristic example, that it has the desirable properties of a linear, measurable characteristic.
17. If the calorie/outlay ratio happened to be the same for both goods, he would presumably choose G_1 for more flavour. Thus we would establish lexicographic ordering. We shall, however, work with the simpler notion of dominance that suffices for all but this case.
18. This of course, because there are only two characteristics. With n characteristics, open satiation of one of them does not lead to dominance because there are still $n-1$ characteristics, rather than just one, that must be considered.

5 Hierarchies in goods–characteristics analysis[1]

The problem with which this chapter is concerned is that of narrowing down the set of all characteristics possessed by goods within a group to a smaller subset of *relevant* characteristics, in terms of which the behaviour of consumers with respect to choices over the group can be fully explained.[2] Relevance is of particular importance in the economist's version of the characteristics model, in which the characteristics are, so to speak, looked at from the goods end rather than the consumer's end and thus consist potentially of all the physical, chemical, biological and other objective properties of the goods. This view was stressed in the original model of Lancaster (1966) and again, more recently, in Ratchford (1975). Behavioural models, looking at characteristics from the consumer end, have generally preselected the apparently relevant characteristics, but may ignore the taken-for-granted properties.

It is worth emphasizing at this point that the economist has always taken a holistic view of the consumer as a decision-maker with a unified overall objective (maximization of utility, or attainment of a preferred state), so that all his decisions should be considered to be interconnected. Both this view and the most common behavioural view of the consumer as fragmented into a complex of more or less independent decision-making particles are obvious oversimplifications, but they are oversimplified from quite different directions. Thus the economist does not take it for granted that a particular group of goods can be separated off and consumer behaviour with respect to the group be analysed without reference to events outside the group, but considers it necessary to specify what special structural properties enable this separation to be made.

Goods may be separated into distinct groups on the basis of horizontal properties. Goods in two groups may, for example, possess the same essential characteristics but may be clustered so that the relative contents of different characteristics are comparatively close within each group, but widely different between groups (sports cars and estate cars, for example). Our main interest here, however, is in vertical separation. This does not mean that the groups themselves are conceived of as standing in a vertical or hierarchical relationship, but that the separation between the groups can be established prior to any detailed investigation of the properties of the group.

UTILITY TREES

One property that permits the division of the consumer's overall decision-making process into a series of smaller decisions is that of separability of the utility function. A function $F(x_1, \ldots, x_n)$ is *separable* into s branches if the n variables can be partitioned into s groups and there exist functions $f^r(x^r)$, $r = 1, \ldots, s$, where x^r is the collection of variables assigned to the rth group, such that F can be written in the form

$$F(f^1(x^1), \ldots, f^r(x^r), \ldots, f^s(x^s))$$

Each f^r is called a branch of the function F.

The importance of the separability property, should it be present, is that maximization of utility can be carried out as a consistent two-stage process, in which the consumer first makes an optimal allocation of his budget among groups, then spends that allocation optimally within each group.[3] Note that if the utility function is separable, it is possible that one or more of the branch utility functions f^r may themselves be separable into subbranch utility functions, and that some of these may in turn be further separable (giving us a real 'utility tree'), implying the existence of a consistent multi-stage optimization.

If utility maximization can be regarded as a multi-stage process, the final stage will consist of choice among a restricted group of goods, subject only to the group budget. Effects arising from, say, price changes within another group will be very indirect and will be apparent only in so far as they affect the budget allocation of the group. Thus separability of the utility function would go a long way towards enabling us to analyse the demand for a group of goods in comparative isolation from events outside the group.

The traditional discussions of separability have been in terms of a utility function on goods, with goods as the arguments of both the overall utility function and the branch functions. In the characteristics approach, the utility function is conceived of as a function of characteristics quantities. Now there is no reason why the utility function on characteristics should not be separable, the groups now being groups of characteristics rather than of goods, but the multi-stage optimization property (which is what we are really interested in) no longer follows from separable utility alone.

The problem is that, although the utility function is defined on characteristics, the budget constraint is in terms of goods. Characteristics can only be obtained by buying them as bundles contained in the goods – they cannot be purchased separately. Characteristics which may be separable in the utility function may not be separable in the budget because they are possessed by the same good. Suppose, for example, that there are three characteristics and the utility function is separable into three branches, one for each characteristic. If all goods possess all three characteristics, no division of the optimization process is possible and the separability of the utility function has no operational significance.

The consumption technology $z = \phi(x)$ $x \epsilon \mathbf{R}^n, z \epsilon \mathbf{R}^m$, where z is the vector of characteristics, is strictly separable into k goods groups if there exists a partitioning of both characteristics and goods into k corresponding groups, $C_1 ... C_k$, and $G_1 ... G_k$, respectively, such that $\dfrac{\partial z_i}{\partial x_j} = 0$ whenever i, j are not in the corresponding groups.

It is obviously sufficient for multi-stage optimization in a characteristics model that (a) the utility function on characteristics be separable into groups of characteristics and (b) that the technological relationship between goods and characteristics be such that for every group of characteristics there be a group of goods which possess no characteristics other than those of the associated characteristics group. This requires not only that the consumption technology can be partitioned into groups of goods having characteristics exclusive to the group, but that this partitioning corresponds to the groups of characteristics into which the utility function is separable.

This double requirement on the partitions may seem to be a very strong one, but it is, of course, satisfied implicitly if the utility function *on goods* can in fact be shown to be separable, since the structure of the utility function on goods is a compound of the structure of the utility function on characteristics and the structure of the consumption technology. Stating the properties in terms of characteristics merely reveals how strong a property is that of separability in terms of goods, it does not of itself create the difficulties.

Separability is, of course, a question of fact. Unfortunately there is little in the corpus of empirical work on demand that provides guidance as to whether individuals act as if their utility functions are separable or not. The two most widely used models in econometric demand studies, the 'Rotterdam' and 'Linear Expenditure' models both implicitly assume strong separability of the utility function, along with a variety of other more or less heroic assumptions, and provide no test of any separability hypothesis. The most that can be said is that the assumption of separability (of goods into broad groups) has not been shown to introduce any identifiable problems.[4]

In spite of the lack of any explicit confirmation from broad econometric studies, some kind of separability assumption is implicit in all attempts to study the demand for closely-related goods, whether by economists or by others concerned with consumer research. It is simply taken for granted that we can sensibly study choices within one appropriately chosen group of goods without reference to the details of choice within other groups.

GROUPS

Following through the discussion of separability in the characteristics model, we can see that the separation of certain goods into a group that can be studied in isolation requires an appropriate coincidence between the way in which the utility function can be separated and the way in which the consumption technology can be partitioned. If the partition boundaries coincide exactly, there is no ambiguity about the division into groups. If the partitions coincide only in some cases, then the groups are defined by a kind of highest common factor logic. That is, if C_1 and C_2 are groups of characteristics which are separable in the utility function, but the characteristics from both groups are possessed by all members of some goods group G_1, then we obtain only a single separable group (provided no goods outside G_1 possess these characteristics), not two. Conversely, if goods groups G_1 and G_2 possess no common characteristics, but the characteristics from the groups are not separable in the utility function, then the true separable group is that of the goods in G_1 and G_2 taken together.

Consider, for example, two food characteristics, flavour (taken to be unidimensional for the sake of illustration) and calorie content. It seems reasonable to suppose that flavour, a direct effect on the senses, and calorie content, related to health and personal appearance, impinge on different branches of a separable utility function. Because of their techno-logical jointness in food, however, the separability of the utility function is not the determining influence in the grouping. Or consider a low calorie dinner and an exercise session in the gym, two goods with no objective characteristics in common but which objective characteristics likely to appear in the same branch of the utility function, and thus not in totally separate groups.

In the worst case situation, the utility function may be separable into many groups of goods with their own sets of characteristics, but there may be no coincidences between the divisions and no groups of goods that can be fully separated from each other.

Due to the role played by the structure of the consumption technology in determining groups, grouping may be changed as a result of technologi-cal innovation, either embodied in new goods or arising from newly-discovered information about the properties of existing goods. Air travel, for example, has consolidated the formerly distinct groups, 'visits to

Europe' and 'two week holiday activities' into a single group, by removing the disparity in time required for the two activities. Discovery of the carcinogenic properties of cigarette smoking was equivalent to a change in technology, even though no change occurred in cigarettes themselves, because it introduced a new relevant characteristic. Technological change may divide groups as well as consolidate them, as modern audio technology permits separation of the activity 'listening to a symphony' from that of 'concert going'.

CONSUMER DIVERSITY

The preceding discussion has been confined to the analysis of how separability of an individual utility function, combined with an appropriate structure of the technology, enables that individual to optimize in stages and thus to consider groups in relative isolation from each other. Obviously, the concept of the group is of no real use in the analysis of market behaviour unless the separation into groups has essentially the same pattern over many, if not all, individuals.

The two-part structure of the characteristics model provides a much firmer basis for the existence of groupings which are common to many consumers than does the traditional economic model which sets up utility as a direct and individual function of goods. In the characteristics model, groups can only be separated along partition lines in the technology and only then if utility is separable in a corresponding way. Since the technology is common to all consumers, the grouping for any consumer is built out of the same basic blocks as those for any other consumer. This does not guarantee the existence of groups which are common to all consumers, since the technology may, for example, be partitioned into blocks A, B, and C, with some consumers' utility functions separable in such a way as to give two groups corresponding to $A \cup B$ and C, and others so as to give A and $B \cup C$. In this case, all consumers see a pattern of two groups, but they are not the same two for all. In spite of examples of this kind, it is apparent that the existence of common building blocks each containing many goods does make the existence of common groupings a reasonable hypothesis, strengthened if some of the properties of separation within utility functions are common to all.

Virtually all econometric demand studies that are based on some underlying model of consumer behaviour and not a set of *ad hoc* equations assume that aggregate demand can be treated as if it resulted from the decisions of a single representative consumer. Such models have no place for consumer diversity, which would nullify some of the properties assigned to aggregate demand functions. Taking goods groupings to be common to all consumers is inherent in such analysis, and provides no test of commonality.

We cannot, of course, analyse the fine structure of demand within a group without supposing that consumers are diverse. The hypothetical representative consumer in the demand studies is someone who brushes his teeth with every brand of toothpaste (in proportion to each brand's market share) and thus reveals nothing about choice among kinds of toothpaste. In so far as economists' traditional demand studies are useful at all, it is in the light they can throw on very broad properties of demand in which 'goods' are really aggregate goods or even complete groups rather than individual products. Although these studies are commonly considered micro rather than macro studies, they are really a kind of halfway micro-macro.

Micro-micro demand theory, that can handle product differentiates and not just aggregates like motor cars, can only exist if account is taken of the real diversity that exists between individuals. The more micro the analysis, however, the greater the dependence on the ability to separate groups of goods. If this cannot be done, we are forced to contemplate a model in which a consumer makes a single stage choice over tens of thousands of different products.

Putting all the above aspects together, we see that a feasible analysis of demand at the most micro level really requires:

1. That all, or most, individuals share a common *structure* of prefer-ences, with utility functions separable in the same way over all indivi-duals. Then any groups arising from a coincidence of separability properties in the consumption technology with those of the utility function will be universal groups.
2. But that the individual preferences are diverse within this common structure, so that different individuals allocate different proportions of their budgets to different groups and make different choices within the groups.

Although the assumption of diversity constrained by a universal structure is presupposing a great deal about the human psyche, this assumption has always been implicit in all fine-structure analysis of demand over small groups of products.

INTRAGROUP ANALYSIS

We have now established the conditions which enable us to single out a group of goods and analyse the demand for goods within the group without explicit reference to goods in other groups, confident that this corresponds to the decision structure common to all individuals in the market yet leaves scope for diversity of choices within the group. Analysis of demand over a relatively small group of goods is clearly a much simpler problem than that of analysis over the set of all possible goods, but remains complex. We remain strongly interested in additional structural or other properties that permit further reduction of the problem.

If we take any set of goods likely to emerge as a group for decision-making purposes, and take the characteristics to be the set of all objective properties possessed by goods within the group, it is obvious enough that the potential number of characteristics can be enormous. The number will vary a great deal – if the group is motor cars (or any subset of this), the number of discernible properties is very large, while if the group is non-alcoholic beverages the number will be much smaller. Nevertheless, analysis in terms of characteristics is potentially most useful if the number of characteristics entering the decision process is a small subset of the total number. We shall refer to these as *relevant* characteristics.

Some of the grounds on which characteristics might be rejected as irrelevant on the basis of a priori criteria have been explored in Lancaster (1971). The criteria include universality (characteristics possessed to the same extent by all the goods in the group), invariance of a characteristic, irrelevance of a characteristic through satiation effects, and redundancy of a characteristic always present in fixed proportion to another. In most cases, however, we can expect that there remain a very large number of potentially relevant characteristics even after the maximum possible use of the preceding criteria.

Now consider the group from the other direction, from the viewpoint of the consumer rather than the technology. We all know that we, as human decision-makers, are very limited as to the number of different variables that we can handle at one time. The work of Miller (1956) and others has validated this introspection experimentally, and come up with five to nine as the maximum number. Fishbein (1970) takes the number of salient outcomes considered by the consumer to lie in this range. If the magic number seven be accepted as representing the limits of human decision-making powers, then we must conclude that either goods possess no more than seven relevant characteristics or that decision-making occurs in such a way that not more than seven characteristics are being considered at any one time.

There are studies which have investigated the number of characteristics (or somewhat equivalent concepts) relevant in particular markets at particular times, using a variety of methods including asking the consumers themselves in one way or another, using perceptual maps or principal component analysis, or analysing brand switching data. Our interest here is not in the actual characteristics chosen as relevant in some context, but in the process by which the decision of relevance or non-relevance is reached.

The simplest hypothesis is that of random selection – the consumer simply becomes aware of certain characteristics in a sequential and random way, then closes his mind when he reaches his information processing limit. This does not require diversity of preferences in order to generate different choices, and it implies that the role of advertising is to ensure that a characteristic believed to be a good selling point is made prominent enough to get in before the door closes. Economists would accept such a view of decision-making only if it were proved to be true universally and beyond any shadow of a doubt, because the foundation of all microeconomic policy is that consumer choice represents the attainment of a preferred or optimal situation, given the constraints. The random model could lead to the conclusion that an expert 'consumption consultant' would make a better choice than the consumer himself and, ultimately, that the market economy would lose its best claim to superiority over a command system.

As an economist, the author is strongly biased in favour of a model that involves purposive behaviour at all stages and thus towards a model in which there is a deliberate sequential choice process, each step of the sequence involving an appropriately small number of characteristics.

HIERARCHICAL STRUCTURES

A decision process in which a choice involving a restricted number of parameters is made, after which a further choice is made using another restricted set of parameters, and so on down the sequence, is necessarily hierarchical if it is not random. The ordering of the hierarchy determines which set of parameters is considered first, second, and so on through the sequence.

The early foundation of the 'Austrian' school of value theory was Carl Menger's view of the consumer[5] as satisfying different wants in a hierarchical sequence. As the consumer increased the consumption of a particular good, successive units of the good were used to satisfy 'wants' of decreasing importance to that individual, so that successive units of the good had declining value to him. This is not exactly the kind of hierarchy that we need in the present context, but comes much closer to it if successive wants are thought of as being satisfied by different characteristics of the same good.

A neo-Mengerian model that is directly comparable with the characteristics model is given in Ironmonger (1972).[6] This analysis is cast in terms of wants rather than characteristics, with the effective variable in the utility function being 'units of satisfaction of want i'. This can be regarded as the view from the consumer's end of the amount of characteristic i. Ironmonger's utility function is strictly hierarchical, with wants completely ordered – a lexicographic preference ordering with satiation. The consumer's decision at each stage is confined to that of satiating the next unsatisfied want in the ordering. Interesting results follow from the analysis solely because goods possess joint multiple characteristics, so that concentration on satisfying the single want at a given stage results nevertheless in some incidental satisfaction of lower order wants through this jointness. The multiple characteristics properties of goods generate many results analogous to those in Lancaster (1966, 1971), in spite of the great differences in the assumed structure of preferences.[7]

Two aspects of the Ironmonger model seem to rule it out as far too extreme for our present purposes – its totally hierarchical structure and its assumption that only one characteristic at a time is under consideration. A fully hierarchical preference ordering would imply that a consumer would never think about clothes until after he had eaten, while separable but non-hierarchical preferences would imply merely that the consumer could think about clothing without thinking about eating and vice versa. The latter seems to be closer to reality.

The utility model that best fits the reality of limited information processing ability and the various criteria for the microanalysis of demand, together with the property that choice reveals preference, is one with a mixed structure. It should be separable in the same general way for all individuals, with no hierarchical relationships between the groups. Within the groups, however, there should be some hierarchical structure so that the final decisions can be made in several stages, each involving a relatively small number of characteristics.

Consider a potential scenario for choosing a motor car, assuming that separability properties between groups have already enabled this choice to be made without reference to goods other than cars themselves. Stage one might consist of assessing the characteristics associated with whether the car actually runs at all – does the engine work? The wheels turn? Cars which do not pass this stage will not be chosen, whatever their other characteristics (repair is assumed impossible). Stage two might consist of considering those characteristics that make the car suitable for family use: How many will it seat? How much baggage space? Finally, stage three might consist of comparing details in aesthetics, convenience, comfort, mechanical operation, and so on.

This scenario illustrates the main features that would have to be taken into account in devising a multi-stage decision model, which we can summarize as follows:

1. How many stages are there, and is some decision about the number of stages itself a first stage of the process?
2. What determines the ordering of the stages, and is the determination of the ordering also part of the decision process?
3. What kind of decision is made at each stage? Simply accept/not accept, or assignment of some weight or subutility?

Once again, the special interest of the economist in the consumer as a whole needs to be stressed. It would be difficult to gain acceptance for an *ad hoc* model of a limited decision process that implied something about the consumer's overall preference structure or utility function that was very different from that usually assumed in economics. To gain such acceptance, it would have to be shown compellingly that the truth and generality of the model justified scrapping accepted economic assumptions.

We should distinguish between the technique and the substance of the decision-making process. Only the latter affects the fundamental structure of the implied utility function. The number of stages, for example, is not important of itself, but the kind of decision made at each stage can have a fundamental bearing on the implied preference ordering.

Consider the pass/fail kind of decision implied in stage one of the scenario given above, in which a subset of characteristics is checked against a minimum acceptable level and the good is not considered further unless it passes on all counts. If this is followed by an optimizing choice over all those goods which have passed, the implied preference ordering is incomplete because goods which fail the first test are not further considered and so not ranked with respect to each other. But the final choice is unambiguously preferred because it is the preferred choice from the final set, all members of which are preferred to any goods which failed the screening. Thus a stage with simple pass/fail criteria can be consistent with full optimization.

Stage two in the example given might be taken as representative of a more sophisticated type of pass/fail decision. Instead of a series of characteristics which must *all* pass the acceptable level, the various characteristics can be seen as jointly contributing to some index of suitability for family transport. A car passes this stage if the index has at least some minimum acceptable value. Again, provided the final stage is a pure maximization stage, the final choice is a true preferred position. Problems of both completeness and continuity can be introduced, however.

Sequential sorting processes have been suggested as appropriate models for market research purposes[8] and so have various models based on threshold effects. For market research purposes, determining which characteristics are taken into account in which stage is, of course, of the highest importance. For our more general approach, it is important only that an individual be consistent in the structure of his decisions. If the group is well defined, the number and specification of the decision stages can be taken to be an individual matter, contributing to the assumed diversity of preferences over the population. A general and universal theory of the order of sorting is not necessary.

In the screening mode, only the last decision stage is a true maximizing stage. In the stage, the consumer is presumed to choose his preferred collection of those characteristics left to this stage from among those goods whose other characteristics have sufficed to pass the previous screening. This process is that of maximizing a (branch) utility function of certain characteristics, subject to minimum values of other characteristics (or other branch utilities).

Although the screening model has many attractions, has been used as the basis for market behaviour models, and can be made to fit in reasonably well with the most important assumptions on preferences usually made by economists, it has some problematic features. One is that levels of screening characteristics above the minimum fail to count in the final decision. If a car is *especially* suitable as a family car, it would seem reasonable that this should count in the final decision.

One potential modification of the screening model is to introduce some amount of carry over, where properties above the minimum in one stage are weighted together with the next stage characteristics. If above minimum amounts of individual characteristics are carried forward at each stage, the purpose of multi-stage decision-making – to limit the number of variables considered at each stage – may be lost. However, the level of some index or subutility might be carried forward and still achieve reduction of variables.

Why not carry forward the whole value of the early stage indices, so that the final decision is a maximization of a function of indices, subject to minimum levels of specific ones? This could be done on the basis of separability of the utility function alone, and would preserve most of the properties liked by economists. But, although it reduces the number of characteristics considered at any one time (since the making of each index is a separate operation), it does not reduce the number of goods – all goods in the group would be considered together in the final judgement. Some elements of a goods screening process should be preserved.

NOTES

1. Originally published in *Recent Advances in Consumer Research*, Volume 5, Association for Consumer Research, 1977.
2. See Lancaster (1971). A somewhat related concept is that of 'salience' in Fishbein (1971).
3. See Strotz (1957). Blackorby *et al.* (1970) established that the Leontief (weak) separability given above was sufficient.
4. See Brown and Deaton (1972) or Phlips (1974).
5. Menger (1871, 1981).
6. Although published several years after the author's 1966 paper, Ironmonger's work was developed independently and was based on his 1961 dissertation.
7. The Lancaster analysis assumes simultaneous rather than sequential effects.
8. See Herniter (1974).

6   The measurement of changes in quality[1]

Although there had been some study of the problem of measuring quality change prior to 1961, the modern work on the problem can be considered to date from the papers by Adelman and Griliches, and by Griliches, published in that year. In the succeeding years, a considerable body of work on the subject has been developed.[2] An important share of this work was carried out, or commissioned, by the Price Statistics Committee of the Federal Reserve Board, and the general emphasis of much of the work has been towards developing methods for *adjusting for* quality change in cost-of-living indexes, rather than towards measuring quality changes as such. Most of the earlier work was concerned with practical problems of econometrics within a relatively simple theoretical framework, but later contributions, especially Fisher and Shell (1967) and Muellbauer (1974), have probed more deeply into the theoretical foundations.

The purpose of this chapter is to investigate the problem of measuring quality change as an objective in itself, not specifically related to such other problems as that of developing a 'true' cost-of-living index. The author proposes to pursue his normal role as a theorist, concerning himself with keeping everyone honest by pointing out all the difficulties while trying to give some judgement as to the practicality of those techniques which appear to have a firm conceptual basis.

WHAT IS MEANT BY 'MEASURING' QUALITY?

We shall take the initial step of assuming that the ordering of comparable varieties of goods in terms of quality is a well-defined operation for an individual consumer, who can unambiguously rank one variety as of higher or lower quality than another. However, we can also presume that an individual would be unable to answer the question: by how much is the quality of one variety greater than that of the other? And thus must regard perceived quality as inherently ordinal, providing no natural basis for a measure. Any numbers we choose to associate with quality or quality change must correctly represent the quality ordering, whenever that ordering is well defined, but the cardinal significance of the numbers can be chosen to be a measure of anything that has the same ordering as quality. It is the purpose of this Chapter to examine the possibilities for such a measure, some obvious candidates being the prices that would be paid for goods of different quality when all were available at the same time, the amount of a lower quality good considered to be 'as good as' a unit of the higher quality good, and some index number of the quantities of the various characteristics of the goods.

What about quality as quantity, the simple repackaging case? If a box of biscuits or a bar of chocolate contains 10 per cent less content this year than last, it has been the practice among economists to refer to this as a quality change. If the term is appropriate, the quality change would be truly measurable. But it would seem likely that a hypothetical consumer would regard the change, correctly enough, as a mere change in the quantity units, having nothing to do with quality in the proper sense.[3]

Thus we conclude that quality is an ordinal concept with no inherent cardinality, and the terms 'measuring quality' or 'measuring quality change' refer to the construction of some numerical index with the following properties:

1.   that it correctly *ranks* goods varieties in terms of quality whenever an unambiguous ranking exists,
2.   that it *measures* something well-defined and useful in the context to which the index is applied.

From these considerations it is clear that there may be many indexes which rank quality, each of which measures something different and is applicable to its own special use.

INDEXES OF RELATIVE QUALITY I: DIVISIBLE GOODS

Before attempting to tackle quality *change* which most often occurs in some context in which goods available in one period are replaced by goods of different specification in the next period, we shall first investigate the conceptually simpler problem of assigning quality indexes to different varieties of a good when all varieties are available simultaneously. In the simultaneous case, the market forces consumers (and producers) to compare the varieties with each other under circumstances which directly affect choice and do not involve hypothetical comparisons or possible preference changes.

We shall carry out all analysis in this chapter in terms of characteristics,[4] assuming that the objects of consumer preference are collections of characteristics and that goods are purchased only to provide characteristics and not for their own sake. We shall also assume that the goods between which quality comparisons are made are members of a separable group,[5] sharing none of their characteristics with members of any other

group, and that the relevant utility functions are separable in the characteristics of the group.

If consumers have identical preferences and identical income levels, and
if the goods in the group have a clearly identifiable natural unit common
to all the goods (such as a gram or a litre), then we can take identical
qualities of all the goods and see how the characteristics collections
associated with various goods are ranked in terms of preference. This
ranking gives the quality ranking.

Even in this highly-simplified context, problems arise. One is that the
quality rankings need not be independent of the quantities chosen for the
comparison, unless either preferences are homothetic or higher-quality
goods do not ever have less of any characteristic per unit than do lower-
quality goods.

Let us assume homotheticity and identical preferences (identical
incomes are not required) so that there is a universally agreed quality
ranking, and concentrate on the construction of a suitable numerical
index. Since the goods are divisible, the most obvious index is one based
on the relative quantities of the various goods required to attain the same
utility level as some specified amount of any one of the goods chosen as
numeraire. The inverse of these quantities would give an appropriate
index, and we can call such a measure a *quality-equivalent* index.

For uniform homothetic preferences, a quantity-equivalent index of
quality has the following properties, all desirable:

1. Its quality ranking will coincide with the true and unambiguous
    ranking.
2. It will be independent of the amount of the numeraire good chosen.
3. Recomputation of the index to make the value for a non-numeraire
    good equal to 100 will give the same results as would making this
    good the new numeraire.
4. The value of the index depends only on the technical properties of the
    goods and the shape of any one indifference curve, and is independent
    of the properties of the market.
5. For goods having all characteristics in the same proportions, the value
    of the index will coincide with that obtained by treating the difference
    between the goods as due to simple repackaging.

Note that, although the quantity-equivalent index is independent of
market conditions, the market will reflect the content of the index. Under
the circumstances assumed above (uniform homothetic preferences), the
relative prices of the goods must be directly proportional to their quality
indices[6] if all goods are available simultaneously and are all actually

purchased, provided the goods are not used in combination. If the goods are combined, the relative costs of the combinations must reflect the qualities of the combinations but the prices of individual goods need not reflect their quality indices.

If preferences are not uniform or homothetic, a quantity-equivalent index can be constructed for a reference group of consumers at a specific income level. The index will not be relevant to other consumer groups, and even the quality ranking may not hold outside the reference group.

As a practical matter, we cannot really expect to possess information as to the exact shape of the typical indifference curve (or surface) of the reference group. It is more reasonable to expect that we can isolate and measure the leading characteristics of the goods, so an obvious alternative to a true quantity-equivalent index would be some kind of fixed weight index number of quantities of characteristics, constructed in the same way a quantity index of a bundle of goods is constructed. If we were to construct such an index, how would its properties compare with those of the quantity-equivalent index?

The essential difference between the true quantity-equivalent index and a fixed weight index number is that the latter takes as equivalent all combinations of characteristics corresponding to points on the same hyperplane, the former combinations corresponding to points on the same indifference surface. It is obvious that, if preferences are strictly convex, the fixed weight number will *overstate* the quality of all goods except that corresponding to the point of tangency between the index hyperplane and an indifference surface, as compared with the quantity-equivalent index. It is easy to construct examples in which the *ranking* of goods in terms of quality is not even the same in the two cases. The degree of divergence between the two measures will increase with increased convexity of the indifference surface and with increased dispersion of the characteristics proportions of the goods in the group.

The slope of the index hyperplane is, of course, determined by the choice of weights for the index, these in turn being shadow prices allocated to the various characteristics.[7] If the characteristics proportions of the various goods are clustered together and/or the indifference surface has little curvature, the fixed weight index will be relatively close to the true quantity-equivalent index if the slope of the index hyperplane is close to the slope of the indifference surface for a good somewhat near the centre of the cluster. In this case, it is clearly worthwhile attempting to obtain the best possible estimates for the true shadow prices on characteristics, in order to use these for the weights. But if there is likely to be considerable divergence between the fixed weight index and the true index, we can only regard the former as a roughly approximate measure and undue concern with estimating shadow prices is not only a waste of resources but tends to give a spurious impression of accuracy in the final index.

INDEXES OF RELATIVE QUALITY II: NON-DIVISIBLE GOODS

Historically, most of the attempts to measure or adjust for quality differences have been carried out on such essentially indivisible goods as motor cars and refrigerators. There are no problems in determining appropriate units for such goods, but we cannot compare different quantities of different goods as in constructing a quantity-equivalent index.

Banking goods in terms of quality presents no more and no less of a problem than in the divisible goods case – if anything, perhaps less, since we will always compare single units and problems of combinability do not arise. A good ranks higher in quality than another if the characteristics collection associated with a unit of the good is preferred to the collection associated with the other, at least by the reference consumer group. We can presume that a Mercedes would be ranked higher in quality than a Volkswagen, but can we associate a numerical index with the quality that conveys any useful information other than the relative ranking?

Since one consumer can use only one car at a time, the characteristics of six Volkswagens are not markedly different from those of one except for increased reliability (they will surely not all fail to start at the same time) and durability, although the ability to provide cars for the family and friends may provide increased utility. Thus someone who really likes the characteristics mix of a Mercedes may prefer one to 20 Volkswagens without implying that he considered the Mercedes to have at least 20 times as much 'quality'.[8]

One way of attempting to solve the indivisibility problem is to introduce hypothetical divisibility. In the Mercedes–Volkswagen example, we take the Volkswagen as quality numeraire and consider a hypothetical good having its characteristics in the same *proportions* as the Mercedes, but at a scale that makes the consumer indifferent between this hypothetical good (a 'Merc-wagen') and the Volkswagen. The ratio of the characteristics of the Mercedes to those of the Merc-wagen is then a potential quality index, which we shall call a *hypothetical quantity-equivalent index*.[9]

Since the comparison on which the hypothetical quantity-equivalent index is based does not correspond to any real choice situation, no real meaning can be ascribed to the numerical value of the index, as opposed to the implied ordering. In particular, there is no reason why the numerical values should be reflected by the market under any circumstances. Let us suppose, purely for the sake of illustration, that a standard Mercedes contains 1.8 times as much of every characteristic as a hypothetical Merc-wagen with characteristics in the same proportions as the Mercedes but which would be ranked equivalent to the Volkswagen. The only market predictions we could make are that *if* the Merc-wagen actually existed, it would have to sell at the same price as the Volkswagen (and then only if there were uniform preferences over all consumers), and that the Mercedes must sell for a higher price than the Volkswagen. The Mercedes might actually sell at a price 20 per cent higher than that of a Volkswagen or it might sell at ten times the price, either being consistent with the sale of both cars and with uniform preferences. There is absolutely no reason for expecting the price ratio to be 1.8, the numerical value of the quality index.

The lack of relationship between market price ratios and the value of the hypothetical quantity-equivalent index is, of course, due to the necessity of comparing good at different expenditure levels for the group under study (e.g., motor cars) and thus involving comparison with expenditure alternatives outside the group. A consumer will be indifferent between a Volkswagen at £6000 and a Mercedes at £15,000 if and only if he is indifferent between a Volkswagen plus £(Y-6000) of other things and Mercedes plus £(Y-15,000) of other things, where Y is his total budget. He may well be indifferent between these two collections even though the quality index of the Mercedes is only 1.8 times that of the Volkswagen on a hypothetical quantity-of-characteristics comparison. It all depends on how he rates the enjoyment of other things as against more quality in a car. Separability of his utility function is not sufficient to avoid this comparison with expenditures outside the group.

We might try to construct an *expenditure-equivalent* index[10] of quality by conducting the following imaginary experiment. Take a particular consumer with a given budget, choose a specific car as numeraire (say, a Volkswagen), and take the price of the Volkswagen and of all goods except other cars as given. The consumer is now asked to buy a Volkswagen, spend the rest of his budget optimally, and note his preference level. We then ask him to return to scratch and calculate how much he would be willing to pay for a Mercedes (or any other variety of car) in place of the Volkswagen under the following conditions:

1. His total budget is to be the same as before.
2. He is to achieve the same level of preference as before after optimal allocation of the remainder of his budget.

With normal assumptions on preferences there will be, in principle, a unique solution for every type of car which, when divided by the price of the numeraire, will give our expenditure-equivalent index. This index will obviously conform to the true quality ranking and the numbers convey information relevant to a real choice situation. As with the quantity-equivalent index, the numbers are applicable only to a particular consumer or group of consumers with identical preferences and may depend on the choice of numeraire. In this case the index depends, in addition, on the budget level chosen, the price of the numeraire good and the prices of all other goods except non-numeraire members of the group of goods being indexed.

INDEXES OF QUALITY CHANGE

Constructing an index of quality change involves the same problems as constructing an index of relative quality, with the addition of problems from two new areas of difficulty. The first is that the new and old goods may not be (and typically are not) available simultaneously, so that comparisons are hypothetical and not real. The second is that preferences, incomes and prices may change at the same time as the specifications of the goods.

Complications due to preference changes will not be taken up in this chapter,[11] since these present the same kind of problem whether there is quality change or not, so we will assume that each consumer maintains the same preferences over the period in which quality change is being investigated. Since we are taking preferences to be defined over characteristics collections, the introduction of new goods varieties does not require new preferences.

In the case of divisible goods, quality change with constant preferences can be handled in essentially the same way as relative quality. Even if the old variety of a good is replaced by a new variety, so that the two varieties are not available at the same time, we can reconstruct the characteristics collection that would have been provided by the old good at the time the new good is available and construct a quantity-equivalent index of the new good in terms of the old, from which we directly obtain the quality change as measured in a well-defined way. In most contexts in which we are likely to wish to measure quality change over a short period, we will be comparing new and old models or varieties of what would be identified as essentially the same good. This implies that we are making comparisons between new and old varieties having similar characteristics proportions and thus that a fixed-weight index of characteristics with appropriate weights will be a close approximation to the true quantity-equivalent index.

With indivisibility, we can base an index of quality change on either the hypothetical quality-equivalent index or the expenditure-equivalent index. In discussing relative quality, we showed that these indexes will be different in general, and that only the expenditure-equivalent index corresponds to a real choice situation or is likely to be reflected by the market. For measuring quality *change*, however, the potential gap between the two indexes in both numerical values and operational foundations is considerably reduced for several reasons.

In the standard context of model replacement, the comparisons between old and new models will be hypothetical in any case, reducing the operational realism of the expenditure-equivalent index. In addition, the dependence of this index on prices in general requires that adjustments be made for price changes among goods outside the group, giving another hypothetical comparison. On the other hand, if the quality change being assessed is that between successive models of the 'same' car (or other typical nondivisible good), the changes in both the characteristics proportions *and* the absolute quantities of characteristics will be relatively small. Under these circumstances, the marginal rate of substitution between a fixed-weight aggregate or characteristics of goods in the quality-changing group and an aggregate of other characteristics can be taken to be constant. Thus for small quality changes of this kind, the expenditure-equivalent index, the hypothetical quantity-equivalent index, and the fixed-weight characteristics index will be approximately equal, all three converging as the quality change becomes sufficiently small.

To prove this last statement, consider a model of consumption that satisfies the conditions of our analysis, namely that the set of goods for which we are indexing quality forms a separable group. This requires that the characteristics of the group are not possessed by any goods outside the group and that the utility function is separable. We shall write the latter in the form

$$U = U[u(z), v(Z)]$$

where z is the m-vector of characteristics possessed by goods within the group and Z is the scalar representing the aggregate of characteristics from other goods, relative prices being constant outside the group. We shall suppose other goods to be normalized with respect to prices, so that the cost of the unit aggregate is unity.

First consider the expenditure-equivalent index. Initially, the consumer is constrained to consume one unit of the indivisible group good with specification $z = b$, for which he must pay P. His utility is then given by

$$U = U[u(b), v(Y - P)]$$

where Y is his total budget. This is fully determined, given that the aggregate Z is already optimal over the prices of non-group goods, and no optimization is involved.

Now suppose the specification of the group good is changed to $z = b + db$, with the expenditure on the good changed to $P + dP$, where dP is to be chosen so as to leave utility unchanged. We have

$$dU = U_1 \Sigma u_i db_i - U_2 v' dP = 0$$

giving

$$dP = \frac{U_1}{U_2 v'} \Sigma u_i db_i$$

The measure of quality change in terms of the expenditure-equivalent index is given by dP/P. To complete our analysis, we need to express P in terms of the same parameters as dP. This can be done by finding the set of shadow prices on characteristics such that, if the consumer was charged these shadow prices and given a budget P for buying characteristics within the group, he would buy exactly the collection of characteristics given by $z = b$. If we denote the vector of these shadow prices by y, they must be such as to give the solution $z = b$, $yz = P$, to the problem:

$$\max U[u(z), v(Z)], \text{ subject to } yz + Z = Y$$

The first order conditions of the optimization give

$$U_1 u_i = \lambda y_i \quad i = 1, \ldots, m$$
$$U_2 v' = \lambda$$

so that $y_i = U_1 u_i / U_2 v'$. Substituting in $yb = P$, we obtain

$$P = \frac{U_1}{U_2 v'} \Sigma u_i b_i$$

and the expenditure-equivalent index of quality change is given by:

$$\frac{dP}{P} = \frac{\Sigma u_i db_i}{\Sigma u_i b_i}$$

Now let us turn to calculation of the hypothetical quantity-equivalent index. We shall make the comparison between the old variety with specification $z = b$ and a hypothetical variety with specification $z = (1 + d\beta)b$, where $d\beta$ is a scalar chosen so that the utility is the same with the hypothetical good as the actual new variety of specification $z = b + db$. If u is the original utility (in the group) and $u + du$ the utility after the quality change, we must have, du (actual) $= du$ (hypothetical), that is $\Sigma u_i db_i = d\beta \Sigma u_i b_i$

The measure of quality change in terms of the hypothetical quantity-equivalent index is given by the value of $d\beta$, that is, by the expression $\dfrac{\Sigma u_i db_i}{\Sigma u_i b_i}$ which is identical with the value given by the expenditure-equivalent index.

Finally, we note that the expression for the measure of quality change is identical with that given by a fixed-weight index of characteristics with weights proportional to the u_i's, giving the third equivalent measure.

Thus an unambiguous measure of quality change, in the sense of a number which has the same value in all three potential indexes, ranks the qualities correctly, and can be given an operational meaning, under the following conditions:

1. The change in characteristics per unit of the good should be small (but characteristics need not change in the same ratio).
2. We are concerned with a single good which changes in specification and which is consumed by itself without co-operating inputs or combinations with other goods.
3. The good belongs to a separable group, one that is separable both in terms of the consumption technology (having no characteristics also possessed by goods outside the group) and the utility function.[12]
4. The quality change is measured from the point of view of a single consumer (or a group of consumers with identical preferences) whose tastes and income do not change.
5. The prices of goods outside the group do not change, nor is there quality change anywhere except for the good under investigation.

Condition 1 is not unduly restrictive for measuring typical year-to-year changes, but implies that long-period changes should be estimated by chaining and not by constant base-period weights. Condition 5 is the most certain to be violated, since it will be normal to expect price and/or quality changes over many goods in a typical year-to-year comparison. The problems are similar to those encountered in many other contexts in which one change is to be measured when many are taking place. If all changes are small and cross-effects can be neglected, the individual contributions to the total change can be treated as additive – otherwise, as in mixed price-quantity changes, there is no 'true' measure of the individual components.

The remaining conditions are technical. Condition 3 is simply a tighter version of the structure we implicitly assume in our ordinary consumption decisions while 2 and 4 are concerned with definitional context of our measurement.

THE QUALITY OF WHAT?

So far, we have concerned ourselves with the measurement of quality change for a well-defined single good with reference to a well-defined consumer or consumer single group, and implicitly assumed that the good was not used in combination with other goods or inputs. We shall now explore some of the problems which arise when we relax these assumptions.

Consider the case of two divisible and linearly combinable goods in the same group which are consumed in combination by the reference consumer, the vectors of characteristics per unit for the goods being b_1, b_2. These are consumed in a linear combination with quantities km_1, $(1-k)m_2$, where m_1 is the budget for the group divided by the price of the ith good, so that the characteristics combination is given by

$$z = km_1b_1 + (1-k)m_2b_2$$

Now suppose that there is a quality change in the first good only, its unit specification becoming $b_1 + db_1$. The measure of quality change for the good in isolation will be given by wdb_1/wb_1, where w is the vector of appropriate shadow prices, while the measure of quality change for the combination of goods will be given by $wdb_1/w < b_1 + \{[(1-k)m_2]/km_1\}b_2)$, smaller than the former expression so long as $k < 1$.

Which is the appropriate measure, the quality change for the good treated as if it were consumed in isolation (a hypothetical comparison) or considered in combination (a real comparison)? It will depend on the context in which the measure of quality change is to be used. If, for example, the measure is to be used to adjust a price index for quality change, the single-good value will be appropriate if the price index is based on single-good prices, the combination value if the price index is based on composite prices of goods combinations.

A kind of inverse problem arises in the common practice of setting out to measure the quality change of, say, motor cars as a group, rather than the quality change in a particular car.[13] In this case we are making comparisons between combinations of goods, although they are consumed separately. The only justification for aggregation would seem to be on an implicit assumption that the 'true' quality change measures are really the same for all cars, and that averaging is used to minimize purely statistical errors.

A deeper problem arises when the good in which we are interested requires co-operating inputs of a kind that breaks down the assumption of separability. One of the more interesting cases falling into this classification is the need for time as an input from the consumer, so that use of the particular good is doubly linked to the rest of his consumption, through both time expenditure and money expenditure.

If time is needed for the use of an indivisible good, like a car, and if a change in specifications does not affect either the time per unit of 'use' or the intensity of utilization,[14] the preceding analysis holds unchanged and we can construct an expenditure-equivalent index in the standard way. But if the change affects time per unit of utilization (greater reliability may reduce the ratio of total time devoted to the car to time spent in use of the car for its desired purpose), or the degree of use (the car may be easier to drive, leading to more driving per year), there is a reduction in time available for other consumption activities. This may make the original collection of characteristics from goods other than cars no longer optimal, and perhaps even technically infeasible, contrary to the assumptions underlying the expenditure-equivalent index.

Let us simplify the problem somewhat by assuming that the primary variable use of time, other than time consumed by activities involving goods in the special group, is in pure leisure which is a single-characteristic good requiring no co-operating inputs. Then any variation in time required for goods in the group is reflected in changes in leisure time only and not in the mix of other characteristics. We shall suppose, as before, that the group is separable with respect to all characteristics other than time. Now let us consider the expenditure-equivalent index for a quality change involving time as well as other characteristics.

For an initial specification $z = b$, $t = t$ of a good sold at price P, utility is given by $U = U[u(z,t),v(Y-P,T-t)]$ where Y is income and T the time available for use of the group good plus leisure. If the specification of the good changes to $b+db, t+dt$ and the price of the good is adjusted to $P+dP$, chosen to leave U unchanged, we obtain:

$$dP = \frac{U_1}{U_2 v_1}(\Sigma u_i db_i + u_t dt) - \frac{v_2}{v_1}dt$$

Note that dP differs from a shadow-price weighted sum of characteristics (including time use) changes by the term $-(v_2/v_1)dt$. This last term represents the marginal valuation of leisure in terms of goods outside the group and can be taken to be the wage rate in typical situations. This suggests that the appropriate index for measuring quality change is not the plain expenditure-equivalent index but an index based on an augmented expenditure concept defined by $\bar{P} = P + wt$, where w is the wage rate and t the time devoted to activities using goods in the group. ($\bar{P}$ corresponds to the 'full price' in the sense of Becker (1965)).

So long as we can assume that $w = v_2/v_1$, it is easy to proceed along the lines of the preceding section analysis and show that

$$\frac{d\bar{P}}{\bar{P}} = \frac{\Sigma u_i db_1 + u_t dt}{\Sigma u_i b_i + u_i t}$$

Thus the augmented expenditure-equivalent index gives the same measure of quality change as the hypothetical quantity-equivalent index and the fixed-weight characteristics index, both with time use included among the characteristics. Clearly it is the augmented expenditure-equivalent index and not the standard expenditure-equivalent index which is the appropriate measure of quality change.

Note that, although time appears in the augmented expenditure with a weight that can be taken to be given by the relevant wage rate, the weight to be given to time in the index of characteristics is different – it is the marginal utility of time *in using the car* relative to the marginal utility in generalized leisure. The former may be greater than the latter (if driving is considered very pleasurable) or less, and the marginal utility of time in use of the car may even be negative if driving is considered an unpleasant chore.

What happens if the assumption of separability must be discarded altogether, there being no characteristics obtainable from goods in the group which cannot also be obtained from other goods? In this case, we cannot find an operational concept corresponding to any number which purports to measure the quality change in a single good. We can measure only the overall 'quality of consumption' change which results from the change in specifications of the various goods in the consumption bundle.[15]

USING MARKET DATA

The various potentially acceptable measures of quality change require information with respect to one or more of the following:

1. Market data showing the relative prices at which the original and quality-changed varieties are being sold to the same consumers at the same time. (For expenditure-equivalent indexes.)
2. Technical data on the quantitative content of relevant characteristics

in the original and quality-changed varieties, plus the shape of the relevant portion of the reference indifference curve. (For quantity-equivalent and hypothetical quantity-equivalent indexes.)

3. The same technical data, plus true shadow prices for characteristics rather than indifference curve shapes. (For fixed-weight indexes of characteristics.)

Since it is separate from the others, let us first consider the use of market data to obtain expenditure equivalents. To read such equivalents directly from the market, we require that the original and changed version of the good be available simultaneously and that there be evidence that the reference consumer is indifferent between the two versions at the going prices, which can then be treated as expenditure equivalents.

In most typical cases (such as motor cars), the new and old models are not really available at the same time. Although there may be some overlap at the commencement of the model year, the new models will not yet have attained the equilibrium price and the old models are usually being discounted heavily to clear inventory, so that the relative prices are not representative of the equilibrium relationship. In addition, depreciation depends on the nominal year of the model rather than the actual data of first use, further distorting relative prices during the changeover period.

One way of trying to avoid the problem of non-simultaneity simultaneity is the Burstein–Cagan–Hall[16] technique of looking at the market for used goods in cases (such as motor cars and houses) in which this market has more than fringe significance. In 1991, the used market will give relative prices for 1989 and 1990 models. These relative prices are presumed to depend on two separable factors, the quality difference between the two models which is presumed to be independent of time, and the difference in age between the two models, the effect of which is presumed to be independent of the characteristics mix. The assumption of separability enables us to determine the effect of pure time depreciation in a variety of ways, adjust for the contribution of this to the price difference between 1973 and 1974 models, and assume that the residual represents the price difference due to quality change. The used-good approach has the advantage of being based on an effective comparison between successive model years, but depends crucially on the separability of time depreciation from other characteristics (implying that the characteristics mix does not change as the good grows older, very dubious) and on the estimation of the effect of this time depreciation. In addition, the quality change measure is not available except with a lag and this quality change is being assessed in terms of the preferences of a later year and not either of the two years in which at least one of the models was actually available new.

Nevertheless, this approach may be the best we have for developing historical series of quality change measures for indivisible goods.[17]

The alternatives to expenditure equivalents both require that we possess information on the characteristics of the good both before and after the quality change. This information is technological rather than market information, although we may use market data to satisfy ourselves as to the set of characteristics which is really relevant to consumer choice. In any case, the presumptive set of relevant characteristics and their quantification is a non-market problem, to be obtained from engineering or testing service data.

As a practical matter, we can rule out the possibility of obtaining the shape of a reference indifference curve from any kinds of data likely to be available in a real situation. Thus the real alternative to an expenditure-equivalent index is a fixed-weight index of characteristics, with weights proportional to the appropriate shadow prices. It is these shadow prices for which we require the market data.

In the section on indexes of quality change (see pp. 87–90) it was shown that the appropriate shadow prices are those proportional to the marginal utilities of the characteristics (or relative shadow prices should equal the marginal rates of substitution between characteristics), and can thus be obtained from the slope of the hyperplane which is tangent to the indifference surface at the point corresponding to the characteristics bundle of the good.

Historically, the slope of this hyperplane has been estimated by regressing price (adjusted for the 'pure' price change) on characteristics content over cross-section and/or time series data for the individual varieties of goods.[18] This technique assumes that the shadow prices on characteristics are the same for all varieties, and it is this assumption that needs close scrutiny.

Although almost all the applications of the above 'hedonic technique' have been to goods which are essentially indivisible and non-combinable, let us examine its foundations by first considering the combinable case. Since combinability implies either divisibility or indivisibility with consumption of many units, we can eliminate direct consideration of price by taking the set of all characteristics bundles that can be obtained by spending a given budget on all possible combinations of goods (in the group). Now if all consumers have identical preferences and incomes or identical homothetic preferences, the only circumstances under which all goods could simultaneously find a place in the market would be when the relative prices of the goods were such as to make all points corresponding to characteristics obtainable from the budget lie on a hyperplane. Under these circumstances, there is a unique hyperplane which is tangent to the indifference surface and the regression method gives the true shadow prices.

It is surely much more realistic to suppose that the existence of many varieties of goods on the market implies the existence of varied preferences over the population. In this case, goods can be sold at prices which do not lead to points on a hyperplane, provided the points lie on the boundary of a convex feasible set of characteristics, with different consumers buying different goods combinations. This is shown in Figure 6.1, where there are

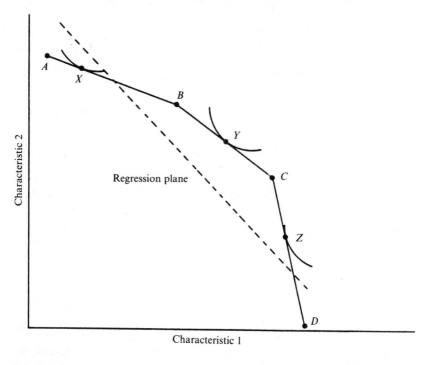

Figure 6.1

three different consumers buying different combinations of goods (two at a time) to achieve their respective optimal characteristics combinations X, Y, Z. If our reference consumer is the one with optimal point X, the relevant shadow prices are given by the slope of BC. A regression will fit a line to all four points, giving shadow prices determined by the broken regression line in the diagram. These are not the appropriate shadow prices for the reference consumer, nor for any of the three consumers.

Given combinability, we can determine the true shadow prices from the slope of the facet *BC*.[19] Note that the facet method uses information about the characteristics of goods *B* and *C* only – it measures quality change only over those goods actually purchased by the reference group of consumers. In many cases we might expect a cluster of goods with very similar characteristics proportions near that part of the spectrum in which our reference consumer is interested, suggesting that a regression through this cluster might be an acceptable estimate of shadow prices with some error-diminishing properties. In any case, the statistically most useful observations (the most divergent from the cluster) would not be used.

The problems outlined above are relatively minor ones compared with those that arise with indivisible and non-combinable goods. Here we are in real trouble because the true shadow prices may not become manifest in any form at all. Let us consider a group of, say, motor cars which differ in characteristics proportions and which, for simplicity, are all sold on the market simultaneously at the same price. If all consumers are identical, these facets are consistent only if the characteristics bundles corresponding to the various cars correspond to points on the (unique) indifference surface. In principle, we could then draw the indifference surface from the data and obtain the shadow prices relevant to quality change measurement for any one of the cars from the slopes at the proper point.

If preferences vary and consumers are not identical, the market tells us very little. Since each consumer chooses only one good, the fact that all are sold implies only that the points corresponding to the characteristics bundles of the goods *not* bought by each particular consumer must all lie on the origin side of the indifference curve through the point corresponding to the good he actually did buy. This imposes some limits on the possible values of the shadow prices, but these limits may be very broad unless there is independent evidence that the indifference curves show very high elasticity of substitution.

The best we can do in the indivisible case – which is the main case in terms of the usefulness of measuring quality change – is to assume relatively flat indifference curves (high elasticity of substitution) and choose a reference consumer whose optimal characteristics collection is in a cluster of goods with similar characteristics proportions. The slope of the indifference curve cannot then differ greatly from the slope of the line joining the points corresponding to the goods closest in specification to that actually chosen by the reference consumer. Since there is simply no way of determining the *exact* shadow prices, even in principle, it would probably be appropriate to take the regression through the cluster as a safe approximation. As in the divisible case, the appropriate regression would ignore points that were not close to the cluster, increasing the theoretical validity at the expense of statistical reliability.

CONCLUSION

We have shown that, if the quality changes are 'small', the numbers derived from all three of the indexes which we might choose as criteria for quality change will coincide, and we can then consider these numbers to give an unambiguous 'measure' of quality change. The choice of index will then be a matter of practical convenience, the two realistic options being the expenditure-equivalent index (especially applicable to vintage and used-good data) and a fixed-weight index of characteristics with properly derived shadow price weights and not regression weights. The major complications which may arise are non-separability, taste changes, and relative price changes among goods not being indexed for quality change.

NOTES

1. Originally published in *Review of Income and Wealth* **23** (1977), 157–72.
2. See the survey in Griliches (1971). The pioneering works were Court (1939), Houthakker (1952) and Stone (1956).
3. Attempts to treat quality change in indivisible goods by a repackaging approach lack even the merit of a well-defined quantitative variable.
4. See Lancaster (1966, 1971).
5. See Lancaster (1971), Chapter 8.
6. A special problem arises if there are no natural units, such as detergents which may be powdered or liquid, or of different degrees of concentration. One should convert to equivalent units, such as the amount required per load of washing.
7. See the section on indexes of quality change (pp. 87–90) for the theoretical determination of the relevant shadow prices, and the section on using market data (pp. 93–7) for the practical problems of estimating these.
8. The customer is, of course, prohibited from trading any of these Volkswagens, directly or indirectly.
9. This is the index actually sought in most applications of the so-called hedonic technique.
10. This is the index implicitly being sought in Cagan (1965) and other studies based on used-goods markets; and also the index implicit in Fisher and Shell (1968). See also Rosen (1974).
11. Discussion of quality change along with preference change is given in Fisher and Shell (1968) and Muellbauer (1975).
12. See Fisher and Shell (1968) for discussion of the non-separable case along rather different lines from this paper.
13. The classic studies, such as Griliches (1961), and official statistics attempt to measure this average change.
14. Note that we have been short-cutting here by taking the characteristics of the durables themselves, rather than the characteristics of the services of the durables, as the arguments of utility functions. The general conclusions are not affected by the more correct analysis in terms of service flows, provided the same separability conditions hold. See, however, Fisher and Shell (1968) for examples suggesting that separability is somewhat less realistic when the analysis is cast in terms of services, and Muellbauer (1974) for a discussion of quality change in a household production context.
15. See also Fisher and Shell (1968) and Muellbauer (1974, 1975).
16. Burstein (1961), Cagan (1965), Hall (1971).
17. See Hall (1971) for discussion of the econometric problems.

18. See Griliches (1961, 1971).
19. See Lancaster (1967, 1971), Muellbauer (1974) and Klevmarken (1973).

PART III

STUDIES IN COLLECTIVE CONSUMPTION

7 The theory of household behaviour: some foundations[1]

For some years now, it has been common to refer to the basic decision-making entity with respect to consumption as the 'household' by those primarily concerned with data collection and analysis and those working mainly with macroeconomic models, and as the 'individual' by those working in microeconomic theory and welfare economics. Although one-person households do exist, they are the exception rather than the rule, and the individual and the household cannot be taken to be identical.

In the total absence of trade between the micro-welfare and macro-empirical branches of the profession, it might not matter that the consumption units were different in the different contexts. But there is trade – perhaps less than there ought to be – and this is where the danger lies. It is not uncommon to take analysis that has been devised to provide a reasonable model of the single individual and then apply that analysis to the household, as if it were the same thing. The most surprising offender is Arrow and Hahn (1971) where, in a book designed to meet the highest standards of analytical rigour, the basic decision-maker in consumption is called the 'household' – and then has ascribed to it a set of properties that are appropriate only for the single individual.

If it could be shown that households did, indeed, behave like the individuals of micro-theory, then there would be no problem, but we know that this can be taken to be evidently true, if at all, only in a household run in a dictatorial fashion by a single decision-maker. If the household does behave like an individual in any other circumstances, we must be able to prove this and be able clearly to state those circumstances.

The purpose of this chapter is to concentrate on the fact that the typical household consists of more than one person and to investigate the extent to which it is (a) entirely or (b) approximately legitimate to ascribe to that household those properties traditionally ascribed to the single consumer.

THE INDIVIDUAL AND THE HOUSEHOLD

Since a household is composed of individuals, we must either construct a theory of the household which is based on and derived from the theory of behaviour of individuals, suitably modified to take account of their association within the household, or ignore those individuals altogether and construct a theory of the household which is *sui generis* and not based on individuals. The theory of the consumption function is of this latter kind, not derivable from standard micro-theory, as are *ad hoc* models such as the stock adjustment model of Houthakker and Taylor (1970).

We shall be entirely concerned here with models of the first kind, based on the theory of individual behaviour and using the results of micro-theory. Remarkably little has been done in this area, although Samuelson (1956) tackled the problem directly in what is probably the fullest discussion in the economics literature of the relation of household decisions to individual preferences. Becker (1965), Muth (1966) and others since have considered the problems associated with production (implicit and explicit) within the household and with time allocation within the household, but assumed away any problems associated with the household's decision function. There is, of course, an extensive literature on both aggregation and the construction of social welfare functions, two problems directly relevant to the theory of the household, but with the emphasis placed on large, rather than small, groups. The marketing literature contains much discussion of intra-household decision processes, primarily from the point of view of trying to influence sales by manipulating these, and there has been considerable recent work in the empirical investigation of who makes what decisions within the household.[2] Finally, there is decision theory, especially the work on teams by Marshak and Radner (1972), which has relevance to the household decision process. For the basic problem with which we are concerned here, however, we cannot draw on any of this literature except that on aggregation and social welfare functions (including the Samuelson article), since we shall confine ourselves to the pure demand properties of households under conditions that do not involve production, time or uncertainty.

The individual

The individual, who will appear both as the typical member of the household and as a reference with whose typical behaviour we shall compare the behaviour of the household, is the standard individual consumer of micro-theory. He/she is assumed to have complete and well-ordered preferences, full information, and to optimize perfectly subject to a budget constraint with exogenous prices and income (or endowments). We shall consider consumption behaviour in two contexts:

1. *Traditional*, in which every good fits into the preference system in a way which is unique to itself, and
2. *The characteristics model*, in which goods possess characteristics

which are typically obtainable also from other goods or their combinations.[3]

In using the characteristics model, we shall confine ourselves to the case in which the act of consumption (that is, of extracting characteristics from goods) is linearly combinable, in the sense that the characteristics obtained from any collection of goods is the sum of the characteristics contained in the specified quantities of the individual goods.

When investigating whether the household can be considered to behave like a single individual, we shall concentrate on the following criteria which are either directly observable or can be derived from observable behaviour:

1. *The individual is efficient.* In the traditional context, this is either trivial or unobservable (how could we know whether a consumer was equating marginal rates of substitution to price ratios or not), but is nontrivial and observable in the characteristics model. In the latter model, a consumer who is efficient will, when faced with choices among collections of M goods possessing between them only R different characteristics ($R < M$), need to consume no more than R different goods.

2. *Substitution predominates in demand.* This basic property, a consequence of choice under a budget constraint with preferences having the generally assumed properties, can be expressed in a variety of different ways. The two we shall be particularly interested in are the alternatives:

   (a) The Slutsky matrix is symmetric and negative semi-definite;
   (b) The strong and weak axioms of revealed preference are satisfied.

(The substantive contents of both (a) and (b) are equivalent.)

A household can be considered to act as if it was a single individual only if the aggregate household consumption vectors (obtained by summing the individual consumption vectors over all members of the household), the aggregate household income, and the price vector for goods, are related in such a way as to satisfy 1 and 2 above.

The household

The household is composed of individuals, but it is clearly more than that. We shall consider the household to possess three leading properties:

1.   The household is a collection of individuals
2.   It is a *small* collection of individuals
3.   It is a *closely-knit* collection of individuals.

In so far as the household is a collection of individuals, a theory of the household can draw on general theoretical results for groups, such as aggregation properties and the properties of social decision rules. Since it is a small collection, we must reject group properties which depend on large numbers and search for properties which depend on smallness of numbers. Since the household is a closely-knit group, we can accept some things – like interpersonal utility comparisons – that we would not over random aggregates, and must be prepared to emphasize others, like joint consumption, that would be peripheral phenomena for large groups.

We shall first investigate the extent to which smallness as such enables us to reach different conclusions about the household as an aggregate than we would reach for a large group, then go on to investigate the effect of close-knitness on the household decision function and on joint consumption phenomena.

HOUSEHOLDS AS SMALL AGGREGATES

It is well known[4] that, if individual consumption vectors x^i chosen subject to prices p and incomes y^i are aggregated into a group consumption vector $X\,(=\Sigma x^i)$, then $X,\ Y\,(=\Sigma y^i),\ p$ do not necessarily bear the same kind of relationship to each other as to the equivalent quantities for the individuals. In particular, the aggregate quantities need not satisfy the weak axiom of revealed preference.

The best known example is the 2×2 case given by Hicks (1956), where two persons facing choices among two goods each choose collections in two different price-income situations which are consistent with all standard assumptions about individual behaviour, but in which the aggregate vectors have the properties $pX' < pX, p'X < p'X'$, contravening the revealed preference axiom.

Since the 2×2 example is particularly clear-cut, it was presumed for many years that the aggregate properties of small groups were, if anything, more divergent from those of the individual than the aggregate properties of large groups. The Hicks example requires that the income consumption curves of the individuals be so related that the consumer choosing the lowest ratio of the first to the second good in the initial situation shows a much greater increase in the consumption of the first good, relative to the second, as income rises, than does the other consumer. Thus it has been argued that this kind of effect will wash out over a large group – an argument which can be found spelt out in detail in Pearce (1964).

It is only recently that it has been realized that it is not the number of consumers, as such, that is relevant, but the number of consumers relative to the number of goods. The failure of the aggregate demand in the Hicks case to possess any well-defined substitution property is now seen to depend, not on the actual number of consumers, but on the fact that the number of individuals is the same as the number of goods.

The number of goods and the size of the group

The particular developments in theory that turn out to be especially relevant to the household as a small group were set in motion by Sonnenschein (1972, 1973) who asked, and gave the first answer to, the following question: If the aggregate excess demand function is continuous and satisfies Walras's Law (essentially an accounting identity), but is otherwise arbitrary, could this excess demand function have been obtained as the aggregation of individual excess demand functions each of which possesses all the properties derived from traditional preference maximizing behaviour? Sonnenschein's affirmative answer was sharpened by Mantel (1974) and given definitive shape by Debreu (1974) who showed that the affirmative answer required that the number of individuals be at least as great as the number of goods. Further clarifications have been made since, but the essential pattern was already established.

If we invert the reasoning of the Sonnenschein–Mantel–Debreu result, it implies that, in a world of N goods, there can exist N consumers with acceptable individual behaviour whose aggregate behaviour does not necessarily exhibit the traditional substitution properties. This explains the Hicks example, but shows that it is a special case because it assumes only two goods, rather than because the group comprises only two people.

Since a single individual exhibits all the standard demand behaviour but an aggregate of N individuals (assuming N goods) may show none, the interesting question – and the crucial one for the theory of the household – is what happens when there are at least two, but less than N, individuals? This question has been answered by Diewert (1974?) whose analysis we shall follow.

Consider first an individual consumer. The Slutsky equations for this individual can be written in the matrix form

$$V = K + bx^T$$

where V is the matrix of uncompensated price partials, K is the Slutsky matrix, b is the column vector of income partials and x the column vector of initially chosen quantities. The demand properties of the individual are usually summarized by noting that K is symmetric and negative semi-definite. For our purposes here, it is more useful to consider the properties of V, the uncompensated matrix.

Let us choose a set of linearly independent vectors A^k, each of which is orthogonal to x. There will be $n - 1$ such vectors, which we assemble into the $n \times (n-1)$ matrix A, where n is the number of goods. From the Slutsky equation we then obtain

$$A^T V A = A^T K A + A^T b x^T A$$
$$= A^T K A$$

since $x^T A = 0$.

Now the properties of symmetry and negative semi-definiteness of K are left unchanged by the transformation $A^T \dots A$, so that the matrix $A^T V A$ possesses these properties. Thus, although the $n \times n$ uncompensated matrix V is not itself necessarily either symmetric or negative semi-definite, there always exists a transformation $A^T \dots A$ such that the $(n-1) \times (n-1)$ matrix $A^T V A$ is symmetric negative semi-definite.

If we think of the compensated demand function as exhibiting 'full' concavity properties (since we can associate with it a negative semi-definite matrix of order n), the uncompensated demand function can be considered to have one degree less concavity, since the negative semi-definite property is associated with a matrix of order $n - 1$. Alternatively, we can note that symmetry imposes $\frac{1}{2}n(n-1)$ restrictions on the compensated matrix K, but only $\frac{1}{2}(n-1)(n-2)$ restrictions on the uncompensated matrix V.

Now consider the aggregation of m consumers, each choosing independently with his own preferences and budget (but all facing the same prices). Denoting aggregates by bars and values for the individuals by superscript $s(s = 1 \dots m)$, we have[5]

$$\bar{V} = \sum_s V^s$$
$$= \sum_s K^s + \sum_s b^s (x^s)^T.$$

Choose a set of linearly independent vectors $\bar{A}^k$, each orthogonal to all the vectors x^s. In general, the vectors x^s will be linearly independent, and thus we can certainly find $n - m$ vectors $\bar{A}^k$ but not, in general, more than that. Assembling the vectors into $n \times (n - m)$ matrix $\bar{A}$, we then obtain

$$\bar{A}^T\bar{V}\bar{A} = \Sigma \bar{A}^T K^s \bar{A} + \Sigma \bar{A}^T b^s (x^s)^T \bar{A}$$
$$= \Sigma \bar{A}^T K^s \bar{A}$$

since $(x^s)^T \bar{A} = 0$, all s.

By the same reasoning as used in the individual case, the matrix $\bar{A}^T\bar{V}\bar{A}$ is symmetric negative semi-definite, but of order $n - m$. Thus aggregate demand exhibits 'less' concavity than individual demand, the divergence increasing as the number of individuals increases. The number of implied symmetry restrictions is $\frac{1}{2}(n - m)(n - m - 1)$, a number which declines as m increases. If $m \geq n$, no matrix $\bar{A}$ can be found (unless there is linear dependence among the vectors x^s) and aggregate demand does not necessarily exhibit any concavity or symmetry properties at all, the Sonnenschein–Mantel–Debreu result. On the other hand, if n is large and m small (two for many households), the properties of $\bar{V}$ do not diverge greatly from those for the individual. Thus we can state the following:

- Result 1
  Even if the individuals in the household receive their own budgets and make totally independent choices, the behaviour of the household will be 'close', in a clearly-defined sense, to that of an individual consumer, provided the number of goods is large relative to the number of members of the household.

This is a statement that could not have been made on any firm basis even two or three years ago.

The characteristics model
In the characteristics model, the individual has preferences over characteristics which are taken to have the same properties as the traditional preferences over goods. The characteristics are obtained, in the case we shall use in this chapter, from goods in such a way that the vector of characteristics is a linear transformation of the vector of goods of the form $z = Bx$, where z is the characteristics vector.

If B is a square non-singular matrix, there is a unique inverse transformation $x = B^{-1}z$ from characteristics into goods. In this case we can aggregate the behaviour of the members of the households over characteristics to obtain an aggregate characteristics vector $\bar{z}$. Since there will be a unique vector $q = pB^{-1}$ of implicit characteristics prices, and since we have assumed behaviour over characteristics to fit the traditional pattern of behaviour over goods, the matrix C of uncompensated partials of charac-

teristics with respect to their implicit prices will have the same properties
as ascribed to V in the traditional case. The matrix of price partials of
goods in this case is equal to BCB^{-1}, which has the same symmetry and
negative semi-definite properties as C and thus as the traditional V. The
characteristics model gives identical results with respect to the demand
properties of goods as the traditional model so long as the matrix B is
square and non-singular, requiring that the number of goods and the
number of characteristics be equal.

But if the number of goods exceeds the number of characteristics, the
matrix B is of order $r \times n$ (where r is the number of distinct characteristics).
From standard optimizing theory, the individual will attain his optimum,
subject to a linear budget constraint on goods by consuming only r goods.
The choice of those r goods will depend on the consumer's optimal
characteristics vector and thus will, in general, vary from consumer to
consumer. The choice of those r goods will then give a basis in B from
which the inverse relationships will be determined. In particular, if B^s is
the $r \times r$ basis chosen from B by the sth consumer, we will have
$x^s = (B^s)^{-1} z^s$ and $q^s = p(B^s)^{-1}$. The latter relationship implies that the
implicit prices on characteristics differ between consumers, ruling out all
standard aggregating procedures for characteristics over individuals.

Solution of the individual's optimization problem over characteristics
gives, of course, a unique solution in terms of goods – typically with the
quantities of $n-r$ of the goods being zero. We cannot use the Slutsky
analysis on the demand for goods because the solution is a corner solution, but the demand for goods satisfies the axioms of revealed preference.[6] Aggregation over consumers whose individual behaviour satisfies
the strong axiom of revealed preference has been shown, in McFadden,
Mantel, Mas-Collel and Richter (1974) to lead to results similar to the
Sonnenschein–Mantel–Debreu conclusions. Although we do not have an
analysis of the case in which $m < n$ which shows a continuous relationship
between the size of the group and the degree of divergence from the
individual pattern, as we do when we can use the Slutsky equations, it can
be conjectured that some relationship of this kind does exist.

The most important, and most observable, effects of the characteristics
model on household behaviour lie in efficiency considerations. An individual consumer will not need to consume more goods than there are
characteristics but, if $r < n$, different individuals may, in general, choose
different collections of r goods. Thus a household, each of whose members
is efficient in consuming only r goods, may consume more than r goods in
the aggregate and thus will appear to be consuming inefficiently. Indeed,
the aggregate characteristics vector may be such that it could be more
efficiently attained by consuming a set of goods different from those

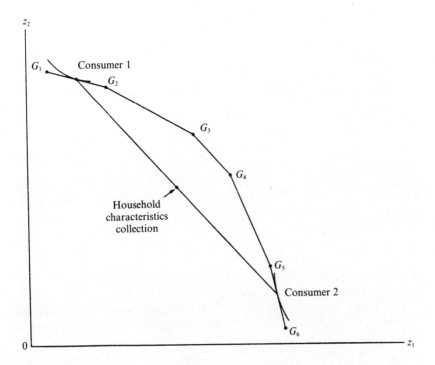

Figure 7.1

chosen by any member of the household. Figure 7.1 shows an example with six goods and two characteristics where the household consumes four goods (G_1, G_2 by one member, G_5, G_6 by the other) when, if the household had really been a single individual, the efficient choice would have been the two goods G_3 and G_4.

It is obvious that, in a general way, the number of goods that the household might be observed to consume in excess of the number that would be consumed by a single individual will increase as the number of goods increases relative to the number of characteristics, and as the number of persons in the household increases. We can state the following:

- Result 2
  If the individuals in the household receive their own budgets and make totally independent choices, and if there are more goods than distinct characteristics, the behaviour of the household may be apparently inefficient, in the sense that it purchases more goods than there are characteristics. The potential divergence between the

number of goods purchased by the household and the number that would be purchased by an individual will be less, the smaller the household and the smaller the number of goods relative to characteristics.

Conclusions on households as simple aggregates

If a household is a simple aggregate of individuals each of whom makes his own choices subject to his own preferences and his own budget (and in the absence of joint and externality effects), then the household cannot, in general, be considered to behave as if it was a single individual. Its observable behaviour will differ from that of the single individual in that demand may show a lesser degree of symmetry and concavity and consumption may appear to be inefficient as evidenced by the purchase of more goods than there are distinct characteristics. In both these respects, however, the household's behaviour will be 'close' to that of an individual if the size of the household is small and the number of characteristics and goods is large. Simple examples in two goods and two individuals vastly overstate the degree of divergence between household and individual behaviour, as compared with the more realistic case of few individuals and many goods.

HOUSEHOLD DECISION FUNCTIONS

We now turn from the model of the household as a mere collection of independent individuals to consider models in which decisions are made by the household as a unit, but in which the individuals still possess their own preferences.

If there is to be a single household decision function which reflects and is based upon the preferences of the individual members of the households, then the Arrow impossibility theorem applies just as it does to larger groups. There can be no rule that will generate, from the preference orderings of the members alone, a household preference ordering that is Paretian, has unrestricted domain, satisfies the condition of independence from irrelevant alternatives, and is non-dictatorial, unless the preferences of the individuals are related in some particular way. To have a household behaving as a single decision-making unit, one or more of the Arrow conditions must be dropped, we must work with a household preference ordering over a restricted domain, we must assume that the preferences of household members are always related in such a way as to always lead to unambiguous household preferences, or we must be willing to have the household decision function based on more information than is contained in individual preference orderings alone.

The traditional approach of simply regarding the household as a single person can be considered to have rested upon one of two implicit assumptions, that the household decision function is dictatorial and reflects the preferences of its 'head', or that the members of the household have identical preferences and unanimity is found on all choices.

Our purpose is, of course, to go beyond this kind of simplification. For the household, we can break out of the Arrow prison by using the 'close-knitness' property that is not applicable in the case of the broader social welfare function. This property makes it reasonable that the household can make decisions on the basis of more information about the effect on its members than is contained in preference orderings alone. In particular, we can contemplate a household decision function which takes account of degrees of preferences and of relative weights to be given to the preferences of different members.

Samuelson households

The household decision function discussed at some length by Samuelson (1956) has the form $U[u^1(x^1), u^2(x^2), \ldots, u^m(x^m)]$ where $u^i(x^i)$ is the utility function of the i-th household member derived from his own consumption vector x^i. There are no externalities, interdependencies or joint effects. U is an increasing function of the u^i's (so the household is Paretian) and the concavity properties of U on the u^i's and of the u^i's on the x^i's are such as to make U a strictly quasi-concave function of the ultimate arguments u_r^i. A sufficient, but not necessary, condition for this is that the u^i's are strictly concave and U is a strictly quasi-concave function of the u^i's. Concavity, not merely quasi-concavity, is appropriate for the u^i's since the household function is assigning cardinal measures to the utilities of all its members.

With a household utility function of this form, the household optimum for given household income Y can be achieved by dividing income among members of the household in such a way as to equalize weighted marginal utilities of income. That is, we must have:

$$U_i \frac{\partial u^i}{\partial y} = U_j \frac{\partial u^j}{\partial y}$$

for all i,j. The individual members then optimize on their personal budgets.

Since U is strictly quasi-concave on the individual goods quantities u_r^i, and since all household members face the same prices, the goods aggregates $X_r = \Sigma_i x_r^i$ satisfy the properties of Hicksian composite goods and thus U is strictly quasi-concave over the household goods vector X. The concavity properties of household demand are identical to those of an individual consumer.

There is, however, one respect in which the behaviour of the household may differ from that of the individual. This will be when there are more goods than characteristics.

Characteristics and Paretian Households

Consider the Samuelson household in the context of the characteristics model, in which we shall assume the consumption technology is such as to have more goods than there are distinct characteristics. The overall structure of the optimizing process is the same as in the traditional model, each member of the household maximising his own utility function subject to his own budget constraint (on goods), the budgets being allocated in accord with the Samuelson rule. The kinds of choices that the individuals will make will be the same as in the aggregate model and the reasoning given in the second section (pp. 106–11) which led to Result 2 will be applicable here. In particular, if members of the household differ sufficiently in their individual preferences, different members may obtain their optimal collections of the same set of characteristics by consuming different bundles of goods. Thus even with a unified household decision rule like that of the Samuelson model, we can still have a situation like that depicted in Figure 7.1, with apparent inefficiency and with the household purchasing more goods than there are characteristics.

The above argument is not applicable only to households of the Samuelson type, but applies for any kind of household decision function which is Paretian (that is, in which U is an increasing function of the u^i's). The optimum for any such household must be such that the utility level attained by any member of the household has been attained with the least possible expenditure on goods from the household budget. For members with sufficiently different preferences, this minimum expenditure criterion will imply different goods in the optimum bundles of different members, giving us once again the situation leading to Result 2 and depicted in Figure 7.1.

We can summarize our findings in this section as follows:

- Result 3
  In the Samuelson model, aggregate household demand will exhibit the same concavity properties as for the individual, whatever the relationship between the number of goods and the number of characteristics.[7]

- Result 4

   If there are more goods than distinct characteristics, neither the Samuelson household nor any other household with a Paretian decision function need necessarily be observed to behave as if it were a single individual, since the household may purchase more goods than there are distinct characteristics, contravening the efficiency condition for the individual.

We should note that Result 4 may be applicable even in a *dictatorial* household. The dictator can get the other members of the household to any utility level he has chosen for them most cheaply by giving each the appropriate optimal goods bundle, leaving the maximum residue for his own use. This will lead to the same kind of results as in the Paretian household.

Conclusions on households with centralized decisions
In the absence of externalities, interdependencies, or joint consumption effects, even a centralized household decision function is not sufficient to guarantee that the household behaves like a single individual in all respects. In particular, although the household may possess the demand substitutability properties of the individual, it may not possess the efficiency properties.

JOINT CONSUMPTION AND RELATED MATTERS

Since a household consists of a small number of individuals with close associations, we can expect every kind of joint and externality effect, including interdependence of utilities, to play a far more significant role than in the case of a large aggregate. A considerable share of typical household activities (meals, recreation, simple occupancy of the home, for example) involve joint consumption in some sense or major consumption externalities. The taxonomy, alone, of all the possible effects would be a considerable task, while a full exploration of territory which has but a few signposts at present would be well beyond the scope of a single chapter.

We shall not take up at all the question of interdependent preferences,[8] but confine our investigation to external interdependence, through joint consumption or otherwise, in which the utilities of other household members do not appear as direct arguments in the utility function of any one. The only direct interrelation between utilities is confined to the formulation of the household decision function.

Joint consumption and externalities

There is an externality effect within the household whenever the utility (preferences) of one member is affected by the quantities consumed of any good by any other member. We shall concentrate on the fullest kind of positive externality, joint consumption, in which the consumption of any quantity of the joint good (or characteristic) by any member of the household has the same effect on other members of the household as if they had directly consumed it themselves. (If someone turns on the radio, everyone hears it). Thus the total quantity consumed within the household appears in everyone's utility function, making the good or characteristic a kind of household public good or public characteristic. It will be convenient to refer to these characteristics or goods as 'public' within the context of the household, although they are private goods from the point of view of society as a whole and are purchased by the household through the market.

The property of being private or public can be taken to reside in the individual characteristic (a food may have a private flavour but a public odour). A true household public good is then one with characteristics which are all public, a private good with characteristics which are all private, and a mixed good with characteristics of both kinds.

If all goods available to the household are either public or private in the above sense, the analysis is precisely the same as if the household was a mini-economy facing a linear transformation curve (the budget line) and the ordinary theory of public goods can be applied. Although the household is small, its size is essentially fixed and phenomena such as 'crowding'[9] are not important. Provided the household has a proper decision function, an optimal solution can be reached by central purchase and allocation, by lump-sum contributions towards purchase of the public goods from members' budgets or even (in a highly sophisticated household!) by a Lindahl solution with the public good sold to different members at different prices.

In the traditional case, where there is a one-to-one relationship between a characteristic and a good, the structural properties of household demand are not changed by the existence of joint consumption within the household, provided the household has a mechanism for attaining an optimum.[10] In particular, if the household decision function has the Samuelson form $U[u^1(x^1,V),\ldots,u^m(x^m,V)]$, with U a strictly quasi-concave function of all the ultimate arguments x^i_j,V_k (V is the vector of public goods), then U is a strictly quasi-concave function of the aggregate household goods quantities X_j,V_k, for the same reasons as in the all-private case. Thus the concavity properties of household demand are not affected by the introduction of the public goods.

More goods than characteristics

If there are more goods than characteristics, the extent to which the household behaviour conforms to the efficiency conditions for the individual depends on the separate relationships between the number of public goods and public characteristics and between the number of private goods and characteristics, in the assumed absence of mixed goods. It is obvious that, since each member's utility from the public characteristics depends on the household totals, those totals should be obtained in the least cost way in order to achieve optimality. Thus the number of public goods will not exceed the number of public characteristics, whatever the size of the household. On the other hand, the relationship between the number of private goods purchased by the household and the number of private characteristics may exceed the number that would be purchased by the single individual, for the same reasons as in the second and third sections of this chapter (pp. 106–12 and 112–15).

Mixed goods

In the overall economy, many of what are regarded as pure public goods undoubtedly have private aspects (defence is not a pure public good to someone living next to an air-base), but these private aspects are scattered and of variable impact in most cases. Thus it is a reasonable first approximation to consider a division of goods into public goods and private goods over the economy as a whole, and only when we consider smaller segments of the economy (especially localities) do we need to consider goods as having a mix of public and private characteristics.

For a unit as small as the household, however, many or most goods that have public characteristics (in the special household sense) will also have private characteristics. The dwelling itself will have a mixture of public characteristics (the areas of joint use) and private (in individual bedrooms). Thus we can regard the mixed good as typical within the household, not an unusual special case.

Since our concern in this chapter is with the extent to which the household can be treated as if it were a single individual, we shall not give any descriptive analysis of the mixed goods case but proceed immediately to consider the effect of mixed goods on the concavity and efficiency properties of household demand.

It is obvious that concavity properties, which are not affected by the presence of pure public goods, will not be affected by the presence of mixed goods. Any effects will be confined to the efficiency criteria. Since pure public goods give efficiency properties identical with those for the individual, while pure private goods lead to a divergence between the properties of the household and the individual, we can expect that mixed goods tend to lower the divergence as compared with pure private goods. Confirmation of our expectations commences with the following theorem.

Theorem
If there are two characteristics, one public (within the household) and one private, a household decision function, and an array of n mixed goods, the household will purchase only two of the goods, however large may be the number of goods and the size of the household.

Denote by $z^s{}_1$ the amount of the private characteristic received by the s-th member of the household, and by z_2 the total household quantity of the public characteristic. Let a_{1j}, a_{2j} be the quantities of the two characteristics contained in unit quantity of the j-th good, and let $x^s{}_j$ denote the quantity of the j-th good consumed by the s-th individual. The household optimum is then the solution of the problem

$$\max \; U[u^1(z^1_1,z_2), u^2(z^2_1,z_2), \ldots]$$

subject to

$$z^s_1 - \sum_s a_{1j} x^s_j = 0 \quad s = 1 \ldots m$$

$$z_2 - \sum_s a_{2j}\left(\sum_s x^s_j\right) = 0$$

$$\sum_j \sum_s x^s_j = I$$

where goods units have been chosen so that prices can be taken as unity, and I is the household income. In addition we have the mn non-negativity restrictions $x^s_j \geq 0$, all s,j.

The dual problem involves the $m+2$ dual variables w^s_j, $s = 1, \ldots, m$ (the shadow price of the private characteristic to each individual), w_2 (the common shadow price of the public characteristic), and v (the shadow marginal valuation of household income). There is a dual constraint for each x^s_j of the form[11]

$$a_{1j} w^s_1 + a_{2j} w_2 \leq v \quad s = 1, \ldots, m; \quad j = 1, \ldots, n$$

such that $x^s_j = 0$ unless the corresponding constraint is satisfied as an equation.

In general, the optimum will involve the consumption of exactly two goods by any individual, and these will be goods which are adjacent along the efficiency frontier (see Figure 7.1). Suppose the optimum for the first individual is consumption of goods j, $j+1$ (the goods are taken to be numbered successively along the frontier), then the following must be true:

$$a_{1j}w_1^1 + a_{2j}w_2 = v$$
$$a_{1j+1}w_1^1 + a_{2j+1}w_2 = v$$
$$a_{1k}w_1^1 + a_{2k}w_2 < v \quad k \neq j, \quad j+1$$

The two equations determine w_1^1 and w_2, the inequalities must hold if j, $j+1$ are truly the optimal pair of goods. Now consider any other consumer for whom the shadow price on the private characteristic is w_1^s. The value of w_2 must be the same as for the first consumer, and the inequalities to be satisfied have the same coefficients a_{1j}, a_{2j} as for the first consumer. Now if we had $w_1^s > w_1^1$, the left-hand sides of the relationships corresponding to the two equations above would be greater than v, contravening the dual constraint. If we had $w_1^s < w_1^1$, then none of the inequalities would be satisfied as an equation and the s-th individual would receive no goods. Thus we must have $w_1^s = w_1^1$, so that the same inequalities are satisfied as equations for the s-th individual as for the first, and his consumption will consist of the same two goods as for the first individual, proving the theorem. The difference between this result and that for the non-joint case, in which every individual may consume a different pair of goods (if there are a sufficient number of goods relative to the number of characteristics), arises from the common shadow price w_2 which would be replaced by individual shadow prices w_2^s in the absence of joint consumption.

Note that the proof of the theorem is based on efficiency conditions alone and is independent of the specific properties of U, u^s, so it holds for any degree of dispersion among the private preferences of household members, provided they can agree on a household decision function which leads to a proper optimum.

If we extend the theorem to cover a situation in which there are r_1 private characteristics and r_2 public characteristics, we can expect any one consumer to consume not more than $r_1 + r_2$ different goods. The appropriate dual relations will give us $r_1 + r_2$ equations in r_1 private shadow prices and r_2 common shadow prices. Now suppose that there are two consumers whose optimal choice of goods differs in r' goods. The total number of dual equations to be satisfied is thus $r_1 + r_2 + r'$, while the number of dual variables is $2r_1 + r_2$. Thus the optimal choices for the two individuals cannot differ in more goods than there are private characteristics.

Consider any individual consuming $r_1 + r_2$ goods and thus whose shadow prices satisfy $r_1 + r_2$ dual equations. The public characteristic shadow prices are common and thus exogenous to the individual. Thus the individual's equation system in his private shadow prices consists of $r_1 + r_2$ equations in r_1 unknowns, so that r_2 of the equations are linearly dependent on the remainder. This means that any other individual who consumes at least r_1 of the same goods, and thus whose private shadow prices satisfy r_1 of the equations, will have the remaining equations also satisfied and thus will consume all $r_1 + r_2$ of the same goods as the first individual.

But we have shown that the two goods collections cannot differ by more than r_1 goods, and thus have a minimum of r_2 goods in common. If $r_2 \geq r_1$, therefore, the individuals will consume identical sets of goods (in types of goods, not necessarily in their proportions).

We can bring together the basic theorem and its extension into a result that also serves to summarize the effect of joint consumption on observed household behaviour.

- Result 5

  Joint consumption effects do not change the concavity properties of household demand, as compared with the situation in their absence, but have important repercussions on the extent to which the household satisfies the efficiency criteria of the single individual. In particular, if goods possess some characteristics that are consumed jointly (public characteristics) and others which effect only the individual directly consuming the good (private characteristics), the effect of the joint consumption is to reduce the divergence between the number of goods that the household would be observed to purchase and the number that would be purchased by an efficient single individual. If the number of public characteristics is at least as great as the number of private characteristics, the household will purchase the same number of goods as would a single individual.

GENERAL CONCLUSIONS

We can summarize the overall results of this chapter as follows:

1. There is no general warrant for considering the household to behave as if it were a single individual. The observable behaviour of the household may differ from the typical behaviour of the individual in two respects:

   (a) the concavity properties of its demand function may differ from that of the individual;

   (b) the efficiency properties (observed as numbers of goods pur-

chased relative to the number of distinct characteristics) may not conform to those of the individual.

2. If the household is an aggregate of independent consumers, the concavity properties of its demand function will be weaker than those for the individual, but will come closer to the individual properties as the size of the household decreases. The efficiency properties will diverge from those of the individual, with the maximum extent of this divergence declining as the size of the household decreases.

3. The existence of a well-behaved household decision function of a Samuelson or similar kind will remove all the divergence in concavity properties between the household and the individual, but will *not* remove the divergence in efficiency properties.

4. The existence of joint consumption effects within the household will not affect the concavity properties of demand but will reduce the divergence in efficiency properties between the household and the individual.

The household that *will* behave as if it were a single individual is either dictatorial or has a well-behaved decision function and joint effects in consumption covering at least half the characteristics relevant to its members.

NOTES

1. Originally published in *Annals of Economic and Social Measurement*, **4** (1975), 5–21.
2. See, for example, Ferber and Nicosia (1973).
3. See Lancaster 1966 or 1971.
4. See, for example, Samuelson 1948b.
5. Note that $\bar{V}$ is the exact aggregate analogue of V^s, but ΣK^s is not the aggregate analogue of the Slutsky matrix. The latter would require a different decomposition of $\bar{V}$ from that given in the text, namely $\bar{V} = S + \bar{b}(\bar{x})^T$ where $\bar{b}_i = (\Sigma x_i)/(\Sigma y)$ and $\bar{x}_i$, Σx_i and S is then the true analogue of the Slutsky matrix for the individual. Since the terms $\bar{b}(\bar{x})^T$ and $\Sigma_s b^s(x^s)^T$ are quite different, so are S and $\Sigma_s K^s$. Note also that we will have a different S for every different rule for distributing the aggregate income.
6. See Lancaster 1971, pp. 58–9.
7. In the characteristics analysis, u^i is taken to be strictly quasi-concave on characteristics but when mapped into a function of goods it becomes quasi-concave only, due to the prevalance of zero goods quantities. Thus we must drop the 'strictly' from the specification of all the concavity properties of the demand for goods, for the individual as well as the household.
8. One could develop the relevant analysis along the lines suggested in Winter (1969).
9. See Buchanan (1965) or Ellickson (1973).
10. Some interesting possibilities arise in the absence of household co-operation, including game-type behaviour based on mutual 'free ride' considerations.
11. These constraints correspond to taking the derivatives of the Lagrangean with respect to the x^s_i's. The value assigned to v can be taken to be essentially arbitrary, but v must be positive.

8   The pure theory of impure public goods[1]

The pure theory of pure public goods, as in Samuelson (1964), is a beautiful piece of analysis, the practicality of which is severely reduced by, among other things, the elusiveness of the 'pure' public good. The good old lighthouse is localized, so that it is at best a local public good; its benefits accrue to a specific section of the community, making it more of a club good; and finally, it is not impossible to devise some techniques of exclusion, making it potentially marketable. As a generalized concept, 'defence' is closer to being a pure public good (provided everyone is agreed on the enemy), but any specific activity in furtherance of defence almost always has some local or special interest property. A ring of defences around London may increase the total defence of the UK, but it may also reduce welfare in other towns which become more likely targets because London is taken off the list. Similar arguments hold for police protection – but not for protection against fires, unless the latter are mainly set by arsonists.

Among other candidates that have been nominated for public good status are weather forecasting, the space programme, the justice system, clean air, an attractive environment, government itself, and a just income distribution. In some of these there is an abstract notion that represents the public good aspect, but any specific measure will involve local effects, special group effects, or clear possibilities of exclusion.

The unwillingness of economists to give up on the idea of the public good in the face of difficulties is due to a firm conviction that 'publicness' is a crucial property of certain types of goods, even though it may not be the only property to be considered.

It is the purpose of this chapter to provide a potentially more practical alternative to the theory of the pure public good by considering instead the 'impure' public good, a good with some properties like those of the pure public good and others like those of an ordinary private good.

GOODS WITH PUBLIC AND PRIVATE CHARACTERISTICS

We shall build our theory of impure public goods (or mixed goods) on the basis of the characteristics analysis of goods which the author has developed elsewhere.[2] The essential features of this analysis is that each good possesses properties or characteristics that are technically determined by the nature of the good, that individuals' preferences and welfare are based only on the characteristics they obtain, and that goods are regarded only as vehicles for supplying characteristics.

In the present context we shall concentrate on the broad division of characteristics into *private* and *public*. The private characteristics have all the properties assumed in the standard characteristics analysis, namely that they are obtainable only by direct consumption of the goods containing them and have no effect on other individuals. Public characteristics, on the other hand, are assumed to have the essential property of the pure public good, that the effect on each individual is determined only by the total amount of the characteristic supplied to the economy as a whole. There will be, in general, a variety of different private and public characteristics, each related to both preferences and to goods in a particular way.

Any good will typically possess a number of characteristics, all of which might be private (making it a regular private good), all public (making it a pure public good, if such exists), or some private and some public, making it a mixed good, or impure public good. Our interest here is in the last kind.

Most, if not all, of the items on the standard list of public goods are better described as mixed goods. Many goods which are not considered true public goods but have been considered to have enough 'publicness' for them to be provided by means other than through the regular market, such as education, can be regarded as mixed goods. Many goods commonly treated as pure private goods may possess some public characteristics that also qualify for treatment as a mixed good. Housing may fall into this category if consumers in general are morally or aesthetically disturbed by the existence of homeless people or substandard housing.

We can consider education a mixed good by noting that the existence of universal literacy can be treated as a public characteristic, while the education of a specific person has a high private content,[3] so that the individual gains both from the general level of education and from his own education. Education of one person, therefore, provides both a private characteristic and a contribution toward the society total of a public characteristic. Somewhat less obviously we might make a similar kind of argument with respect to public transport, that the existence of a well-travelled transport network benefits even those not using it at a particular time. Each user thus gives himself an immediate private benefit and makes a contribution towards the public benefit.[4] The same considerations apply to communication (both telephone and postal networks) and even to housing if, as suggested earlier, the general level of housing impinges on the sensibilities of all. Health services may be an even better example.

Thus the mixed good concept can be considered to cover a wide range of goods, from those generally considered as public goods to others not generally so considered, and from goods generally supplied through the market to those generally supplied direct by government.

The mixed good concept is, of course, similar to that of the private good plus externalities. The main differences between the analysis here and the standard analysis of externalities lie in two special features:

1. The externalities are themselves externalized by being treated as objective characteristics of the goods rather than as properties of individual preferences. This permits us to separate the technical relationships (how much does a specific model of car contribute to air pollution?) from the subjective aspects, such as the extent to which the public characteristic air pollution has weight in preferences.
2. We are concerned here with only one class of externalities, those that can be classified as true public characteristics. It is obvious that there are other situations for which it would be appropriate to introduce the concept of a characteristic that impinges on individuals other than the direct consumer, but in which the effect is too restricted in scope to be considered a public characteristic.[5]

THE TWO GOOD ANALYSIS

The simplest model incorporating the essential features of the mixed good analysis is one involving two goods, one of which is taken to be a pure private good, the other a mixed good. This is then comparable to the simplest public good analysis, which is based on one private and one public good. Two characteristics only are assumed, one private and one public.

The private good x possesses only the private characteristic z, while the mixed good X possesses a public characteristic Z in addition to the private characteristic. The amounts of private and public characteristics per unit of mixed good, and of private characteristic per unit of private good, are taken to be constant, technologically given, and the same for all n agents.

Formal specification of the model is then as follows:

$$u^i = u^i(z_i, Z) \; i = 1, \ldots, n \tag{8.1}$$
$$z_i = x_i + aX_i \; i = 1, \ldots, n \tag{8.2}$$

$$Z = \sum_1^n X_i + X_G \tag{8.3}$$

$$V = T(\Sigma x_i, Z) \tag{8.4}$$

The typical individual i consumes x_i of the private good and X_i of the mixed good, obtaining one unit of the private characteristic from each unit of the former and β units of the private characteristic from each unit of the latter. One unit of public characteristic is obtained from each unit of mixed good. It is assumed that some of the mixed good might be supplied directly by the government (like a pure public good), so the total amount of the public characteristic is equal to the total quantity of the mixed good purchased by individuals and supplied by government. Each individual's utility $u^i (.,.)$ is a function of the amount of private characteristic he receives from both the private and mixed goods he consumes himself and the amount of public characteristic present in society. The production relationship $V = T(.,.)$ gives the amount of the single scarce resource required to produce the given aggregate levels of the two goods.

Any socially efficient configuration of the economy must be a solution of the problem

$$\min V, \text{ subject to } u^i = \bar{u}^i, i = 1,..., n$$

given the structure above and the implied non-negativity constraints.

Necessary conditions for the optimum are then given by

$$T_1 \geq \lambda_i u^i_1 \ (i = 1,..., n) \tag{8.5}$$

$$T_2 \geq \beta \lambda_i u^i_1 + \sum_1^n \lambda_j u^j_2 \ (i = 1,..., n) \tag{8.6}$$

$$T_2 \geq \sum_1^n \lambda_j u^j_2 \tag{8.7}$$

where $x_i = 0$ if the strict inequality holds in (8.5), $X_i = 0$ if it holds in (8.6), and $X_G = 0$ if it holds in (8.7). The derivatives u^i_1, u^i_2 are with respect to the natural arguments z_i, Z respectively, while T_1, T_2 are derivatives of V with respect to the private and the mixed good, respectively.

It is obvious that (8.6) and (8.7) can both be satisfied only by the strict inequality in (8.7) and thus with $X_G = 0$.[6] The system can be solved by considering only the $2n$ relationships (8.5) and (8.6). It will be assumed that none of the individuals will be at a boundary optimum with strict inequality in either (8.5) or (8.6), so that the system can be regarded as a system of equations. If preferences are widely dispersed, this may be unrealistic, since some individuals with very strong biases towards either the public or the private characteristics may be on the boundary.

From any of the equations (8.6) in conjunction with all of the equations (8.5), we obtain

$$\frac{T_2}{T_1} = \beta + \sum_i^n \frac{u^j_2}{u^j_1}$$

(8.8)

where the ratios being summed on the right-hand side are the marginal rates of substitution between *characteristics* for the *j*'th individual ($MRSC_j$). The left-hand side is the marginal rate of transformation between the private and mixed goods, which we shall henceforth denote by *MRT*.

COMPARISON WITH OTHER CASES

The optimal solution for the mixed goods case bears some resemblance to the standard Samuelson solution for the pure public good case, in that the marginal rate of transformation is equated to a sum of marginal rates of substitution rather than to individual marginal rates. The solution for the mixed goods case differs from the pure public goods case in the appearance of the parameter β and the fact that the marginal rates of substitution are between characteristics rather than goods.

It is easier to compare the mixed goods solution with other cases if we convert the results into marginal rates of substitution between goods rather than characteristics. From (8.1), (8.2) and (8.3):

$$\frac{\partial u^i}{\partial x_i} = u^i_1$$

(8.9)

$$\frac{\partial u^i}{\partial X_i} = \beta u^i_1 + u^i_2$$

(8.10)

$$\frac{\partial u^i}{\partial X_G} = u^i_2$$

(8.11)

Thus the marginal rate of substitution between X_i and x_i, which we shall write as *MRSG*, is given by

$$MRSG_i = \beta + MRSC_i$$

(8.12)

The marginal rate of substitution between X_G *and* x_i is simply equal to $MRSC_i$.

We are now in a position to compare the optimal mixed good solution, which we shall refer to as OPT, with two suboptimal solutions of particular significance, one in which both goods are treated as pure private goods (PRIV) and the other in which the mixed good is treated as a pure public good (PUB). If the goods are treated simply as private goods, the apparent efficient solution (which will be the competitive market solution) will equate the marginal rate of transformation between X_i and x_i and thus the price ratio with the marginal rate of substitution of goods in consumption, necessarily the same for all individuals. Thus we have

Solution PRIV: $MRT = MRSG_i = MRSG_j$ for all i,j (8.13)

Treating X as a pure public good means that $X_i = 0$ for all i, the public characteristic being entirely supplied through X_G. The standard Samuelson condition then implies that the marginal rate of transformation should equal the sum of the $MRSG$'s, which in this case are the same as the $MRSC$'s.

$$\text{Solution PUB:} \quad MRT = \sum_{j=1}^{n} MRSC_j \quad\quad (8.14)$$

Finally we can use (8.12) to rewrite the optimal solution in terms of the $MRSG$'s:

$$\text{Solution OPT:} \quad MRT = \sum_{j=1}^{n} MRSG_j - (n-1)\beta \quad\quad (8.15)$$

Suppose initially that the transformation curve is linear so that MRT is constant and the same for all solutions. Comparing solutions $PRIV$ and the modified version of OPT, we have

$$MRSG_i(PRIV) = \sum_{j=1}^{n} MRSG_j(OPT) - (n-1)\beta \forall i \quad\quad (8.16)$$

Now $MRSG = \beta + MRSC$ so that $MRSG_j > \beta$ for all j. Thus the right-hand side of (8.16) is necessarily greater than any $MRSG_j$, so that

$$MRSG_i(PRIV) > \max_{j} MRSG_j(OPT) \quad\quad (8.17)$$

This implies that the private good solution will have *every* individual consuming more of the private good, and less of the mixed good, than at the optimum.

Comparing the public good solution with the optimum, we have

$$\Sigma MRSC_j(PUB) = \beta + \Sigma MRSC_j(OPT) \qquad (8.18)$$

so that

$$\Sigma MRSC_j(PUB) > \Sigma MRSC_j(OPT) \qquad (8.19)$$

The implication of (8.19), initially surprising perhaps, is that the public good solution will provide the average individual with *less* of the public characteristic than will the optimal solution. The reason for this is that part of the supply of the private characteristic is obtained from individual consumption of the mixed good in the optimal solution. In the public good solution, on the other hand, all of the private characteristic must be obtained from the private good, partly at the expense of the public good and thus of the public characteristic.

A NUMERICAL EXAMPLE

Since the relationship between the optimal solution and the public good solution is surprising, it seems worthwhile to illustrate with a simple example. The society consists of ten consumers, all with the same utility function $z_i^{1/2}Z^{1/2}$ and a linear transformation of the form $V = \Sigma x_i + \Sigma X_i + X_G$. The parameter β is taken to have the value 0.2. The solutions are for maximum utility, equally distributed over individuals, from a resource base of 100.

The distribution of both private and mixed goods will be uniform over individuals, with $MRSC_i = MRSC_j \forall i,j$. The common value of $MRSC$ will be given by:

$$MRSC = \frac{x + \beta X}{nX}(\text{OPT and PRIV})$$

$$= \frac{x}{X_G}\ (\text{PUB})$$

MRT is constant and equal to unity.

In this particular case, the amount of private characteristic per individual is the same in both the optimal and public good solutions, but achieving this via the public good solution requires relatively more of the private good, leaving less resources available for the mixed good (which is being treated as a pure public good), and thus a smaller amount of the public characteristic, so that the welfare level is less than the full optimum.

The pure private good solution here gives more of the private characteristic but much less of the public one than either of the other two, and gives the lowest welfare level.

Although we initially assumed a constant marginal rate of transformation in order to simplify comparison of the three solutions, the relative ordering of the solutions is not changed if the transformation relationship is that of a strictly convex production possibility set. Such curvature brings the solutions closer together (in terms of ratios of the two goods), but it remains true that the ratio of public to private characteristic will be largest for the full optimum, next largest for the PUB solution, and smallest for PRIV.

POLICY IMPLICATIONS

Since it is not optimal to treat both goods as private goods and rely on the operation of the competitive market system, nor to supply the mixed good as if it were a pure public good and thereby throw away its potential content of private characteristic, it is obvious that the optimal solution requires that individuals actually purchase the goods themselves, but not at relative prices corresponding to marginal production costs. Optimal policy requires some form of subsidy on the mixed good, tax on the private good, or both.

If both goods are sold through the market, the individual purchaser will buy the two goods in proportions which equate the marginal rate of substitution (between goods) to the buyer price ratio. Denote the buyer price ratio for the j'th consumer by R_j and the producer price ratio by r. Then the optimum condition requires that $r = MRT$ and that

$$r = \Sigma \ MRSG_j - (n-1)\beta = \Sigma \ R_j - (n-1)\beta \qquad (8.20)$$

Noting that $R_j = MRSG_j > \beta$ for all j, it follows that

$$r > \max_j R_j \qquad (8.21)$$

so that a subsidy-tax combination in favour of the mixed good will be required for every individual. In general, the optimum will require a different value of R_j and thus a different tax-subsidy combination for every individual.

Let us remove the complication of individually-tailored subsidy-tax combinations by assuming all individuals have identical homothetic preferences, giving $R_i = R_j$ for all i,j. The subsidy-tax formula then takes a simple form:

$$r = nR - (n-1)a$$

or

$$R - a = \frac{1}{n}(r - a)$$

(8.22)

That is, the difference between R and ß is less than that between r and β, with R converging to β as $n \neq \infty$. For the numerical value given in the last section, $a = 0.2$ and $R = 0.28$. If the population were 100 instead of 10, the optimal value of R would be 0.208.

Thus the optimal solution for the mixed good case can be attained by the sale of both goods in the market, but with policy intervention in the form of a subsidy-tax arrangement which reduces the buyer price of the mixed good in terms of the private good, relative to the producer price ratio. If the consumers have identical preferences or can be represented by a typical consumer, the required difference between the price ratios is given by (8.22) above. Whatever the producer price ratio, the optimal buyer price ratio will be very close to (but greater than) β when the population is large.

The crucial quantitative information for policy purposes in the mixed-good analysis is the value of the parameter β. This is a technical para-meter, here taken to be constant over the economy (an assumption that is dropped in the next section). Whatever the conceptual or measurement problems associated with β, they are insignificant compared with the problem of estimating the sum of the marginal rates of substitution required for the pure public good case.

TECHNICAL VARIATIONS

It is possible that the ratio of private to public characteristics in the mixed good may vary between groups because of local or other *objectively* identifiable causes. To a rural dweller, the existence of a well-developed urban transport network may be a public characteristic (as a guarantee that he will be able to move around easily if and when he visits the city), but the private content to him is small. To a family with adult children, the public characteristic content of an education system may be important, the private characteristic content negligible.

We must be careful to distinguish between the *subjective* preferences of individuals for private versus public characteristics, and the *objective* differences between groups as to how much private versus public characteristic is present in the mixed good, as expressed in the parameter β. An individual may have a small interest in the public characteristic relative to the private, but be able to obtain a high ratio of private to public characteristic from the mixed good.

Assume there are three groups in the economy, G_1, G_2, G_3 each homogeneous within itself, facing different values of the parameter β. Denote the values by $\beta_1 > \beta^2 > \beta_3$ so that the least amount of private characteristic per mixed good unit is obtained by persons in the first group, the greatest by persons in the third group.

Formal specification and optimization of the model follows the same lines as before, modified to account for the different values of β. The inequalities (8.5) are unchanged, but the inequalities (8.6) become divided into three:

$$T_2 \geq \beta_1 \lambda_i u_1^i + \sum_{j=1}^{n} \lambda_j u_2^j \quad (i \epsilon G_1) \qquad (8.23)$$

$$T_2 \geq \beta_2 \lambda_i u_1^i + \sum_{j=1}^{n} \lambda_j u_2^j \quad (i \epsilon G_2) \qquad (8.24)$$

$$T_2 \geq \beta_3 \lambda_i u_1^i + \sum_{j=1}^{n} \lambda_j u_2^j \quad (i \epsilon G_3) \qquad (8.25)$$

It is immediately obvious that the inequalities $T_1 \geq \lambda_i u_1^i$ (from (8.5) and the inequalities (8.23) to (8.25) cannot all be satisfied as equations. What we can regard as the typical solution will have the form:

For $i \epsilon G_1$: $\quad T_1 = \lambda_i u_1^i$
$\qquad\qquad\quad T_2 > \beta_1 \lambda_i u_1^i + \sum \lambda_j u_2^j$

For $i \epsilon G_2$: $\quad T_1 = \lambda_i u_1^i$
$\qquad\qquad\quad T_2 > \beta_2 \lambda_i u_1^i + \sum \lambda_j u_2^j$

For $i \epsilon G_3$: $\quad T_1 = \lambda_i u_1^i > \lambda_i u_1^i \ (\Rightarrow x_i = 0)$
$\qquad\qquad\quad T_2 > \beta_1 \lambda_i u_1^i + \sum \lambda_j u_2^j$

Individuals in G_1 will consume none of the mixed good, obtaining all their public characteristic from the mixed good consumed by other groups. Individuals in G_3 will consume none of the private good, but will obtain all their private characteristics from consuming the mixed good. Only individuals in G_2 will consume both goods.

The optimum condition, combining the relationships above, is

$$MRS = \beta_2 + \sum_{j \in G_1 \cup G_2} MRSC_j + \frac{\beta_2}{\beta_3} \sum_{k \in G_3} MRSC_k \qquad (8.26)$$

This solution has a generic similarity to the solution (8.8) for the fixed parameter case, the median parameter β_2 playing the role of the former single parameter. It differs in that the marginal rates of substitution for individuals in G_3 are added in with weights of less than unity.

In this case an assumption of identical preferences over all individuals does not lead to so direct a simplification as before, because of the differences in the ß's. Consumers in different groups will, in general, have different marginal rates of substitution between characteristics at equilibrium. Denote the value for members of G_2 at the optimum by $MRSC^*$. Then (8.26) can be written as

$$MRT = \beta_2 + nk.MRSC^* \qquad (8.27)$$

where k is given by

$$k = \frac{\sum_{j \in G1 \cup G2} MRSC_j + \frac{\beta_2}{\beta_3} \sum_{k \in G3} MRSC_k}{nMRSC^*}$$

'Now we will have $MRSC < MRSC^*$ for individuals in G_1 and $MRSC^* > MRSC$ for individuals in G_3. The value of k may thus be greater or less than unity, and its value will depend on the distribution of population among the three groups. Thus we can consider k to be substantially independent of the population *size* if the distribution among groups is constant and all members of a group have identical preferences. Due to the effect of the public characteristic, a change in population size will change all $MRSC$'s, but we shall assume that changes in the ratios of these between different groups are small.

Now consider the determination of an optimal policy. Since only members of G_2 buy both goods, the appropriate buyer price ratio is equal to $MRSC^*$. Denote this ratio by R, then from (8.12)

$$R - \beta_2 = MRSC^* \qquad (8.28)$$

If the producer price ratio is r, then (8.27) and (8.28) give

$$R - \beta_2 = \frac{1}{nk}(r - \beta_2)$$

(8.29)

This differs from the single parameter tax-subsidy formula only in the presence of k. Since we have argued that k can be expected to be substantially independent of n, we reach the same conclusion as in the earlier case, that the optimum value of R will be close to, but slightly larger than, the value of β_2 for a large population. Thus the existence of multiple value of the parameter β does not substantially affect the policy prescriptions – the median value being used.

CONCLUSION

By analysing 'impure' public goods as mixed goods possessing both public and private *characteristics* in technically-determined proportions, we reach an important conclusion – that treating such goods as pure public goods will not only be suboptimal but will result in supplying *too little* of the specifically public content. Treating education, for example, as a pure public good could be expected to result in too little 'general literacy' relative to an optimal solution that would be generated by selling education through the market at an appropriately *subsidized* rate. Without the appropriate tax-subsidy policy, however, a pure market solution would, in general, be further from the optimum than the public good solution.

The analysis in this chapter gives some guidelines as to how the policy makers might commence to estimate appropriate subsidization values. For a large population, the appropriate consumer price in terms of pure private goods can be shown to be determined by a parameter which is, in principle at least, *technical* and not behavioural.

NOTES

1. Originally published in Grieson, R. (ed.) (1976), *Public Finance and Urban Economics: Essays in Honor of William S. Vickrey*, Boston, D. C: Heath-Lexington.
2. Lancaster (1966a, 1971)
3. We are ignoring here both the merit argument (Musgrave (1959)) and the human capital approach, in which the consumption aspect of education is treated as of minor importance.
4. This assumes no congestion problems. It seems a pity to be ignoring one of William Vickrey's favourite problems in an essay originally written for a volume in his honour.
5. A classification of most of the possible externality combinations is given by Shoup (1969). For a discussion of externalities that can be considered as public characteristics within a household, see Lancaster (1975a).
6. Since the mixed good has private characteristics, it is clearly inefficient to supply it as a pure public good and waste those characteristics.

9 Optimal variety in the provision of public services[1]

Public goods and services, like private ones, can often be producd in many forms. Public education, for example, can follow different curricula and use different teaching methods. The schools not only embody these variations in education but also possess another characteristic, that of location, adding a further element of potential variety. Schools in different places are like different schools to an individual located at one specific point, even if the educational services are otherwise identical. Education, of course, has many of the properties of a private good, but even defence, which approaches the properties of the textbook public good, can be produced in various different forms. One defence package, for example, may give a high level of expected protection against a certain type of threat and little against another, while a different defence package may protect against the latter threat better than against the former. If both packages represent the same resource cost, each can be considered as the same 'amount' of defence but a different variety, like different models of cars.

The problem of the optimal degree of variety in the supply of private goods has attracted considerable interest in recent years,[2] and the purpose of this paper is to consider the extent to which a comparable problem can be identified with respect to the supply of public services, including public goods in the strict sense. In other words, are there cases in which a public service should be provided in more than single form, and, if so, what determines the number of varieties in which it should be produced? The fact that the public service can be produced in many forms does not, of course, necessarily mean that more than one form should be supplied – the problem may turn out to be that of optimal choice of form, rather than number of forms.

In the case of private goods, the interest in investigating optimal variety is less to arrive at a particular number than to provide a bench-mark against which the performance of various market structures can be assessed. Similarly, for goods which are publicly provided, our interest in the optimal degree of variety (defined in accordance with some appropriate criterion) lies especially in making comparisons with the variety that would result from typical public decision processes, such as voting.

VARIETY IN THE PRIVATE SECTOR

Although there are models of product differentiated markets[3] in which identical individuals have a pure 'taste for variety' (that is, every individual consumes all the varieties available), the more typical models seek to explain the existence of many varieties even when a particular individual consumes only one. The most obvious starting point is to assume the existence of diversity in consumer preferences. By this we mean that, if offered a choice over all the models of some product class that are (or could be) produced with the same resources (and thus can be considered of equivalent 'quality'), different individuals would choose different models.

The first element in determining the degree of variety in the output of some industry is thus the extent of diversity in consumer tastes. There is a second element, of equal importance – the extent of economies of scale in the production of the good. If there are constant returns to scale (no economies or diseconomies) then it is clear that the market will produce all varieties which are wanted and that this is the optimal degree of variety on all reasonable criteria. This is illustrated by the historical existence of extensive custom tailoring and custom dressmaking services when there were no special scale economies accruing to ready-made clothing for technological or management reasons. When such scale economies became dominant, apparent variety was reduced.

If there are economies of scale, however, lesser variety permits more production of each model and thus lower average costs per model. The optimum degree of variety is that for which the welfare losses to those consumers not receiving the models they prefer is just balanced by the saving in resource use which results from fewer models in larger production runs. Too little variety means that too many people fail to obtain their preferred model, even though the models available can be produced at a low average cost. Too much variety means that there are potential cost gains from economies of scale that more than outweigh the welfare loss to those who would suffer from discontinuance of certain models.

The degree of variety that will be produced in the market depends on the type of competitive structure which it possesses, and the two extreme cases, monopoly and monopolistic competition, have been well studied.[4] The relationship between the degree of variety produced by the market and the optimal variety turns out to be a much more complex matter than was once thought. The best that can be said is that, in the absence of knowledge concerning the relevant system parameters, monopoly is likely to produce less variety than is optimal and monopolistic competition, more.

A point of the highest importance concerning variety in the supply of private goods is this: the market will not produce the optimal solution if left to itself when it is technically feasible always to vary product design. This is because, if products can be differentiated in a continuous way, perfect competition will not be a possible market structure. The 'most competitive' market structure will be monopolistic competition, which is not optimal with respect to either price or variety. Thus the common belief that all problems which do not involve externalities or major indivisibilities can be solved by some kind of non-collusive market, does not hold when there is continuously variable product differentiation. This remains true even when cost curves are U-shaped in the traditional way, a cost structure that is certainly consistent with textbook perfect competition.

Everything concerning the degree of variety which results from the existence of consumer diversity necessarily involves *distribution*. A reduction in the degree of variety, by stopping production of certain models in order to gain scale economies by increased production of others, brings losses to those whose preferred models are dropped and gains to those who always preferred the other models which now become cheaper. These distributional aspects will be a dominant theme in the discussion of variety in the public sector.

THE COSTS OF DIVERSITY

If there are any scale economies of any kind in the economy (and a pure public good can be regarded as a good with unlimited economies of scale in consumption), diversity in consumer tastes is almost always costly, in the sense that an economy identical in all relevant respects except that there is uniformity in consumer preferences can obtain higher welfare levels for its members from the same resources. This is because fewer different models will be produced if preferences are uniform, and thus there will be fuller exploitation of economies of scale. The problem of optimal variety is that of making the most efficient use of resourses, *given the diversity in tastes*, but there would always be a further saving in resources if the diversity itself vanished or diminished.

The argument is obvious enough if there are two sorts of people, tall and short, and there are economies of scale in the clothing industry. The same population could be clothed at lower cost if they were all the same size. In the well-known legend, Procrustes concluded that it was simpler to cut everyone to the same size than to have a variety of beds – a drastic solution, perhaps, but cutting everyone to the same psychological size still attracts central planners.

The costs of diversity in the private goods case are due to economies of scale, but there can be costs of diversity when public goods are involved, even when there are no economies of scale in production. This can be demonstrated by considering a simple economy with one public good and one private good, the traditional textbook model on which public good theory is constructed, in which both public and private goods are produced under constant returns to scale. The efficient solution to the public good problem case is then the quantity Y^* of the public good and the quantities x_1^* ,..., x_n^* of the private good which are the solutions to the optimizing problem:

$$min \ V = mY = \sum_{i=1}^{n} x_i \qquad (9.1)$$

subject to

$$U_i(Y,x_i) = U_i * \ i = 1,..., \qquad (9.2)$$

where V is the value of resources required to attain the utility levels U_1^* ,..., U_n^* for consumers 1 ,..., n, respectively, and m is the unit cost of the public good in terms of the private good.

The solution to this problem is identical to that of the following problem in which y is a private good having a unit cost equal to m/n times that of the other private good x:

$$min \ V = \frac{m}{n} \sum_{i=1}^{n} y_i + \sum_{i=1}^{n} x_i \qquad (9.3)$$

subject to:

$$U_i(y_i,x_i) = U_1^* \ i = 1,...,n \qquad (9.4)$$
$$y_i = y_j = Y \ \text{all} \ i,j \qquad (9.5)$$

In comparing the two isomorphic problems, the differences are that (a) in the second case, the unit cost of the private good must be $1/n$th that of the public good in the first, and (b) the existence of the constraint that all consumers must receive the same amount of good y. These differences illustrate the effect of the economies of scale in consumption which are of the essence of a public good – equivalent to reducing the unit production cost by the factor $1/n$. They also show that, as compared with an all-private good economy with the equivalent reduction in cost, there is an additional implicit constraint (8.5), due to the necessary equality of the amount of public good supplied to everyone.

The economies of scale in consumption represent a potential gain from public goods, but the implicit constraint of equal consumption implies – like any constraint – the possibility of loss. This potential loss vanishes, however, if all consumers have identical preferences and are to be given identical utility levels, since then all consumers would choose equal amounts of y_i and thus the constraint (8.5) would be irrelevant. If consumers did not have identical preferences, however, the constraint would be effective and, in this sense, lead to a loss. The costs of diversity are the effects of the constraint. The cost of diversity can be illustrated by considering a two-person economy in which both individuals have Cobb–Douglas (log–linear) utility functions, but not necessarily with the same parameter values. In particular, the individual identified by parameter value a is assumed to have a utility function of the form

$$U(a) = C(a)X(a)^a Y^{1-a} \tag{9.6}$$

where $X(a)$ is the amount of the private good consumed by the individual and Y is the amount of public good supplied to the economy.

The function C(a) is given by

$$C(a) = 2^a m^{1-a} a^{-a}(1 - a)^{-(1-a)}c \tag{9.7}$$

where c is a scale constant, the same for both consumers. Taking $C(a)$ to be a function of a instead of a constant, normalizes the utility functions so that the minimum amount of resources required to put each of two identical consumers on a given level of utility remains the same for all values of a. Without such normalization, two identical consumers with a high value of a (less weight to the public good) will require more resources to achieve a given utility level than will consumers having the same value of C with a lower value of a, because the latter value the public good relatively more and thus make more use of economies of scale in consumption.

For the particular choices $a = 1/3$ for one consumer and $2/3$ for the other, the optimum problem given by (9.1) and (9.2) earlier, with m taken as unity, can be solved directly and the optimum value of V calculated. If the base value of U^* is such as to require 100 resource units when the individuals have identical tastes, the solution for the above diversity example gives 105.28 as the mimimum resources required. The extra 5 per cent of resources represent the pure costs of diversity in this case.

Before leaving this example, it is useful to consider the equity properties, real and apparent, of the solution in the diversity case. If we assume that all the payments for resources goes to the two individuals, and is divided equally between them, then the optimal solution requires that they be taxed at different rates, since all disposable income will be spent on the private good and the optimal consumption of that good differs between the individuals. In the example given, the consumer for whom $a = 1/3$ should pay 57.4 per cent of his income in tax, the other consumer, with $a' = 2/3$, should pay 51.8 per cent. That is, identical money incomes and identical utility levels require *different* tax rates between individuals. *True equity requires apparent inequity* because the value of the common public good differs between the individuals. If both individuals received the same incomes and paid taxes at the same rates (apparent equity), one of the individuals would actually be better off than the other. This is a recurrent theme in all problems which involve diversity of preferences, that true equity may require apparent inequity and, conversely, apparent equity may give rise to true inequity. I have referred to this difficulty elsewhere[5] as that of 'manifest equity'.

A LOCATIONAL EXAMPLE

A simple case of diversity in preferences arises when goods or services and consumer preferences both contain locational elements, and it is useful to approach the problems of distribution and possible conflict between optimality and voting criteria in a context in which the diversity itself is easily mapped. Consider the case of a typical public service, fire-fighting. It is obvious that both the firestation and the premises of a particular individual possess location, and that the views of an individual as to the relative desirability of two different potential firestations will depend on their locations relative to himself.

Consider the problem of the optimal distribution of firestations in a linear city. The population is uniformly distributed along the High Street, which is very long (so the ends can be neglected) and divided into blocks of equal size. Each individual judges his welfare from the provision of fire protection in terms of the fastest response time to a fire alarm. We shall assume that the response time is directly poportional to the distance x between the firestation and the individual's premises and inversely proportional to the speed s of the fire equipment, so that $t = x/s$. We will suppose that the cost of operating a firestation depends on the number of houses it must serve and on its equipment, and that there are economies of scale. Constant returns to scale would imply that the same expenditure per household would buy equipment of the same speed, whatever the number of households. We will assume here that the scale economies are such that the more households are covered by a station, the faster the equipment for a given outlay per head. In particular, we shall assume initially that increasing the scale by a factor r will permit an increase in equipment speed by the same factor, for an unchanged outlay per head.

Now fix the per capita fire department budget and consider whether this should be spent on a few large firestations a long distance apart or many small firestations close together. Since it is obvious that they should be evenly spaced in either case because of the uniform distribution of population, let us compare a system of small firestations spaced R blocks apart with a consolidation into a system of large firestations spaced NR blocks apart. Under the assumed technology and costs, the per capita costs of the two systems will be the same. The speed of the equipment will be N times as fast in the consolidated case, but the average distance from houses to the nearest fire station will be N times as great, so that the *average response time* will remain unchanged, as will the longest response time.

If the criterion for performance were the average response time, then there would be nothing to choose between the two systems, both giving equivalent performance for equivalent cost. For particular individuals, however, the performances are not equivalent – some gain and some lose in each case.

Consider the effect on a particular individual of a consolidation of firestations such that every second firestation is closed and the remainder doubled in capacity and speed, as above. If the individual is at a distance x from the nearest firestation after consolidation, then his nearest firestation beforehand would have been at a distance x or $x - R$, according to whether his original local station was or was not the one closed. The response time with the consolidated system will be $x/2s$ as compared with x/s or $(R-x)/s$ for the original. The individual will prefer the consolidated system if the response time is less, that is if $x/2s < (R-x)/s$, with a break-even at $x = 2R/3$. Thus two-thirds of the individuals would prefer the consolidated system, because the response time to fires in their premises would be shorter.

What if every three firestations were consolidated into one? In that case, an individual at distance u from the nearest consolidated station would be at a distance x, $R - x$, or $x - R$, from the nearest site in the decentralized system, according as x lies in the range $[0, R/2]$, $[R/2, R]$, or $[R, 3R/2]$. There are now two break-even values of x, one for which $x = 3(R-x)$, the other for which $x = 3(x - R)$, giving $x = 3R/4$ and $x = 3R/2$. Since the *closest* consolidated firestation cannot be at a distance greater than $3R/2$, in this case exactly half the individuals gain from the consolidation (those living at a distance up to $3R/4$ from the consolidated station), and half lose.

Since there is a clear majority for consolidation when $N = 2$ and a 50/50 split when $N = 3$, extrapolation might suggest that a majority would be against any consolidation in which N was greater than 3. Actually the analysis for a general value of N is a little less simple than it may appear, but the results can be shown to be as follows:

1. If N is odd, the proportion who gain by consolidation is exactly 50 per cent for all N.
2. If N is even, the proportion who gain by consolidation is given by $N^2/2(N^2-1)$, which is always greater than one half and converges to that value as N increases.

Thus there is always a majority for consolidation provided it involves an even number of firestations, but there is a larger majority for the simple consolidation involving pairs of firestations than for one involving larger numbers. Since this relationship holds at every stage of the consolidation process, we have the interesting result that, starting with four adjacent firestations, there is a majority of only eight to seven for a direct consolidation into one, against a majority of two to one for consolidation into two. Once the consolidation into two has been achieved, however, there is then a two to one majority for further consolidation of those two into one. There is a non-transitivity in the voting, similar to that in the well-known voting paradox, which arises from the fact that every consolidation involves different households in different ways.

To see what is happening, which is important in appreciating the complexities of distribution effects often present in public service supply decisions, let us assume that the streets in our linear town are numbered north and south from Center Street, and that firestations are initially spaced along Central Avenue at Center Street, north 15th, 30th, 45th, 60th and so one every 15 blocks, with a symmetric arrangement to the south. If now the 15th Street and 45th Street stations, north and south, are closed down and the scale of the remaining stations doubled, with equipment operating twice as fast, it is easy to see that, of the householders living in the first 60 blocks north, those living between Center and 10th streets, 20th and 40th streets, and 50th and 60th streets will all gain from lower response times, while those living between 10th and 20th street (near the closed 15th street station), and 40th and 50th street (near the old 45th street station) will all lose.

Now consider a further consolidation, with the 30th street station (and 90th street) closed and the Center and 60th street stations doubled in scale (to four times their original scale). In this consolidation, the gainers are those living up to 20th street, and then from 40th and to 60th streets. Looking at the gainers and losers in each consolidation, those living up to

10th street and from 50th to 60th streets (one-third of the total) gain in both consolidations; those living between 20th and 40th streets gain from the first and lose from the second; while those living between 10th and 20th, and between 40th and 50th lose in the first and gain in the second. Only one-third of the population gains in both consolidations, but at each step it can form a coalition with the one-third who will gain from the next consolidation, a different group each time.

OPTIMALITY CRITERIA

It is obvious that, in the firestation example above, most normal voting procedures will lead to consolidation, ultimately into a single large-scale firestation. Is this the optimal choice? The degree of scale economies in the example was chosen specifically to ensure that the average and maximum response times remained the same after consolidation as before. Indeed, the average expected welfare is the same at every level of consolidation for any loss function that depends only on the response time, whatever its form.[6] Thus one apparently rational criterion suggests that the community should be indifferent to plans for consolidation. The enthusiasm for consolidation revealed by voting behaviour is because the gains and losses from implementing it, although averaging out, are not distributed evenly – there are fewer losers than gainers, but their average loss is greater than the average gain of the majority. For a consolidation of two firestations into one, the maximum saving in response time for any household is equal to the average response time $\bar{t}$, while the maximum increase in response time is twice that.

In this example, there is a strong majority for consolidation, although the average response time and average loss would not really be changed, the gap between the voting and welfare criteria being due to the distribution of potential gains and losses. To have a decision-making procedure reflect these distributional effects, a traditional solution is to require that the gainers should compensate the losers, and that a vote be taken only when it is clear that such compensation will be taken into account. In the firestation case, the average response time (or any loss depending only on it) is unchanged by consolidation, so the gainers could just compensate the losers. If required to pay such compensation, the former gainers would now just come out even, as would the former losers. A vote would no longer necessarily show a majority for consolidation but would result in a tie or a random outcome, reflecting the welfare equivalence of the pre- and post- consolidation situations.

When the diversity in individual preferences comes from some objectively ascertainable difference, such as location, the use of some compensation technique for decision-making seems attractive. For any change in the location of firestations, the change in response time to any particular household can be objectively assessed, and any compensation arrangements (such as reducing property taxes for the losers and raising them for the gainers) will also be objective. There is no real problem of manifest equity, since the potential gainers can easily visualize themselves in the loser's location, and appreciate the justice of the compensation. The situation is very different if the diversity in preferences cannot be perceived as due to objective causes, in which case manifest equity problems are almost certain to arise. Suppose that a majority of the citizens wanted the town lamp-posts painted blue, and a minority wanted them red. How far would one get with the suggestion that they should not be painted blue unless those that preferred them so should compensate those who liked them red? And who would decide how much compensation to pay? The red/blue example can be used to make one or two passing comments, relevant to later discussion. First is that variety does not necessarily solve problems in taste differences when consumption is not fully private – painting the lamp-posts alternately red and blue might make both groups worse off. However, if those who preferred red tended to live on the north side of town, and those who preferred blue on the south side, decentralized decision-making might give a better result.

The firestation example showed a case in which there could be a firm majority for a policy, although there was neither a loss nor a gain in welfare. This was a special example. To consider a more general case, return once more to the example, but generalize degree of returns to scale so that, for a consolidation of two firestations into one large one, the equipment that can be purchased with unchanged expenditure per head now has a speed k times that of the equipment in the smaller stations. If k equals 1, there are no economies of scale, the same outlay per capita buying the same equipment, while if k equals 2 we have the example already discussed.

First of all, let us take note of who would gain and who would lose from consolidation. For a household at a distance x from the nearest station after consolidation, the post-consolidation response time would be x/k (for convenience, the base speed will be taken to be unity). The pre-consolidation response time would be $\min[x, R - x]$, and the households gaining from consolidation would be those for which x/k did not exceed $R - x$. The marginal household is that at distance $\hat{x}$, where

$$\hat{x} = kR/(k + 1)$$

so that the proportion of households which gain from consolidation, $\hat{x}R$, is equal to $k/(k + 1)$. Note that this is greater than one half for all k

greater than unity, that is, for all situations in which there are economies of scale. The size of the majority increases with k, and is very small if k is close to one. So long as there are any scale economies, however, there can be a majority vote to consolidate.

In this case the average response time is $R/4$ before consolidation and $R/2k$ after, so that the response time is higher after consolidation for all values of k less than 2. If the overall welfare criterion is that of minimizing average response time, then the unconsolidated system is optimal for any k less than 2. So long as there are some economies of scale, but k remains less than 2, there is a clear conflict between the optimal degree of variety, based on a reasonable welfare criterion, and the actual degree of variety as generated by a reasonable public choice method. This can be considered the analogue of the conflict that may arise in the private goods case between the optimal degree of variety on some welfare criterion and the amount of variety generated by the market.

As before, the conflict between the average loss level and the direction of the vote is due to the distributional effects. If $\bar{t}$ is the average response time in the unconsolidated system, the maximum gain from consolidation (obtained by households midway between the pre-consolidation locations of stations) is $2(k-1)\bar{t}/k$ while the maximum loss (accruing to households at the sites of the stations abolished for consolidation) is $4\bar{t}/k$. For $k = 2$, the maximum gain is $\bar{t}$ and the maximum loss $2\bar{t}$, as shown previously. The less the economies of scale, the smaller the maximum gain and the larger the maximum loss, the limiting values being 0 and $4\bar{t}$, respectively, as k becomes unity and the economies of scale vanish. For $k = 5/4$, the majority in favour of consolidation would be $5/9$, although the average response time would rise from $\bar{t}$ to $9\bar{t}/5$. Furthermore, the maximum gain from consolidation would be only $2\bar{t}/5$, while the maximum loss would be $16\bar{t}/5$. If the expected loss is a convex function of response time, giving more weight to high values of the response time, then the loss in welfare from consolidation might be considerable.

The requirement that compensation be paid would, of course, solve the conflict between the voting and welfare criteria. For k less than 2, the cost of compensating the losers would be greater than the benefits accruing to the gainers. Those who would gain without compensation would, in fact, be worse off after consolidation when the compensation payments were taken into account. Certainty that compensation would be required would then reverse the votes of this majority, and thus consolidation would be voted down. Another way of looking at the relationships is to observe that the potential losers could bribe the potential gainers to vote against the change, since the losers' total prospective losses are larger than the gainers' prospective gains.

Note that coincidence of voting and welfare criteria through the compensation principle requires voters to perceive the certainty that compensation will actually be paid after the move. There is a long tradition in welfare economics,[7] although not universally accepted, that a policy move should be made if the potential gainers could compensate the potential losers and if the potential losers could not bribe the potential gainers to preserve the status quo, even when it is certain the compensation payments will not be made. It is obvious that a paper computation that the gainers could compensate the losers (or would be unable to) will not solve the voting problem. For k less than 2 in the example, the traditional compensation principle requires that the firestations be left unconsolidated, yet the vote will be to the contrary unless actual payment is required.

VARIETY AND THE THEORY OF PUBLIC GOODS

A pure public good in the textbook sense (which is almost always a service rather than a physical good) possesses two fundamental properties which can be expressed in several different ways but which we can refer to as non-diminishability and non-excludability. That is, it is a good or service, (a) the amount of which available to any individual depends only on the quantity supplied and is independent of the number of other individuals participating in its consumption, and (b) from the enjoyment of which no individual can be excluded. The original example was that of a lighthouse, the warning services of which are not diminished for any vessel by their availability to many others, and from the use of which no vessel can be excluded. It is more common these days to use 'defence', treated as an overall service to the community, as the basic example.

Although, as was suggested in the introductory remarks, even pure public goods can be produced in different 'models' as well as in different quantities, there does not seem to be any question of the degree of variety in relation to textbook public goods because of their special properties. Suppose there were two kinds of defence, one especially good for protection against attack from the land and the other for protection against attack from the sea. Ignoring locational effects, everyone would receive the benefits of whichever defence was chosen. Pursuing both policies at the same time does not provide *greater variety* in the sense of alternatives that different individuals may choose, but *greater quantity* of defence to everyone because of the public good properties which imply additivity. There may be great differences of opinion between individuals as to which kind of defence is most desirable, given that there are insufficient resources to provide all kinds together, but this is not a problem in variety but in choice between alternatives. The same is true as to differences over the desired mix of public and private goods, and both these problems fall under standard public good analysis.

Many (perhaps most) services or goods actually provided by government or other collective action are not pure public goods in the above sense, nor are they pure private goods, but represent something in between the two. Consider education, for example. In many respects this is like a private good, and yet it is not without reason that some form of education is publicly provided almost everywhere, because the existence of literacy and of some common culture increases the welfare of all. The education case can be analysed as that of a private good with externalities in consumption, but I prefer to think of it as a mixed good, or an impure public good, which has several characteristics, some of them public and some private.

A simple analysis of impure public goods in the above sense, confined to goods having one public and one private characteristic was made by the author some years ago.[8] In this analysis, the private characteristic could also be obtained from a pure private good, but the public characteristic could be obtained only from the mixed good. The conclusions of this study were as follows:

1. If the mixed good is treated as a private good (the pure market solution with no intervention), the economy will produce too little of the public good, and thus of the public characteristic, compared with the optimum.
2. If the mixed good is treated as a pure public good and provided in quantity determined by the Samuelson formula,[9] then there is also less of the public characteristic than is optimal.

The first result is not surprising, but the second may be. The reason is that, by treating the mixed good as only containing a public characteristic, its true cost in terms of potential welfare is overstated and too little is produced. It can be shown that the optimum will be attained by providing both goods through the market, but with an appropriate subsidy for the mixed good.

Variety in such mixed goods becomes possible if the assumptions in the original analysis, that the proportions between the private and public characteristics are technologically fixed and that there is but a single private characteristic, be relaxed. There is potential variety in the private/public characteristics proportions, and there is potential variation in the proportions between the private characteristics, if more than one. These two types of variety might be superimposed, if there are several private characteristics and the ratios of these to each other and to the public characteristics can be varied.

As a simple example, consider the mixed good to be education, with a public characteristic (literacy and common culture) and private characteristics, relating to other aspects of the curriculum. Reduce the private aspects of the curriculum to two characteristics – culture and athletics, say. Then educational programmes might be offered with various proportions of the public to combined private characteristics and, for each such variant in the public/private mix, different proportions of culture to athletics in the private characteristics.

Such a model of potential variety in mixed goods is little more than an agenda for study at this stage. We can, however, draw on results already obtained in other contexts to sketch out some expectations about optimal variety in such a case. Provided there are economies of scale sufficient to rule out one-on-one tutoring, these expectations are:

1. If education were left entirely to a non-collusive profit- maximizing private sector, there would be (a) a less than optimal proportion of public to private characteristics, (b) a more than optimal degree of variety in the number of culture/athletic mixes offered, and (c) there would be too little education in general as compared with other things (because price would be above marginal cost).

2. If education were entirely public, the outcome in this case is not necessarily that of the simple mixed good model quoted above. In that model, the private characteristics were assumed to be ignored in the treatment of the mixed good as a public good. Here, however, the public/private proportions can be varied and the existence of the latter cannot be ignored. One assumption might be that the public authority would provide the minimum ratio of private to public characteristics, tending to result in (a) a more than optimal proportion of public to private characteristics, and (b) a less than optimal amount of education because its non-optimal programme design leads to undervaluation.

3. Ensuring both the optimal private/public characteristics mix and the optimal variety in private characteristics offerings would require some quite complex policy mix of direct supply, regulation and tax/subsidy arrangements. The outcome would depend heavily on the exact nature of the production technology. If the public and private characteristics could be produced separately at no extra cost, then the solution would presumably be one in which education was received partly from public supply and partly on the market, possibly with regulation and tax/subsidy arrangements.

DECENTRALIZATION AND FEDERALISM

One answer often suggested to the problem of variety in public services, or at least to the problem of variety in the relative mix of public and private goods, is that of decentralization into smaller governmental units or assignment of more decision-making to community-level units in a multi-layered system. There is a current political tide in the United States in favour of such an approach, on the grounds that decentralization will bring better government because it is 'closer to the people'. The last phrase implies the existence of potential variety arising from diversity among communities–if there were no such diversity, it is difficult to see why a central government would differ from a local one in terms of policy decisions. A well-known economic argument in favour of this solution is set out in a 1956 paper by Tiebout.

There are two fundamental problems which arise in relation to the centralization versus decentralization debate. One is the relationship between individual diversity and community diversity, and the other is the extent of the scale economies in the provision of public goods and services. The case in which it is totally obvious that decision making at the local community level can achieve a full optimum is when the four following criteria are satisfied:

1.   Each community is made up of identical individuals.
2.   There are no potential economies of scale in the provision of public goods and services which could be obtained by consolidating production between two or more communities.
3.   There are no consumption externalities between communities and no public goods common to all communities, or, if there are, their effects are separable and can be handled at a central level independent of decisions at the local level.
4.   The overall social welfare criterion does not call for any inter-community distribution.

If any of the above criteria fail to be satisfied, the case for decision making at the local community level is no longer beyond question, although it may still be valid. In the usual analysis, conditions 3 and 4 are not mentioned, but are implicitly assumed, while 1 and 2 are assumed explicitly. Economies of potential consolidation are assumed away by confining the analysis to that of 'local' public goods, the concept of which suffers from some lack of clarity, but which are such that no community can use the local public good of another. It has been asserted by one worker in the field of public goods theory, Bryan Ellickson,[10] that there is no concept of a local public good which is at all comparable to that of the Samuelson pure public good, and that the former should be treated as private goods with strong indivisibilities.

Ellickson gives a formal analysis of the Tiebout model, using the above concept of a local public good as equivalent to an indivisible private good, and shows that an approximate competitive equilibrium can be attained. But Ellickson requires that the local public good be excludable, and that economies of scale in production can be completely exhausted at the level of output appropriate to the size of the community. The types of goods and services which satisfy these requirements are education (due to possible scale economies, the smaller the community, the more elementary the level of education which conforms), parks and beaches, and most of the things actually supplied at the community level almost everywhere. Some local services, such as law enforcement, do not provide for complete exclusion of non-participants, even if the police turn their backs when they see a non-buyer of their services being attacked in the street. A model of this kind does not seem to throw much light on the extent to which decentralization may be useful in solving the problem of variety and diversity with goods closer to the true public good.

Let us concentrate on the deeper problem, which is whether diversity over individuals is better served by decisions at the community level or at a more central level. This will obviously depend to a considerable extent on the relationship between *intra*-community diversity and *inter*-community diversity. One limiting case is that in which each community is homogeneous, and all heterogeneity in the overall society is reflected in inter-community differences. Provided there are no inter-community economies in the provision of public goods, a mix of public and private goods which is determined uniquely for each community will clearly be optimal as compared with a single mix applied to every community by a central decision. On the other hand, if there is diversity within each community, distributed so that the proportions of each consumer type are the same in every community, there is no superiority of local over central decision-making, and the latter will be preferable if potential scale economies exist.

Between these two extremes, it seems plausible that the case for decentralization should increase if intra-community diversity falls relative to inter-community diversity. So far as I know, no general theorem of this kind exists that has been proved, but it is certainly true that the costs of variety will, in general, increase with the degree of diversity within the community. In the example given earlier to illustrate these costs, it was shown that a community consisting of two individuals whose preference parameters were one-third and two-thirds, would require 5 per cent more resources to give its members a specified welfare level than would be required if both had the same preferences. It can be shown, in the same way, that a more diverse community, with parameters one-sixth and five-sixths would require 15 per cent more resources than the homogeneous case – a clear increase resulting from greater diversity.

Although policy tailored to the community may often be superior to a uniform policy if compensation is actually paid or the decisions are based on a social welfare function, problems may arise from the method of decision making at the community level. Suppose there are three types of individuals, each type having distinct preferences, and they are represented equally in the society at large, but the overall society is divided into two parts: north, containing all the As and half of the Cs, and south, containing all of the Bs and the other half of the Cs. The preferences of the Cs may be ignored altogether in both parts, even though there are as many Cs in the society as a whole as any other group. This example summarizes one of the two fundamental arguments against decentralized decision-making, the other being the distributional problems that will arise if income variations are large between communities and small within them.

VARIETY IN PUBLIC UTILITY OUTPUT

Since regulation of the output of public utilities is one of the traditional public services, it is a natural part of this study to consider the appropriate approach to regulators to variety in public utility output. Such variety can consist of the number of different types of telephones available, the frequency of service and/or number of localities served by public transport, or the number of different tariff plans available to the electricity consumer.

The starting point is the degree of variety that will be made available by an unregulated monopoly, as compared with the optimal degree of variety in that same product class. This problem has been examined elsewhere,[11] and the results can be summarized as follows:

1. The degree of product variety under unregulated monopoly will always be less than it would be under the most competitive comparable market situation, that of monopolistic competition.
2. The degree of product variety under monopoly will be less than at the true optimum, if consumers are compensated in both cases to keep them all at the same welfare level whatever the variety.
3. A more realistic comparison, between monopoly without compensation and a second-best optimum (also uncompensated), shows that monopoly will almost always produce too little variety.

On the basis of these relationships, it would appear that the regulatory agency should be putting on pressure for variety in services. It is not at all certain that regulators pay as much heed as they should to the question of product or service variety, nor if they do, whether they view the problem from the correct perspective. The point has already been made several times that diversity of tastes imposes costs in industries with scale economies, in the sense that the optimal level of product variety will result in less gains from economies of scale than if the diversity in tastes were absent. The regulators may be strongly influenced by averages, and may easily neglect the distributional inequities that arise from too little variety, with the result that it may seem both popular and good practice to favour a solution in which average costs (and thus average tariffs) can be lowered by reducing variety of services.

There is, however, one very well-known situation in which there is pressure on regulators to provide too much variety. This is in respect of transport services to localities that generate little traffic. As in the fire-station analysis, the demand for variety based on locational diversity is much more easily voiced, since the reason is clearly visible to all, than that for variety due to taste differences. Thus air, bus, or train services to some locality may be required of long-haul carriers, even though it might be cheaper to pay for, or subsidize, taxi or other services instead. It should be noted, however, that clear examples of such inefficiencies are often due to particular political pressures or to piecemeal regulation that prevents the regulator of one service insisting on the use of another service which comes under other authority.

NOTES

1. This paper, previously unpublished, was delivered as the Rand Chair Lecture at the University of Buffalo in 1982.
2. See Dixit and Stiglitz (1977), Lancaster (1975b, 1979) and Spence (1976a).
3. The Dixit–Stiglitz model, most notably.
4. See Spence (1976a,b) and Lancaster (1979).
5. Lancaster (1979).
6. This is because the particular degree of economies of scale chosen results in consolidation being mathematically equivalent to a pure change in units.
7. Springing from the work by Hicks and Kaldor in the late 1930s and early 1940s.
8. Lancaster (1976).
9. That the marginal rate of transformation should equal the sum of the marginal rates of substitution over all individuals.
10. Ellickson (1979). Note that Ellickson is incorrect in asserting that the public good analysis is not required if individuals are identical. The optimal condition then becomes that the marginal rate of transformation should equal N times the marginal rate of substitution, where N is the population, not the marginal rate of substitution itself.
11. Lancaster (1979), Chapter 9.

PART IV

STUDIES IN PRODUCT VARIETY

10 Socially optimal product differentiation[1]

This chapter sets out to investigate the extent to which we can reach broad general conclusions concerning the social optimality of different degrees of product differentiation. The chapter is concerned with consumer preferences and production conditions only, and it abstracts from such problems as search and information costs, and disutilities of uncertainty or consumer confusion in the face of variety. It examines the problem of optimal variety in a world in which every consumer knows exactly what he prefers and exactly how to achieve personal optimality in the face of the constraints upon his actions.

Product differentiation exists when, within a group of goods so similarly related to consumers that they can be considered to form a product class, there is a variety of similar but not identical goods. The theory of product differentiation has been historically associated with the theory of monopolistic competition, and has been analysed primarily from the point of view of the firm. Although some social policy conclusions have been drawn from this approach to the subject, there does not exist a firmly-based analysis leading to an answer to the question: How many different product variants should society provide?

One cannot go very far in answering this question within the framework of conventional or 'direct' consumer theory, in which preferences are assumed to be given directly in terms of goods. For this reason, I shall turn to the 'characteristics' or 'indirect' analysis of consumer behaviour, based on my earlier work (1966a,b, 1971), in which the consumer is assumed to derive his actual utility or satisfaction from characteristics which cannot in general be purchased directly, but are incorporated in goods. The consumer obtains his optimum bundle of characteristics by purchasing a collection of goods so chosen as to possess *in toto* the desired characteristics.

Use of the characteristics framework provides a clear definition of a product class (those goods possessing a particular set of characteristics) and permits quantitative definition and measurement of product differentiation (by comparing the proportions in which the various characteristics are possessed by different goods within the product class), both of which properties are necessary for the analysis of optimum product variety. The characteristics framework enables us to cast the problem into a spatial setting and proceed along lines reminiscent of the pioneer work by Harold

Hotelling.

The structure of the chapter is as follows. In the first section, I shall set up some special tools of analysis that will be basic to the remainder of the analysis. Then, in the second section, I shall state and prove two basic theorems concerning optimal product differentiation and returns to scale, after which section three examines the conditions that must be satisfied by an optimal choice for the number and type of products. In the fourth section, I shall state and prove four theorems concerned with optimal pricing and the effects of imperfect competition and, finally, summarize the results with special reference to policy conclusions.

The analysis will be carried out for product classes defined on two characteristics only. It will be apparent from the analysis itself and the results obtained that generalization to any number of characteristics is simply a question of additional arithmetical complexity, a complexity that does not seem justified in a pioneer investigation of the problem.

TOOLS OF ANALYSIS

The production–consumption link

Consumers derive their ultimate utility or welfare from characteristics which in turn are obtained from the specific product differentiates which are available. Each product is assumed to possess those characteristics in fixed proportions. The product differentiates are themselves no more than a *transfer mechanism* by which fixed bundles of characteristics are assembled at the production end and then made available to ultimate consumers, the goods playing the role of intermediaries rather than being either primary resources or ultimate objects of consumption. If we view the system as a whole, consumer welfare is determined by the characteristics available for consumption, while the ultimate constraints are those on resources, the two linked by the transfer through goods. The transfer mechanism depends on both the way in which the resources may be used to produce goods having characteristics in different proportions and on the way in which the specific bundles of characteristics so produced are related to consumers' preferences as between all possible characteristics bundles.

For a given level of resources, the level of welfare that can be attained by the various consumers will depend on:

1. The production conditions that determine how much of each characteristic can be supplied from given resources, when embodied in a good with specific characteristics proportions.

2. The preferences of the consumers, which determine the relative welfare levels associated with various bundles of characteristics.
3. The consumption process, which determines what characteristics combinations the consumer can actually obtain from different collections of goods.
4. The number and types of goods that determine the transfer link between production and consumption.

In this chapter we shall take the production and consumption possibilities as given, and be concerned primarily with the transfer mechanism. It is obvious that transfer can be efficient or not, depending on the choice of the good used for the transfer. Suppose, for example, that existing resources can be used to produce a unit of either good G_1 (embodying two units of characteristic z_1, and one of z_2) or good G_2 (one unit of z_1, two of z_2). If there is a single consumer whose preferences are for high z_1-content, a lower welfare level will be attained by producing G_2 than by producing G_1. In this case, G_2 represents inefficient transfer relative to G_1, but if the consumer's preferences are biased toward z_2, the relative efficiencies of the two transfer modes will be reversed. And what if there are some consumers with preferences biased towards z_1, some towards z_2, and others in between? That is the essence of the problem we shall be solving.

Production conditions
Differentiation possibilities
We assume that it is possible in principle, to produce goods having all possible ratios of the two characteristics, so that the producer can plan to produce a good anywhere in the characteristics spectrum. Having chosen the proportions in which his particular product will contain the two characteristics, there will be a unique maximum quantity of those characteristics that can be produced with given resources when incorporated in that particular good. For a given level of resources, we can take any ratio of the two characteristics, determine the maximum output of the good with that specification from the given resources and thus the maximum quantities of the two characteristics that can be produced from the resources when embodied in the appropriate good. The set of all characteristics combinations producible from a given level of resources by incorporation in a good can be plotted as a curve in characteristics space. We shall refer to this curve as a *product differentiation curve* and abbreviate it to *PDC*. Of particular interest will be the *PDC* corresponding to unit resource use, the *unit PDC*.
Assume the *PDC* has geometric properties similar to those of the

conventional transformation curve or production possibility curve, namely:

1. it is continuous;
2. it slopes downward from left to right;
3. it is either a straight line or a curve which is concave toward the origin.

I shall make the following additional assumption:
4. *PDCs* for different resource levels are positive homothetic expansions or contractions of the *unit PDC*.

Figure 10.1 illustrates the assumed properties of the *PDCs*.

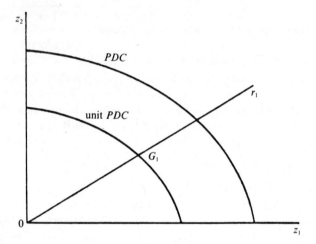

Figure 10.1

Note that I assume only a homothetic relationship between *PDCs* for different resource levels and particularly avoid any suggestion of linear homogeneity, which would imply constant returns to scale. Most of this chapter is devoted to production under *non-constant* returns to scale, but restricted to the homothetic case which implies the same returns to scale properties for all goods in the product class.[2]

Measurement and comparability

The greatest single obstacle in the path of formal analysis of product differentiation is that of making quantitative comparisons between goods which are not identical. Since prices are endogenous, monetary measures cannot be used. One can only choose between comparing goods in terms of their final utility or their resource content. Since it is essential to the later analysis that there be many consumers with differing preferences, final utility measures are quite unsuitable. I shall, therefore, use a modified input measure that requires only that all firms face the same *PDC*s, an assumption that would be made in any case.

I shall therefore define and measure goods in the following way:

1. A good is defined by its characteristics ratio, goods with identical characteristics ratios being identical goods.
2. We bring *different* goods to the same measure by defining the unit quantity of any good to be that quantity which can be produced with unit resources.
3. Different quantities of the same good are scaled in proportion to the content of either characteristic (since the characteristics are in fixed proportions) relative to the content of that characteristic in a unit of the good as defined above.
4. As a consequence of 1–3, plus the assumed homotheticity of the *PDC*s, quantities of different goods will receive the same measure if and only if those quantities require the same level of resources. Figure 10.2 illustrates the measurement system.

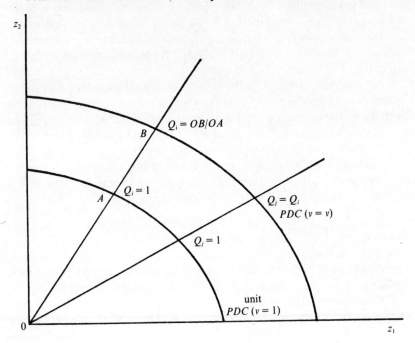

Figure 10.2

Note that a unit of a good is defined as requiring a unit of resources, but q units of a good do not necessarily require q units of resources since there may not be constant returns to scale. Resource content is used to relate quantities of *different* goods but quantities of the same good are scaled linearly from the resource content. Given the unit *PDC*, the characteristics content of unit quantities of different goods can be read straight off the curve and other quantities by linear scaling from these. Thus quantities of different goods are directly comparable, are in equivalent units, and can be arithmetically combined.

The input function

Once the choice has been made to produce a particular good with a specific characteristics ratio, there will be a defined functional relationship between the quantity of that good and the inputs required. It is convenient to use this production function in the inverse form, $v_i = F(Q_i)$, where v_i is the resource requirement for the quantity Q_i of the good whose identity is defined by characteristics ratio $r_i (= z_2^i/z_1^i)$. I shall refer to $F(Q_i)$ as the input function, to stress its inverse nature.

Due to the way in which we have defined our quantity measure and to the assumed homotheticity of the *PDC*, F has the following very important property: the input function is the same for all goods. That is, the functional relationship between v_i and Q_i will be the same as the functional relationship between v_j and Q_j, for all i, j. (We assume, of course, that i, j are in the same product class.)

Since the input function is the inverse of a production function, $F(Q)$ increases in proportion to Q for constant returns to scale, less than in proportion for increasing returns to scale, and more than in proportion for decreasing returns. Since we shall be interested in variations in the degree of returns to scale, we note that $F(Q')/F(Q) > 1$ for all $Q' > Q$ but that the ratio approaches unity as the degree of increasing returns to scale increases without limit and the ratio increases without limit as the degree of returns to scale becomes more and more decreasing.

Consumption

Consumers

Consumers have preferences defined on characteristics. Preferences with respect to goods are indirect and derived from preferences on characteristics. These are assumed to have the same general properties with respect to characteristics as conventional preferences with respect to goods. They may be represented by preference maps with indifference curves of the conventional kind, except that we do not rule out indifference curves which are linear or piecewise linear. We shall be more interested than usual in the elasticity of substitution (curvature of the indifference curves) and sometimes concern ourselves with indifference curves showing infinite elasticity of substitution (straight lines) or zero elasticity (fixed proportions). In the latter case, excess amounts of either characteristic beyond the appropriate fixed proportion will have no effect, so that zero elasticity indifference curves can be considered to extend vertically and horizontally away from the point of optimum proportions.

We shall generally assume that the population consists of a very large number of consumers with different preference patterns, so that there is a continuous spectrum of preferences. Later, we shall refer to a 'uniform' distribution of preferences, a term that will be defined in the appropriate context. We shall also make a special assumption about the distribution of preferences, which we introduce at the appropriate point.

The consumption process

Consumption involves the extraction of the characteristics embodied in the goods at the production end. There are two major technical possibilities: we may have *combinable* consumption in which goods may be combined in the consumption process to obtain some combination of the characteristics contents of the individual goods. Combinable consumption will be taken to be *linear*, the characteristics of the combination being the sum of the characteristics contents of the individual goods. On the other hand, we may have *non-combinable* consumption in which only one good can be consumed at a time and characteristics can be obtained only in those proportions represented by an available good.

Both types of consumption are realistic in different contexts. Food nutrients fit the linear combinable case, but the services of many consumer durables fit the non-combinable pattern. The emphasis in this chapter will be on non-combinable cases.

Optimal and suboptimal transfer

If we take a single individual in isolation and set out to minimize the resources required to attain a specified utility level, it is obvious which transfer good will achieve the optimum; it will be the good having a characteristics ratio r^* which corresponds to the point at which the relevant indifference curve for the consumer is tangent to a *PDC* (or at the corner of the indifference curve in the zero elasticity case). Figure 10.3 shows optimal transfer in diagrammatic form, and needs no further comment.

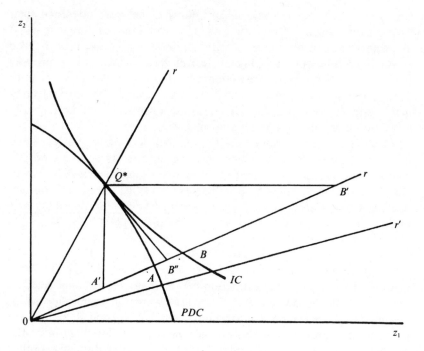

Figure 10.3

Compensation for suboptimal transfer

If the consumer's optimal good (that which would give him optimal transfer) is not available, there is some quantity of the 'next best' good[3] that will enable him to achieve the utility level he would have attained with some specific quantity of the optimal good. If Q^* is the quantity of optimal good (characteristics ratio r^*) that enables the consumer to attain a specified welfare level, and Q is the quantity of a good with characteristics ratio r that enables him to achieve the same level, we can regard Q as the *compensating* quantity corresponding to Q^*. Since Q, Q^* are in comparable units, we can take the ratio Q/Q^* and refer to it as the *compensating ratio* for good r as compared with optimal good r^*.

Figure 10.3 shows a consumer for whom the optimal good is r^* and another good $r(r < r^*)$ which is suboptimal for this consumer. In order to bring the consumer to the same indifference level as attained with Q^*, he must be given an amount of good r which corresponds to point B on the diagram. From the properties of the quantity measure we are using, the compensating ratio is OB/OA.

It is obvious that the compensating ratio depends on three factors, the degree of curvature of the utility function, the degree of curvature of the *PDC*, and the difference between r and r^*. The ratio will increase with increased curvature of either curve and with an increase in the difference between r and r^*. The maximum possible value for the compensating ratio will be when B is at B' and A is at A' (corresponding to right-angled indifference and *PDC* curves with corners coincident at Q^*) and will be equal to r^*/r. In the case in which we have $r > r^*$, the maximum value of the compensating ratio will be r/r^*.

The compensating ratio will be one of the main tools of our subsequent analysis. Since it depends on r, r^* as well as on underlying preference and production conditions, it is useful to write the ratio as a function of r, r^*. We shall refer to the ratio in the form $h(r,r^*)$ as the *compensating function*, and it will have the following properties:

1. $h(r^*,r^*) = 1$
2. $1 \le h(r,r^*) \le \max(r^*/r, r/r^*)$, for all r
3. $h_r(r,r^*) \ge 0$ for $r > r^*$, ≤ 0 for $r \le r^*$
4. $h_{r^*}(r,r^*) \le 0$ for $r \ge r^*$, ≥ 0 for $r \le r^*$
5. $h_{rr}(r,r^*) > 0$, unless both the indifference curve and *PDC* are linear,[4] at least for r within a 'reasonable' distance of r^*.

TWO BASIC THEOREMS ON DIFFERENTIATION AND RETURNS TO SCALE

Using the tools we have developed, it is possible to enunciate two basic theorems on the relationship between optimal product differentiation and returns to scale.

Theorem 1
If production is subject to constant or decreasing returns to scale, it will be socially optimal to produce every good which represents optimal transfer for any consumer. If and only if there are constant returns to scale in production, a linear product differentiation curve, and linearly combinable consumption processes, the social optimum can also be achieved with a number of goods in each product class not greater than the number of separate characteristics in the product class. Under decreasing returns to scale, it may be optimal to produce even more goods than under constant returns to scale with the same distribution of preferences, and certainly not less.

Under constant returns to scale, the resources used to produce any quantity of any good are directly proportional to the quantity as measured, with the same constant of proportionality for all goods, because of the homotheticity assumption and the definition of the quantity measure. Any consumer who must consume a suboptimal good is therefore using more resources than would be needed for him to attain the same welfare level with an optimal good, and it is necessarily optimal to provide every consumer with his optimal good.

If, in addition to constant returns to scale, there is linearly combinable consumption and a linear *PDC*, then production of the two extreme goods (each containing one of the characteristics only) will enable any consumer to attain the same welfare level by a combination of those goods as with his optimal good, for the same level of resource utilization.

Now consider the case in which there are decreasing returns to scale. In this case more goods, each produced in smaller quantities, will use less resources than fewer goods produced in larger quantities. It is obvious that it will never be optimal not to produce every consumer's optimal good. But now it may be optimal to have a consumer derive some of his welfare from a non-optimal good, so as to reduce the average level of output of all goods.

Suppose that there is a linear *PDC* with equation $z_1 + z_2 = 1$, and that there are two consumers whose preferences show zero elasticity of substitution and whose optimal goods are given by $r_1 = 3$, $r_2 = 1/3$. The input function has the form $v = Q^a$ ($a > 1$ for decreasing returns to scale), and the consumers initially each receive one unit of their respective optimal goods for a total resource use of two.

Now introduce a third good with characteristics ratio $r = 1$, and suppose that each consumer receives some quantity of his optimal good, plus enough of the third good to bring him to his original welfare level. In this particular example the compensating ratios for the third good are equal at 1.5 and since the example is symmetrical we suppose each consumer receives an amount $(1 - x)$ of his optimal good and an amount $1.5x$ of the third good, bringing each consumer to his original welfare level.[5]

Total resources used in the three-good case will then be given by

$$V = 2(1 - x)^a + (3x)^a$$

If we choose x so as to minimize V, we obtain

$$x^* = [1 + 3(3/2)^b]^{-1}$$

where $b = 1/(a - 1)$ which gives $x^* > 0$ for all $a > 1$, and thus it is optimal to produce some of the third good for all degrees of decreasing returns to scale. For $a = 2$, we have $x = 2/11$ and $V = 18/11$, a saving of $4/11$

resource units. Thus it will be optimal to produce goods which are not the optimal goods of any consumers, if there are decreasing returns to scale.

It is interesting to consider the pricing associated with the above case. Since the compensating ratio is 1.5, a consumer will be induced to buy both the third good and his optimal good if the price of the third good is 2/3 that of the optimal good. Since the cost function for any good has the form $C = AQ^a$, where A is the same for all goods, we can compute the marginal costs of the goods at the optimum. It turns out that the ratio of the marginal cost of the third good to that of either optimal good is 2/3 for all values of a, when x is given its optimum value. Thus competitive prices are appropriate.

Increasing returns to scale
Economic intuition suggests that the effect of increasing returns to scale will be to reduce the socially optimal number of goods below what it would be under constant returns to scale, at least for a sufficient degree of increasing returns. For a sufficiently well-behaved case, the socially optimal number of goods will be a function of the degree of increasing returns and will decrease as this degree increases. Finally, intuition suggests that a solution for the optimal number of goods will necessarily involve solving for the optimal choice of those goods in terms of characteristics ratios. A grand theorem incorporating all these possible results is not easy to produce, so we shall start with a simple but basic theorem.

Theorem 2
There is some degree of increasing returns to scale, sufficiently large, for which the socially optimal number of goods is one.

Consider a situation in which the consumers are supplied with N goods, the amount consumed of the ith good being Q_i. We make no assumptions about the specification of these goods or the distribution of preferences except that there are non-zero quantities of at least two goods. We shall consider the effect of replacing these goods by a single good, arbitrarily chosen with respect to characteristics. The quantity of the single good is denoted by Q and, if it is just sufficient to enable all consumers to attain the same welfare levels as with the N goods, it is obvious that $Q \geq \Sigma_1^N Q_i$. Write $Q = k\Sigma_1^N Q_i$, where $k \geq 1$.

We need first to prove that k is bounded above. Now, among all the consumers in the initial (N-good) situation, there must be one who consumes the greatest amount of characteristic z_1 per unit of whatever good he consumes; denote this maximal amount by $\bar{z}_1$. There will be a maximal z_2, denoted by $\bar{z}_2$, derived in a comparable fashion. Suppose the amounts of the two characteristics in unit quantity of the single good are $z_1^{\bullet}$, $z_2^{\bullet}$ (note we restrict the single good to having some of both characteristics), then the maximal value for the compensating ratio cannot exceed max $(\bar{z}_1/z_1^{\bullet}, \bar{z}_2/z_2^{\bullet})$ for any consumer. The value of k cannot exceed the maximum compensating ratio for a single consumer, hence k is bounded.

Resource use in the N-good case is given by

$$V_N = \sum_1^N F(Q_i)$$

Since there are increasing returns to scale, $\Sigma F(Q_i) > F(\Sigma Q_i)$, with the ratio $\Sigma F(Q_i)/F(\Sigma Q_i)$ increasing as the degree of increasing returns increases.

If the N goods are replaced by a single good, produced in a quantity just sufficient to enable consumers to attain original welfare levels, resource use will be given by

$$V = F(Q = F(k\Sigma Q_i)$$

With increasing returns, the ratio $F(k\Sigma Q_i)/F(\Sigma Q_i)$ is greater than unity, but approaches unity as the degree of increasing returns is increased without limit.

Thus we have the following situation. V_N is greater than $F(\Sigma Q_i)$ and recedes from $F(\Sigma Q_i)$ as the degree of increasing returns increases, while V is also greater than $F(\Sigma Q_i)$ but approaches it more and more closely as the degree of increasing returns increases. Thus there is some degree of increasing returns sufficiently great to give $V \leq V_N$, and the single good is then optimal for increasing returns of this or any greater degree, as compared with the specific N goods of the initial situation. Since no restrictions were placed on N or on the specification of the N goods, it follows that there is some degree of increasing returns for which the single good is optimal as compared with any choice of N goods, for all $N \geq 2$.

This theorem gives only a part of the overall picture with respect to increasing returns to scale, but firmly establishes the basic proposition that increasing returns will be associated with an optimal number of goods that is less than with constant returns to scale, and does this with the minimum of assumptions about preferences and their distribution or about the *PDC*.

THE CONDITIONS FOR OPTIMAL DIFFERENTIATION

Under constant returns to scale, the optimal number of product differentiates will be finite only if the number of distinct preferences represented in the society is finite, and is essentially unbounded if preferences form a continuum. Under decreasing returns to scale, the optimal number of goods will not generally be bounded even if the number of distinct preferences is finite. These are the conclusions to be drawn from Theorem 1. For increasing returns to scale, on the other hand, Theorem 2 shows the optimal number to be bounded for a sufficient degree of increasing returns. Thus the study of optimal differentiation is confined to the cases in which there are increasing returns.

Determining the optimal number of goods under increasing returns to scale is not a simple matter. We cannot merely consider the N-good case, then add an $(N+1)$th good, because there will be a total structural change in passing from N goods to $N+1$ goods. It is obvious that, since we are seeking optimality, we must find the specifications, quantities, and distribution of N goods which provide given welfare levels for minimum use of resources, then find specifications, quantities, and distribution of $N+1$ goods that achieve the same welfare levels as before for minimum resource use. In general, the goods in the $N+1$ case will be entirely different goods from those in the N-good case. The only thing that will be comparable between them will be the minimum resources required to attain the given welfare level in the two cases, and it is direct comparison of this that will indicate whether $N+1$ goods are better or worse than N. Thus solving for the optimal number of goods is a two-part process, first solving the optimum configuration for each possible number of goods, then comparing the resources required between different numbers of goods to find the optimum number. Since the number of goods is an integer variable and the configuration changes between different numbers of goods are discrete, the second stage is simple once the first has been completed.

The optimum configuration
The most difficult and interesting part of the overall problem is that of finding the optimum configuration for a specified number of goods. This involves finding characteristics ratios for the goods and the distribution of those goods over the consumers, such that the given welfare levels for all consumers are achieved with minimum use of resources. It is obvious that opportunities for ill-behaviour abound in a general model, so we shall make the two following assumptions on the distribution of preferences which are designed to give a minimum level of good behaviour:

1. *Continuum assumption.* The distribution of preferences is such that the set of all points along the *PDC* that represent optimal transfer for some individual forms a continuum.
2. *Anticrossover assumption.* The distribution and form of preferences is

such that, if it is optimal to supply two consumers whose optimal transfer goods would have characteristics ratios r_i, r_j ($\leq r_i$) with the same good Q_k, then it will be optimal to supply Q_k to all consumers whose optimal good would have a characteristics ratio r such that $r_j \leq r \leq r_i$.

The two assumptions between them ensure that the set of all consumers being supplied with the same good is compact. It is possible to visualize cases, such as two consumers with the same optimal good, one with zero elasticity of substitution and the other with infinite elasticity, in which it just might sometimes be optimal to supply them with different goods. We rule this out by the anticrossover assumption, which implies that the shape of preferences as between individuals with closely similar optimal transfer goods does not vary too much.

To determine the optimal configuration for N goods we proceed as follows. First we note that, as a consequence of the above assumptions, the continuum of consumers (identified by the characteristics ratios of their optimal transfer goods) will be divided into N segments, each segment supplied by one of the N goods. Denote by $R_1, \ldots, R_{N-1}$ the characteristics ratios which divide the segments from each other, and by $r_1, \ldots, r_N$ the characteristics ratios of the N goods. For given preference and population distributions and given production conditions, the quantity of the ith good (characteristic ratio r_i) required to bring all consumers in the segment bounded by R_i, R_{i-1} to specified welfare levels will be a function of r_i, R_i, R_{i-1} only, so that we can write Q_i as $Q_i(r_i, R_i, R_{i-1})$.

Let us take R as given, and consider the optimal choice for r_i. Since Q_i is not a function of r_j, nor Q_j of r_i, and since R is held constant, Q_i is independent of Q_j (all i,j) and thus the optimal choice for r_i must be that which minimizes Q_i. This gives us our first optimum condition.

$$\partial Q_i(r_i, R_i, R_{i-1}) / \ \partial r_i = 0 \tag{10.1}$$

If $Q_i^* = Q_i^*$ optimized with respect to r_i, then $Q_i^* = Q_i^*(R_i, R_{i-1})$. We can now find the optimal value for R. The Q^*, considered as functions of R, are no longer independent of each other because each R_i appears as an argument in two of the Q^*s. To optimize we must minimize total resources, given by

$$V = \Sigma F_i(Q_i^*) = V(R_1, \ldots, R_{N-1})$$

Because R_j appears as an argument in Q_j^*, Q_{j+1}^* only, the optimum conditions for R takes the form

$$\frac{\partial V}{\partial R_i} = -\frac{\partial Q_{i+1}}{\partial R_i} F'_{i+1} + \frac{\partial Q_i}{\partial R_i} F'_i = 0 \tag{10.2}$$

Interpretation of the optimum conditions

We can give the optimum conditions an interpretation with more direct economic appeal by expressing them in terms which involve the compensating ratios. To do this we shall make the additional assumption, that all consumers having the same optimal transfer good have identical preferences.

Consider the segment of consumers bounded by optimal transfer ratios R_i, R_{i-1}, all supplied by good G_i with characteristics ratio r_i. Consider those consumers whose optimal good would have characteristics ratio r ($R_i \geq r \geq R_{i-1}$), and let the quantity of that good that would bring all these consumers to the specified welfare levels be denoted by $s(r)$. Since the consumers are being supplied with a good having characteristics ratio r_i, not necessarily their optimal good, the total quantity of this good needed to achieve the welfare level is given by $h(r_i,r)s(r)$, where h is the compensating function as discussed in the first section (see pp. 162–3). The total quantity of good G_i required to bring all consumers in this segment up to specified utility levels is then given by

$$Q_i = \int_{R_{i-1}}^{R_i} h(r_i,r)s(r)dr$$

Since R_i, R_{i-1} appear only as limits of integration, we thus have

$$\partial Q_i / \partial R_i = h(r_i,R_i)s(R_i)$$
$$\partial Q_i / \partial R_{i-1} = -h(r_i,R_{i-1})s(R_{i-1})$$

Inserting these values in the optimum conditions (10.2) gives

$$\frac{F'_i}{F'_{i+1}} = \frac{h(r_{i+1},R_i)}{h(r_i,R_i)} \tag{10.3}$$

Now F'_i, F'_{i+1} are the marginal resource costs of producing goods G_i, G_{i+1}, respectively. The right-hand side of (10.3) is the ratio of the compensating ratios for the dividing consumer (whose optimal transfer good is on the boundary between the two adjacent segments) with respect to being supplied with G_{i+1} as compared with G_i.

Thus the second optimum condition, in the case in which consumers having identical optimal transfer goods have identical preferences, has the following easily interpretable form: the ratio of the marginal resource costs of two adjacent goods will be the inverse of the ratio of the compensating ratios with respect to the two goods, for the dividing consumer. No special insights are given by this formulation into optimum condition (10.1) or into the optimality of N goods relative to M goods.

A well-behaved example

To show that intuitive notions about well-behaved relationships between the optimal number of goods and the degree of returns to scale are valid in appropriate cases, we shall sketch out and give the results for a simple example.

On the production side we assume a linear *PDC* of the form $z_i + z_2 = 1$ and an input function of the form $V = Q^{1/b}$ where the degree of increasing returns increases with b. We assume that consumers show zero elasticity of substitution, have optimal goods distributed with uniform line density along the *PDC*, are to be maintained on welfare levels corresponding to unit quantities of their optimal goods, and that the total population is unity.

It can be shown that, under these assumptions, the compensating function h and the density function s have the following forms:

$$h(r_i, r) = \frac{r(1 + r_i)}{r_i(1 + r)} \quad r \geq r_i$$

$$= \frac{1 + r_i}{1 + r} \quad r \leq r_i$$

$$s(r) = \frac{1}{(1 + r)^2}$$

where r is the characteristics ratio of the optimal good and r_i the characteristics ratio of the good actually supplied to consumers with optimal good r.

Confining our investigations to the cases $N = 3, 2, 1$, we obtain the following optimal configurations for the three cases:

$N = 3$:	$r_1 = 1/3,$	$Q_1 = 7/18$		
	$r_2 = 1,$	$Q_2 = 7/18$	$R_1 = 1/2,$	$R_2 = 2$
	$r_3 = 3,$	$Q_3 = 7/18$		
$N = 2$:	$r_1 = 1/2,$	$Q_1 = 5/8$	$R_1 = 1$	
	$r_2 = 2,$	$Q_2 = 5/8$		
$N = 1$:	$r_1 = 1,$	$Q_1 = 3/2$		

Denoting by $V(N)$ the resources required to achieve the given utility levels with N goods of optimal configuration, we obtain $V(3) = 3(7/18)^{1/b}$, $V(2) = 2(5/8)^{1/b}$, $V(1) = (3/2)^{1/b}$. By solving for the values of b at which the various pairs are equal, we obtain our final result. The optimal number of goods is three for $b \leq 1.169$ (relative to the choice between 3 and a lesser number of goods), two for $1.169 \leq b \leq 1.263$, and one for $b \geq 1.263$. Note that the total quantity of goods (ΣQ_i) increases from 7/6 with three goods to 5/4 with two goods to 3/2 with one good (it is 1 for $b = 1$, the constant returns to scale case). If this were not so, the optimal number of goods would never be greater than unity, if there were any degree of increasing returns.

This example shows that, for a sufficiently well-behaved model, we do find the optimal number of goods decreasing steadily as the degree of increasing returns increases.

FOUR THEOREMS ON PRICING AND IMPERFECT COMPETITION

The conditions for optimal configuration at the optimum number of goods lead directly to the following theorem:

Theorem 3
If the optimal number of goods is some number $N > 1$, then the optimal prices for those goods will be such that prices stand in the same ratio to marginal costs for all goods in the group. This can be shown to hold for any *PDC*, any forms of the preference functions, and any forms for the input functions, provided there is a proper interior optimum at N goods.

Consider the optimal distribution of the goods through a market mechanism (where each consumer has an income appropriate to the specified welfare levels), and consider the consumer whose optimal transfer good would have characteristics ratio R_i, the dividing point between the market segments supplied by G_i and G_{i+1}. If he is to be the dividing consumer, he must find that the £1 expenditures on G_i or G_{i+1} which are equivalent to a unit of his (unavailable) optimal good are the same. Thus the ratio P_i/P_{i+1} must be inverse to the ratio of the two compensating ratios $h(r_i, R_i)$, $h(r_{i+1}, R_i)$ for the dividing consumer. But we have already shown in equation (10.3) that the ratio of marginal costs, F'_i/F'_{i+1}, must also equal the inverse of the ratio of the compensating ratios at the optimum configuration for N goods. Thus the ratio of prices between adjacent goods must equal the ratio of their marginal costs. By chain reasoning, the same relationship must then hold for all pairs of goods, proving the theorem.

Note that the theorem requires only that all prices bear the same ratio to marginal costs for goods within the group, and does not require equality of prices and marginal costs. However, if we consider the group embedded in the larger economy then the usual arguments will lead to the requirement of equality in order to achieve optimality over the economy as a whole.

Equalization of the ratios of prices to marginal costs within the group is necessary but not sufficient for optimal configuration, and certainly not sufficient to guarantee that the number of goods is optimal (as we shall see in Theorem 6). It is, of course, easily possible to have the economy operating in an optimal configuration for N goods but be suboptimal because the optimal *number* of goods is really M.

Achieving the optimum

Since the interesting problems with respect to the optimum number of goods arise with increasing returns to scale, and since the optimum pricing system is that of perfect competition, a problem arises in achieving that optimum. The competitive system will not work, first because obtaining the potential scale economies for each good requires a single producer for that good (unless the economies are all industry externalities) and, second, because all firms will make losses when price is equated to marginal cost. Furthermore, even marginal cost pricing cannot guarantee that the *number* of goods is optimal.

One possibility is a managed economy with single firm control of the production of each good and each firm constrained to adopt marginal cost pricing. This would then require a subsidy to cover the gap between total costs and total revenue for each firm. The subsidy itself would be a control variable however, since the optimum number of goods would require the minimum subsidy over the group. A subsidy set at this minimum level for the group as a whole should then induce the group to produce the optimum number of goods, given appropriate institutional rules.

Imperfect competition

The remainder of this chapter is concerned with imperfect competition and its effects on the optimal number, quantity, and specification of goods. We have different cases to consider, but in each case we shall commence from the optimum position and consider the changes introduced by the relevant type of imperfect competition. First we shall clear the air by disposing of a simple but important case.

Theorem 4 (constant returns to scale)

Under constant returns to scale, market imperfection will not cause the number or specification of goods to diverge from the optimum.

If we commence at the optimum and there are constant returns to scale, no form of market imperfection will make it profitable for any firm to eliminate anyone's optimal transfer good because (a) there is no saving in costs from changing the number of goods produced, and (b) the maximum revenue that can be extracted from any one consumer for a given quantity of good supplied will be when he has sold his optimal transfer good. Thus the same goods will be sold, with the same characteristics ratios, as at the optimum. If there are any gains to be made by the monopolist, they will be by increasing prices and reducing quantities of the same goods which are produced at the optimum, not by changing the number of goods or their characteristics ratios. The remaining theorems are all presumed to refer to a context of increasing returns to scale.

Theorem 5 (single good monopoly)
Monopoly control of the production of any one good when firms producing other goods do not behave as monopolists will in general lead to a non-optimal choice for the characteristics ratio of that good and, if other firms adopt marginal cost pricing, to a restriction of the output of the monopoly good.

The second part of the theorem should surprise no one, but the first part represents a new kind of result for imperfect competition theory.

To prove the theorem, consider a particular good (characteristics ratio r) in the overall spectrum. Next to this good in the spectrum will be an 'upper' good (characteristics ratio $r_U > r$) and a 'lower' adjacent good (characteristics ratio $r_L > r$). The dividing consumers between the markets for the good in question and the upper and lower adjacent goods have optimal transfer goods with characteristics ratios R_U, R_L. We start from the optimal configuration and consider the changes that will be made by a monopolist taking control of the good.

We assume that over the range of variations being considered, there are no acceptable substitutes for the good from outside the group. If the price of the good increases, consumers in the centre of the market will simply have to buy the same quantity of the good and spend more in order to remain at the same welfare level. Consumers at the market fringes, however, may switch to the purchase of adjacent goods if it is advantageous to do so. The market boundaries will adjust so that the dividing consumer is the one for whom the ratio of compensating ratios is inversely proportional to the price ratio. Thus the quantity of the good will be given by

$$Q = \int_{R_L}^{R_U} h(r,x)s(x)dx \qquad (10.4)$$
$$= Q(r, R_U, R_L)$$

where $h(r,x)$ is the compensating ratio for the consumer whose optimal good has characteristics ratio x, and $s(x)$ is the market density at x. The effect of price changes operates through changes in R_U, R_L.

By definition of the dividing ratios, the following conditions must be satisfied everywhere:

$$h(r,R_U)P = h(r_U,R_U)P_U \qquad (10.5)$$
$$h(r,R_L)P = h(r_L,R_L)P_L \qquad (10.6)$$

where P, P_U, P_L are the prices of the good in question and the upper and lower adjacent goods, respectively.

Relationships (10.4), (10.5), (10.6), together with the profit definition

$$\pi = PQ - C(Q) \qquad (10.7)$$

(where $C(Q)$ is the cost function) form a set of four relationships that must be satisfied everywhere by the six variables π, P, Q, r, R_U, R_L. There are two degrees of freedom in the system, which we shall take to be the choice of r and the choice of Q.

To prove the first part of the theorem, hold Q constant and consider the effect of variations in r on the firm's profit. Using standard comparative static methods and noting that $\partial Q/\partial r=0$ at the optimum (optimum condition (10.1)), we obtain

$$\frac{\partial \pi}{\partial r} = \frac{Q_L M_U h^L_r + Q_U M_L h^U_r}{Q_U M_L h^U + Q_L M_U h^L} PQ \qquad (10.8)$$

at the optimum point, where

$$h^U = h(r,R_U), \quad h^L = h(r,R_L)$$
$$h^U{}_r = \partial h^U/\delta r, \quad h^L{}_r = \partial h^L/\delta r$$
$$M_U = \partial [Ph^U - P_U h(r_U,R_U)]/\partial R_U$$
$$M_L = \partial [Ph^L - P_L h(r_L,R_L)]/\partial R_L$$
$$Q_U = \partial Q/\delta R_U = h^U s(R_U)$$
$$Q_L = \partial G/\delta R_L = -h^L s(R)$$

The h-functions always decrease as the two arguments move closer together and always increase as they diverge, so that M_U,h^L_r are positive and M_L,h^U_r are negative, while h^U, h^L are essentially non-negative; Q_U is positive, and Q_L negative. Thus the denominator in (10.8) is always negative, but the numerator consists of two terms of opposite sign. Thus $\delta\pi/\delta r$ may have any sign (or be zero but only by coincidence), and the monopolist will in general find it profitable to change the characteristics ratio of his good away from the optimum.

The reason why the monopolist will not generally be satisfied with the socially optimum specification of the good is not difficult to see. From his point of view, the central consumers are locked into his market and it is only at the edges where he must compete with adjacent goods. Thus his actions in the market will be based on the properties at the market fringes, as shown by (10.8) where $\delta\pi/\delta r$ is seen to depend only on the properties at R_U, R_L. The socially optimal choice of r, on the other hand, is given by:

$$\frac{\partial Q}{\partial r} = \int_{RL}^{RU} \frac{\partial h(r,x)}{\partial r} s(x) \ \partial x = 0$$

a condition which gives weight to all consumers in the market segment.

To prove the second part of the theorem, we hold r constant and consider variations in Q. Proceeding as before, we obtain

$$\frac{\partial \pi}{\partial Q} = (P - C') - \frac{QM_U M_L}{D} \qquad (10.9)$$

where D is the same as the denominator in (10.8).

If, as assumed, we have marginal cost pricing at the optimum, then $P - C' = 0$ and we have

$$\frac{\partial \pi}{\partial Q} = -\frac{QM_U M_L}{D} \qquad (10.10)$$

Since M_U, M_L have opposite signs and D has already been shown to be negative, $\partial\pi/\partial Q < 0$ and the monopolist will find it profitable to reduce output (necessarily involving an increase in price and a shrinking of the market boundaries), completing proof of the theorem.

The next theorem is similar in its policy conclusions to the well-known 'excess capacity' theorem of monopolistic competition, although it is based on a different process of reasoning and does not depend in any way on the ambiguous notion of 'capacity'.

Theorem 6 (Monopolistic competition)

Under increasing returns to scale and with a sufficiently uniform and evenly distributed market, 'monopolistic competition' will lead to a greater degree of product differentiation than is socially optimal.

Quotation marks have been placed around monopolistic competition here because one of the most basic assumptions of the Chamberlin model, that the effects of a behaviour change by any one firm will be spread evenly over all other firms, most emphatically does not hold in this case. Here, the behaviour of a firm affects very much those firms producing adjacent goods in the spectrum, and very little those producing goods remote from it in the spectrum. We make the remaining assumptions of monopolistic competition, that each firm produces one product, no other firm produces the same product, and there is free entry into the group that will continue so long as positive profits can be made. Thus, although the dynamics of the group cannot conform to the Chamberlin model because of the oligo-polistic elements present, the equilibrium (if attained) will be of the Chamberlin kind – for a sufficiently evenly distributed total market, all firms will be of the same size, with marginal revenues equal to marginal costs and prices equal to average costs. Thus we shall consider the term *monopolistic competition* to be the most appropriate for the model being considered.

A 'uniform' market is taken here to mean that, after a possible transformation of co-ordinates, the compensating ratio for a consumer whose optimal good has characteristics ratio corresponding to x, with respect to a good having characteristics ratio corresponding to x^*, depends only on the absolute value of the difference between x and x^*. That is, the compensating function has the particular form $h(x^*,x) = h(|x-x^*|)$. If the upper and lower dividing consumers for the market for the good represented by x^* have optimal goods with characteristics ratios x^*+c_2, x^*-c_1, and the market density is constant (taken to be unity), total demand for the good represented by x^* is given from:

$$Q = \int_{z^*-c_1}^{z^*+c_2} h(|x-x^*|) \, \partial x \qquad (10.11)$$

$$= H(c_1) + H(c_2)$$

where $\partial H/\partial x = h$.

Given this uniformity and uniform density, it is obvious that goods and firms will be arranged, both at the social optimum and at monopolistic competition equilibrium, so that $c_1 = c_2$ for every good, and c and Q are equal for all goods. Thus we can write $h(c) = H'(c)$ and $Q = 2H(c)$ for all goods.

Since the whole spectrum is to be covered by goods with equal market areas (in the coordinates being used), there is an inverse relationship between the number of goods n, and the market area measure c, which we can write as $n = A/c$ where A is an appropriate constant.

Now consider the optimum number of goods, and suppose it is sufficiently large to treat n as closely approximated by a continuous variable. For n goods, total resource use is given by

$$V = nF(Q) \qquad (10.12)$$

where $F(Q)$ is the input function for the single good. Since both n and Q are functions of c only, we minimize V with respect to c to obtain the condition for the optimum

$$F' = F/2ch \qquad (10.13)$$

where the second-order conditions are satisfied for increasing returns to scale.

Having established the optimum conditions, we turn to consider the monopolistic competition equilibrium, which will consist of firms facing identical conditions. Each firm will face the same considerations as the firm of Theorem 5, since we assume no oligopolistic elements and thus that other prices are taken as given. Due to the special uniformity assumptions, the expressions that appear in Theorem 5 have the following simplified forms here

$$h^U = h^L = h \ (= h(c))$$
$$M_U = -M_L = 2Ph'$$
$$Q_U = -Q_L = h$$

Inserting these values in (10.9) of Theorem 5, together with the value of $Q(=2H)$ from above, and noting that $h=H'$, $h'=H''$, we obtain

$$\frac{\partial \pi}{\partial Q} = P - C' - 2P\frac{HH''}{(H')^2} \qquad (10.14)$$

We shall suppose prices to be measured in resource units, so that $C = F$, $C' = F'$. We commence at the optimum and thus assume that the condition (10.13), $F' = F/2cH'$ is satisfied.

There are two equilibrium conditions for the monopolistic competition group:

1. that all firms are at individual profit maximizing equilibria; and
2. that there are just sufficient firms to equate price and average cost everywhere.

We shall proceed by supposing that we have the socially optimal number of goods and that price is equal to average cost for all firms, then investigate whether the firms are at profit maximizing equilibria.

Inserting the values $C' = F' = F/2cH'$, $P = F/2H$, in (10.14) we obtain, after some manipulation,

$$\frac{\partial \pi}{\partial Q} = \frac{F}{2H}\left[\frac{H'}{H} - \frac{H''}{H'} - \frac{1}{c}\right] - \frac{FH''}{2(H')^2} \qquad (10.15)$$

Since H'' is positive (the compensating ratio is an increasing function of c), the last term above is clearly negative. Now consider the expression in brackets. This is equal to $\partial(log\ G/\ \partial c = G'/G$, where $G = H/cH'$ and is thus equal to the ratio of the average to the marginal compensating ratio over the half market from $x = x^*$ to $x = x^* + c$. Due to the assumed shape of the compensating function, G is a decreasing function of c so that G' is negative, the bracketed expression is negative, and $\partial\pi/\ \partial Q$ is negative.

Thus a configuration with the optimal number of goods and zero profits will not be profit maximizing for the individual firms. These can increase their profits by contracting output, leading to positive profits and the entry of more firms. The final monopolistic competition equilibrium will therefore result in a greater number of goods than at the social optimum.

Finally, we shall consider the effect of monopolization of a market sector, that is control of the outputs of several goods (taken to be adjacent in the spectrum) by a single monopolist.

Theorem 7 (Monopoly control of a market sector)
Under increasing returns to scale, monopoly control of a market sector will lead to a lesser degree of product differentiation over that sector than is socially optimal.

Consider an optimal configuration over an optimal number of goods, and consider the effect of monopoly control over several adjacent goods in the market. We shall suppose that the monopolist takes over control of the $(j-1)$th, jth and $(j+1)$th goods. Although not essential, it simplifies the argument to suppose that there is uniform distribution over this sector so that, at the social optimum, the prices of all three goods are the same.

Consider the effect of taking the jth good out of production. This will not affect those consumers who originally purchased the other two goods and, if prices are unchanged, will have no effect on consumers purchasing goods outside the monopolized sector. Since we assume throughout that there are no acceptably close substitutes for goods within the general product class from outside the class, those consumers who originally purchased the jth good will now purchase either the $(j-1)$th or the $(j+1)$th. If their incomes are fixed, they will obtain the same amount and the same quantity of the substitute as of their original good (since prices are the same), but will be somewhat worse off. If they are compensated, they will buy more of the substitute than of the original good. Thus the monopolist's average revenue will be unchanged on total sales no less than with all three goods.

Since there are increasing returns to scale, however, the increased output of the $(j-1)$th and $(j+1)$th goods will reduce average costs and thus the monopolist's profits will be increased as a result of closing down production of the *j*th good. Simply closing down the production of the *j*th good does not represent the monopolist's final equilibrium position, of course, but the profitability of this move is sufficient to prove the theorem.

POLICY CONCLUSIONS

The policy conclusions to be drawn from the analysis can best be put in the form of answers to five questions which the policy maker must inevitably ask.

1. *Is there a socially optimal degree of product differentiation?* The answer to this basic question is yes, there is a socially optimal degree of product differentiation, divergence from which will increase the resources needed to enable consumers to attain specified levels of welfare.

2. *Can the optimum, or divergences from it, be easily recognized in the economy or in a particular industry?* The answer to this question seems, alas, to be no. Although there are clearly-defined conditions that must be satisfied for the optimal configuration for a specific number of product differentiates, there are no easily recognizable conditions with respect to the actual number of goods.

3. *Would perfect competition throughout the economy result in attainment of the optimum?* The pricing system appropriate to the optimal configuration would be established under perfect competition. However, the problem of optimal differentiation is most important and most interesting under increasing returns to scale. Perfect competition, under these circumstances, could not take advantage of the scale economies and thus would not generate the optimum, which would require marginal cost pricing and single firm output for each good. Thus we cannot look to perfect competition to solve the optimum differentiation problem.

4. *Will market imperfections tend to give a non-optimal degree of product differentiation?* Under constant returns to scale, no. Under increasing returns to scale, yes.

5. *Does market imperfection give a consistent bias in the degree of product differentiation, always too little or always too much?* Under increasing returns to scale, when imperfect competition tends to give non-optimal differentiation, the direction of bias depends on the exact market structure. Monopolistic competition will lead to too much differentiation, monopolization of a market sector, to too little. More

complex, and thus more realistic, market structures may be expected to show effects of both kinds, leaving the direction of bias uncertain.

NOTES

1. Originally published in *American Economic Review*, **65** (1975), 567–85.
2. This is clearly a restrictive assumption, since it is reasonable enough to suppose that there are cases in which the returns to scale properties differ between goods in the same product class. Many of the observed differences in productivity between goods in the same product class, such as between mass-produced and custom-built cars, are differences in *scale* but not necessarily in the degree of *returns to scale*.
3. It is assumed throughout the analysis that the substitution of characteristics from other product classes can be ignored, so that the 'next best' good is always within the same product class as the 'best' good.
4. This property may not hold for r sufficiently different from r^*, even in cases which would appear to be very well-behaved. For a linear PDC of the form $z_1 + z_2 = 1$ and a Cobb-Douglas utility function of the form $u = z_1^{1/2} z_2^{1/2}$ (for which $r^* = 1$), $h(r)$ has the form $h(r) = \frac{1}{2}(r^{1/2} + r^{-1/2})$, giving $h'' = (3 - r)/8r^{5/2}$. In this case $h'' \geq 0$ only within the range $3r^* \geq r \geq 1/3r^*$.
5. Rather than having a single consumer with split consumption, which is somewhat unrealistic, we can suppose each 'consumer' is actually an aggregate of consumers with identical tastes, some of whom consume one good and some the other.

11 Competition and product variety[1]

Three results of the study which are of general interest are the following:

1. It is never optimal to produce any good at minimum average cost, but always better to increase variety at the expense of average cost when any good reaches this level of output.
2. A structure very similar to that of Chamberlin's monopolistic competition is the 'most perfect' market structure that can be generated, being the Nash equilibrium of firms under conditions of perfect information, non-collusion, perfect flexibility, and free and willing entry. Thus, this structure cannot be regarded as 'imperfect competition' and is here referred to as 'perfect monopolistic competition'. The traditional 'perfect competition' structure cannot exist under the conditions posited for the economy, but could be attained by imposing constraints (in particular by requiring all goods to be produced to the same specification within some range), in which case the apparently perfectly competitive structure would result in a welfare loss as compared with monopolistic competition.
3. Monopolistic competition does not lead inevitably to a greater-than-optimal degree of variety – the traditional view[2] – but may give less than optimal variety under some circumstances.

THE ANALYTICAL FRAMEWORK

The basic analytical structure is that of a two-sector economy, the sector of special attention consisting of the group of goods within which product differentiation takes place, and the other sector being the rest of the economy. The product-differentiated sector consists of a single group – that is, all goods within it possess the same characteristics – but goods can possess these in variable proportions and do not share any of these characteristics with goods in the rest of the economy. Preferences are assumed to have appropriate separability properties so that choice within the group is independent of choice over the remaining goods. The goods in the rest of the economy are lumped together as 'outside goods' (as contrasted with group goods), and prices and specifications of these goods are assumed constant, so that they can be treated as a single aggregate good.

Within the group, the possession of the same characteristics is presumed to imply similarities at the production end, so that a smooth 'product-differentiation curve' can be drawn relating the various characteristics quantities that can be produced when embodied in the output of a good of any specification, given a fixed level of resources to be devoted entirely to the production of that single good. The product-differentiation possibilities are assumed to be homothetic, so that if V resource units can give characteristics vector z^1 when used to produce a good of specification (characteristics proportions) S_1, or vector z^2 when used to produce a good of specification S_2, the resources required to produce a characteristics vector kz^1 from good S_1 will be the same as the resources required to produce a characteristics vector kz^2 from good S_2, although the resources in each case will not necessarily be equal to kV since returns to scale are not assumed to be constant. This property is used to define a unit of a good of arbitrary specification as that quantity that can be produced with a unit resource level. The unit level is arbitrary, but relative quantities of goods of different specifications are then clearly defined. These ideas are identical with their equivalents given in Lancaster (1975b), where the treatment is more expanded.

Once the specification of a good has been chosen and the unit quantity defined as above, the resources required to produce a level of output Q are given by an input function $F(Q)$. It is assumed that resources can be treated as a single aggregate and thus that the input function $V = F(Q)$ is a single valued function, the unique inverse of the conventional production function. In a market context, $F(Q)$ becomes the cost function. The properties of the input or cost function will appear in the analysis mainly as the 'degree of economies of scale' parameter θ, defined as

$$\theta = F/QF' \tag{11.1}$$

That is, θ is the ratio of average to marginal cost, or average to marginal resource requirement. If $\theta > 1$, there are economies of scale; if $\theta < 1$, diseconomies of scale; and $\theta = 1$ if there are constant returns to scale or output is at minimum average cost with a U-shaped cost curve.[3]

It is assumed throughout that production within the group shows some initial economies of scale, so that $\theta(Q) > 1$ for $0 \leq Q \leq Q_o$, where $Q_o > 0$. If there are true increasing returns to scale, θ will be a constant greater than unity, equal to the degree of homogeneity of the production function. In general, θ will be a function of Q, and it is assumed that $\theta' \leq 0$ everywhere so that the degree of returns to scale does not increase with output.[4] (This turns out also to be a requirement for satisfaction of second-order conditions.) The restrictions on production are consistent with a wide variety of production conditions, including homogeneity of degree greater than one and fixed costs combined with constant or even rising marginal cost, the last giving a U-shaped cost curve. It will be assumed that the production of the aggregate outside good, representing the rest of the economy, is subject to constant returns to scale.

An individual consumer is assumed to have preferences over characteristics of goods within the group. Because of the assumed separability, the choice within the group is essentially independent of the quantities or prices of outside goods, the latter having effects only of an 'income' type as far as group characteristics are concerned. If this economy consisted only of a single individual, there would be a particular specification for a good within the group such that the consumer could attain a given utility or welfare level with a minimum use of resources. This specification would be given by the tangency between a product-differentiation curve, and a good of that specification will be referred to henceforth as the 'most preferred good' of that consumer. Figure 11.1 illustrates the idea, and a more

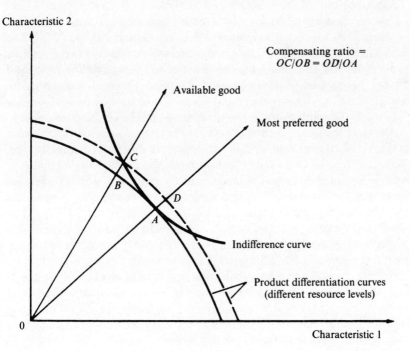

Figure 11.1

detailed treatment is given in Lancaster (1975b), where the term 'optimal good' is used, a nomenclature that has been changed to avoid overuse of the word 'optimal'.

A consumer supplied with an arbitrary 'available' good, not to the specification of his most preferred good, will require more resources to attain a given welfare level. Since equal quantities of different goods require equal resources (by the quantity definition), a consumer will require a larger quantity of an arbitrary available good than of his most preferred good to attain a given welfare level. The ratio of the quantity of available good to the quantity of most preferred good giving the same welfare level will be called the 'compensating ratio' for that consumer with respect to that available good. It will be assumed that preferences can be regarded as homothetic over the relevant range, so that the compensating ratio can be treated as independent of the level of welfare chosen within the range.

Due to the assumed strict quasi-concavity of preferences and the assumed shape of the product differentiation curves (non-convex toward the origin), the compensating ratio will increase as the difference between the specifications of the available and most preferred goods increases.[5] Let μ be some measure of distance between the two specifications, so that the compensating ratio can be written as a compensating function $h(u)$. The $h(u)$ will be taken to be strictly convex, and will possess the two boundary properties $h(O) = 1$ (from the definition of the compensating ratio) and $h'(O) = 0$ (because of the tangency at the most-preferred-good specification). Thus $h'' > 0$ everywhere and $h(u) > 1$, $h'(u) > 0$ for $u > 0$.

If there are many consumers with diverse preferences, as is assumed to be the case, then each consumer will have his own compensating function and his own compensating ratio with respect to any given available good. To bring some order to the potential chaos, the fundamental simplifying assumption of the analysis is made, that of uniformity of the preference spectrum. It is assumed that preferences vary over individuals in such a way that, for a suitable choice of the distance measure between specifications of different good, the compensating ratio for any individual with respect to any available good is the same as that for any other individual with respect to any available good (the same as for the first individual, or different), if the distance in specification between the most preferred goods and the available goods is the same for both individuals. That is, a uniform compensating function $h(u)$ gives the compensating ratio for any individual anywhere on the preference spectrum with respect to an available good at distance u from his most preferred good.[6]

The uniformity assumption is a heroic simplification, but no apologies are made for it. It has some resemblances to, and plays much the same role as, the assumption of a featureless plain in location theory, providing a background of regularity against which variations in other features of the system can be studied.

Implicit in the idea of uniformity is that preferences are, in some sense, similar between individuals except as to specifications of most preferred goods. The preference spectrum can be visualized as made up of geometrically similar indifference curves, shifted in one direction or the other along the spectrum as shown in Figure 11.2. Thus the specification of the most

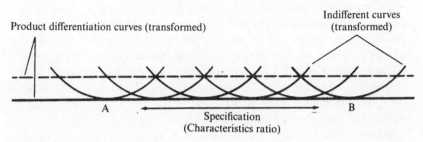

Figure 11.2

preferred good is sufficient identification of an individual or of a group of individuals with identical preferences.

It will be assumed that there is a continuum of preferences – that is, every small region of the spectrum contains individuals having most preferred goods with specifications falling within that region, at least over a portion of the spectrum of possible characteristics combinations which will be called the range of preference diversity.

Uniformity of the spectrum in the above sense refers to the properties of preferences and stipulates nothing concerning the relative numbers of individuals having most preferred goods in different parts of the spectrum or concerning the distribution of incomes or market weights over the spectrum. The central analysis is conducted for the particular case of uniform density of consumers over the spectrum, but this assumption can be relaxed to study the effect of density variations over the spectrum. In any case, 'uniformity' and 'uniform density' are totally independent and unrelated properties.

Optimum choice for an individual among whatever goods in the group are available depends on a basic property of the consumption technology, namely, whether goods are combinable or non-combinable. If goods are combinable, the individual can obtain characteristics in any proportions by combining goods: he can always make his own most preferred combination in this way. If goods are non-combinable and his most preferred good is not available, he cannot attain his most preferred combination and must settle for the best available good, which will be determined by closeness in specification to his most preferred combination in conjunction with relative prices. The emphasis here is on the analysis of the non-combinable case, which is the most interesting, but the combinable case can also be treated. In the non-combinable case, the individual consumes a single good within the group.

Attention has so far been concentrated on events within the group. As pointed out earlier, however, it is the embedding of the group within an economy that is the most important single contribution of the present analysis. This embedding involves taking account of the role of outside goods, which appear as a single aggregate good. It is greatly simplified by the assumption of uniformity, which makes it entirely reasonable to assume that consumers have a uniform view of outside goods; this is interpreted to mean that the substitutability between outside goods and their most preferred good is the same for all consumers. This does not mean that the substitutability between an arbitrary available good and outside goods is the same for all individuals. On the contrary, the substitutability between the available good and an outside good is compounded of the substitutability between the available and the individual's most preferred good (determined by the properties of the compensating function) and the substitutability between the most preferred good and the outside good, so that outside goods become better substitutes for available group goods as the difference between the specifications of the available and most preferred goods increases. The outside substitution concept is modelled by assuming a constant elasticity of substitution between outside goods and the most preferred group good, the elasticity being the same for all individuals. The relationship of the group to the rest of the economy is then fully parameterized by two parameters, the elasticity of substitution (σ) and a parameter expressing the relative importance of the group in the total, the latter being the ratio of expenditure on group goods to total expenditure when in a market context.

The utility function (w) for an individual given quantity q of an available good which is distant by a measure u from his most preferred good, and quantity y of the aggregate outside goods, is given by

$$w(q,y,u) = T\{aq^s[h(u)]^{-s} + (1 - a)y^s\} \qquad (11.2)$$

where $\sigma = -1/(s - 1)$ is the elasticity of substitution and a the parameter expressing the importance of group goods, T being any monotone increasing function.

For a consumer choosing freely in a market context defined by an outside good and a single good having specification distance u from his most preferred good, at income I and group good price P (both in units of outside good), his utility is given by

$$w(I,P,u) = T(I^sP^{-s}h^{-h}m^{1-s}) \qquad (11.3)$$

where m is the proportion of total expenditure devoted to group goods and is related to a but also a function of P, u, and σ.

THE OPTIMUM CONFIGURATION

Before introducing market analysis, it is necessary to establish the optimum configuration as a reference. It is obvious that if there were constant returns to scale everywhere, an arbitrarily determined distribution of welfare over individuals would always be attained optimally (that is, with the minimum use of resources) by producing every individual's most preferred good. This proposition is inherent in the definition of the most-preferred-good concept.

If there are economies of scale, however, resources can always be saved by producing a smaller number of goods, each at a larger output level. In so doing, there will be individuals whose most preferred goods are no longer available and these individuals will be worse off if given a quantity of the available good only equal to the quantity of most preferred good they received before the elimination of that good from the production schedule. In order to maintain them at the original welfare level, they must be compensated by being given an increased quantity of the available good or of outside goods or both. The compensation will require additional resources in whatever form it is received, and the cost of compensation must be weighed against the resource saving from producing fewer goods. The optimum is determined by the appropriate balance between the saving from economies of scale and the compensation costs.

Before proceeding further, it should be noted that there is an optimal compensation mix for any individual – that is, a mix of available group good and outside goods that requires the least resources for fully compensating that individual. This optimal mix can be determined from his preferences, the distance between the available group good and his most preferred good, and the marginal resource costs of producing the two goods. It will be the mix that he himself would choose if compensated appropriately with additional income and permitted to buy the goods at prices proportional to marginal resource costs. (A special case arises if the group goods are indivisible, like motor cars, so that compensation must be entirely in outside goods and marginal optimal conditions cannot be satisfied.)

The reader will find no difficulty in accepting that a formal analysis of the relationship between the quantity and composition of optimal compensation and the distance u between the available good and an individual's most preferred good will show (a) that the value of the total compensation, at marginal resource cost prices, will be an increasing function of u: and (b) that the ratio of the quantity of outside good to that of the available group good in the mix can be an increasing or a decreasing function of u, depending on the value of the elasticity of substitution.[7]

If there is a continuum of preferences over the spectrum and there is to be a finite number of goods produced, there will be a set of individuals to be supplied with each good. Under the assumption of uniformity over the spectrum, each set will be a segment of the spectrum since if it is optimal (that is, compensation is minimal) to supply any individual whose most preferred good is distant u from a specific available good, it will be optimal to supply any other individual whose most preferred good is at a distance less than u from this good. Given the compensation properties for each individual as a function of the distance u from the available good and the welfare level to be associated with each individual (strictly the welfare density for a small subsegment of the spectrum), the aggregate quantities of both the available good and the outside good required to supply both the 'base' and the compensation for all individuals having most preferred goods at a distance up to and including u from the available good can be determined as a function of u.

For the basic model it is assumed that the welfare density is uniform – that is, if there were no economies of scale so that it would be optimal to supply everyone with his most preferred good, then the target welfare distribution would call for all goods to be produced in equal quantities. With economies of scale this same welfare distribution is to be maintained by compensation. It is easy to appreciate that under a uniform density assumption it will be optimal to divide the spectrum into equal segments, whatever the number of goods, and supply each segment with a good having its specification centred in the segment. If the distance of the edge of the segment from the specification of the available good is Δ, the segment will be of width 2Δ. All segments will be of the same width, so that the optimum can be determined by considering the typical segment.

From the properties of individual compensation and the uniform-density assumption, the aggregate quantity of goods (available group plus outside) required to maintain all individuals in a segment at the base welfare level will increase more than in proportion to the segment half-width Δ and, furthermore, will increase at an increasing rate. While it is certain that the quantity of outside goods required will rise more than proportionally to Δ, the quantity of the group good need not do so.[8] Denote by $Q(\Delta)$ the aggregate quantity of the group good to be provided to all individuals within the segment and by $Y(\Delta)$ the aggregate quantity of outside good, the respective elasticities of Q, Y with respect to Δ being denoted by e_Q, e_Y. Both e_Q and e_Y will vary with Δ, and will depend on the properties of the compensating function $h(u)$, the elasticity of substitution between group goods and outside goods σ, and the relative importance of the group in total expenditure m. While e_q will be less than unity for high values of σ.

As the width of the segment is varied, the quantities of group and outside goods will change and so will the average resource cost of providing them due to the economies of scale in the production of the group good, even though there are assumed to be no scale economies for the outside good. The optimum configuration will be such that the scale economies and the compensation costs balance each other at the margin.

The formal solution of the optimal problem can be shown to be such that the segment width (the same for all segments) satisfies the optimum equation

$$me_Q(\Delta) + (1 - m)e_Y(\Delta) = m\theta[Q(\Delta)] + (1 - m) \qquad (11.4)$$

The meaning of this equation can be appreciated intuitively by considering the effect of a 1 per cent change in the segment width 2Δ. The elasticities e_Q, e_Y then give the percentage change in the group and outside goods, respectively, necessary to maintain welfare for every individual at the constant target level. Since the parameter m represents the proportion of the value of group goods to total goods, the left-hand side represents the percentage change in the value of total goods which is necessary to maintain constant welfare when the segment width is changed by 1 per cent. On the right-hand side, the function θ is the elasticity of the production function for the group good, giving the percentage change in output from a 1 per cent change in resources. Since there are assumed to be constant returns to scale in the production of the outside good, the equivalent elasticity for the outside good is unity. Thus, the right-hand side represents the percentage change in the value of total output at marginal-resource-cost shadow prices and when group and outside goods are produced in a mix of proportions $m, 1 - m$, when there is a 1 per cent change in resources.

Thus, when equation (11.4) is satisfied, a 1 per cent change in segment size will require a change of exactly 1 per cent in resources. That is, the equation represents the segment width at which the total resource use per unit of segment width is stationary. Since the sum of segment widths is equal to the total spectrum (fixed) and all segments are equal in size with equal use of resources, a stationary value of resources per unit of segment width is equivalent to a stationary value of total resource use. Thus, equation (11.4) gives the segment width at which resources are minimized for the given welfare distribution, subject to second-order conditions being satisfied (which can be shown to be the case).

It can be shown that the left-hand side of (11.4) is a strictly increasing function of Δ, while the right-hand side is constant or decreasing,[9] so that an optimum solution always exists. It can also be shown that the weighted elasticity, $me_Q + (1 - m)e_Y$, is always greater than unity[10] (that is, the value of total goods to be provided to a segment always increases more than proportionally to the segment width), so that the right-hand side must be greater than unity. But this necessarily implies that $\theta > 1$ – that is, that production of the group is always at a level at which average resource cost exceeds marginal resource cost, so that the group goods are never produced at the minimum average cost output level even when the cost curves are U-shaped.

Given that the range of the preference spectrum is constant, the optimum segment width is inverse to the number of group goods being produced, and it is convenient to discuss the properties of the optimum configuration in terms of the 'degree of product differentiation', the number of goods produced. Obviously, the optimum degree of product differentiation will be a function of the system parameters, including the degree of convexity of the compensating function, the degree of economies of scale, the elasticity of substitution with respect to outside goods, and the relative importance of the group in the economy. The effect of some of these parameters on the optimal degree of product differentiation is both easy to determine and in conformity with intuitive expectations, such as, that the optimum degree of product differentiation will be lower if the degree of scale economies is higher and will be lower if the degree of convexity of the compensating function is lower – that is, if individuals are less sensitive to differences in specification between their most preferred good and the available good.

The effect of other parameters on the optimal degree of product differentiation is much more difficult to determine and the results less intuitive. In particular, the effect of the elasticity of substitution on the optimal degree of product differentiation – which is important for comparing market and optimal solutions – falls into this category. It can be shown that the optimal degree of product differentiation first decreases as the elasticity of substitution increases, to reach a mimimum at unit elasticity, and then increases with the elasticity. Although no simple explanation can be given for the full shape of the relationship, the reasons for a high degree of product differentiation at high elasticity are clear enough. When the elasticity of substitution is high, outside goods are good substitutes for group goods so that optimal compensation will result in a rapidly increasing ratio of outside goods to group goods as the segment width is increased. But there are no economies of scale in outside goods, so that the average scale economies over the total goods mix fall rapidly as the segment width increases. (In the extreme case of infinite elasticity of substitution, only consumers for whom the available good meets most preferred specifications will be supplied with that good, and there are no potential gains from economies of scale at all.) Thus the optimal segment widths will be relatively small and the number of products relatively large.

COMPENSATION PROBLEMS AND THE SECOND BEST

The preceding welfare analysis is strictly Paretian in the sense that every individual is maintained on his same indifference contour throughout as the number of goods is varied until the configuration which uses resources to the minimum extent is determined. There is no trading off one individual's welfare against that of another. Although the analysis is given for a specific welfare distribution, the principles apply to an arbitrary distribution.

In order to maintain every individual's welfare at a constant level, it is necessary to compensate for specification as the number and thus the specification of available goods changes. Apart from the information problem implicit in knowing the preferences of every single individual and not merely the distribution of preferences in an anonymous fashion, there is a special problem of what can best be termed 'manifest equity'. Consider two individuals, labelled as I_1 and I_2, whose preferences are such that both will be supplied with the same group good at the optimum. This good happens to be the most preferred good for I_1 but not for I_2, so that I_2 will be compensated by being given more of the good and/or more outside good, even when the desired welfare distribution is one of equality.[11] Now I_1 may well find it difficult to accept that he is not being treated inequitably when he sees I_2 being compensated for receiving the very good that I_1 considers to have an ideal specification. Compensation for specification inevitably results in truly equal treatment appearing to be inequitable.

Because of practical and manifest equity problems associated with the full optimum, it seems desirable to investigate also a second-best optimum in which the constraint is imposed that all individuals are to receive the same income, so that there is no compensation for specification. Since the distribution of welfare then changes as the number of goods is increased or decreased, it is necessary to assume the existence of a social welfare criterion that weighs welfare gains by some individuals against welfare losses by others. Since the uniformity assumption implies that preferences vary over individuals with respect to the specification of the most preferred good but are 'similar' in other respects, a naïve utilitarian criterion does not seem inappropriate for such a simple model.

It is assumed that individuals supplied with the same quantities of their respective most preferred goods and with the same amounts of outside good will derive the same welfare and that a person supplied with a good which is not his most preferred derives welfare that can be assessed by converting the available good to its 'most-preferred-good equivalent' by dividing by the compensating ratio. The criterion used in the analysis is the average welfare per capita derived in this way. The second-best solution is the number of goods which minimizes the resource use per capita for a target level of per capita welfare.

The second-best solution can be shown to give a smaller degree of product differentiation than does the full optimum solution. The intuitive explanation for this is that while the average value of output per head required to maintain a constant level of average welfare per capita rises as the segment width increases, just as does the average output per head required to maintain every individual on a constant welfare level in the full optimum case, it rises more slowly in the second-best case. This is because the effect of the individuals at the margin is partly balanced by averaging with individuals at the centre in the second-best, but not in the full optimum. Thus, in the second-best, the segments will be larger and the number of goods smaller.

MARKET DEMAND

In order to lay the foundation for a market analysis under the same general conditions for which the optimal configuration of the economy was determined, it is necessary to derive the properties of market demand from the properties of individual preferences, the distribution of those preferences, and the distribution of income.

The analysis will be confined to the case in which the consumption technology is of the non-combinable kind (within the group), so that the individual will consume only one of the group goods. The individual's decisions then consist of the following:

1.   which of the group goods to purchase;
2.   how much of that good to purchase; and
3.   how much of the outside good to purchase.

The individual is assumed to have full information concerning all goods and their specifications, to know his own preferences fully, and to choose freely within the market subject to his budget constraint while taking prices and his income as given.

An individual's choice concerning which of the group goods to purchase will depend only on the specifications of the available good, the specification of his most preferred good, and the relative prices of the available goods. It will be independent of the quantity of that good he will subsequently choose to purchase and, thus, of his income and the price of outside goods. If the group is defined by only two characteristics, so that specification is determined by a single parameter (the ratio of the characteristics or some transform of this), then the spectrum of specifications is a segment of a line. In general, the choice for any particular consumer will be between two goods, those having specifications closest in each direction to the specification of his most preferred good.[12] The quantity of either of the goods which is equivalent to any specified quantity of his most preferred good is given by application of the compensating function. Obviously, he will buy whichever of the goods provides a given most-preferred-good equivalent at the lowest cost. If the two goods have specifications which differ from the specification of his most preferred good by distance measures u_1, u_2, and sell at prices P_1, P_2, the relative costs of attaining the equivalent of $\bar{q}$ units of his most preferred good will be $\bar{q}P_1h(u_1)$ and $\bar{q}P_2h(u_2)$, respectively. He will choose that good for which the product $Ph(u)$ is the least and will be indifferent between the goods if P_1, P_2 and u_1, u_2, are related in such a way that $P_1h(u_1(= P_2h(u_2)$.

Once the best available group good has been chosen, the quantity of that good and of the outside good will be determined in the usual way, by maximization of this utility subject to the budget constraint. The utility function is assumed to have the constant-elasticity-of-substitution form given in (11.2).

Because of the uniformity assumption, the demand functions for all individuals are fully determined by the distance of the chosen group good from their most preferred good (u), and particular individuals do not need to be identified. If q represents the quantity of the chosen group good and y the quantity of outside good, the demand functions for individuals are given by:

$$q(u,P,I) = IP^{-1} [1 + AP^{\sigma-1} h(u)^{\sigma-1}]^{-1} \qquad (11.5a)$$

$$y(u,P,I) = IAP^{\sigma-1}h(u)^{\sigma-1} [1 + AP^{\sigma-1} h(u)^{\sigma-1}]^{-1} \qquad (11.5b)$$

where A is a constant reflecting the importance of the group in total utility.[13]

The market demand for any available good depends on the market width, or the highest value of u for which individuals will buy that good at the going relative prices of group goods, and the market depth or average quantity purchased per unit of market width. The market width depends only on the individual choice concerning which good to buy and thus only on relative prices of goods within the group and the difference in specification between goods in the market. The market depth depends on the individual demand functions (11.5a) and thus on the price of the good relative to the price of outside goods and on the distribution of incomes over consumers buying the good. The market depth also depends on the market width through the compensating function $h(u)$ which appears in the demand equation.

The market width is determined by the following dividing condition. Denote the price of the jth good by P_j and assume that the goods are numbered in sequence along the spectrum, so that the $(j + 1)$th good is the adjacent good in one direction, sold at price P_{j+1}. If the spacing between the goods is 2Δ, the dividing consumer (the consumer who is indifferent between the goods) will be the consumer whose most preferred good is at distance u from the jth good, where u satisfies the dividing condition:

$$P_j h(u) = P_{j+1} h(2\Delta - u) \qquad (11.6)$$

Note that the division between the markets for the two goods depends only on the properties of the compensating function, the difference in specification between the goods (2Δ), and their relative prices. There will also be a dividing condition for the jth good relative to the $(j - 1)$th, the total market width for the jth good being the sum of the widths of the two half-markets. The analysis here will be confined to symmetrical situations in which the half-markets are identical, but they may differ in width and other respects in the general case, and there will be more than two dividing conditions if there are more than two characteristics. Note also that $P_j = P_{j+1}$ implies $u = \Delta$ – that is, the dividing consumer's most preferred good has a specification midway between the specifications of the two available goods when the prices of the adjacent good are the same.

A change in the price of P_j has the following effects:

1. It changes the width of the market by changing the price of the jth good relative to the prices of adjacent goods.
2. It changes the quantity of the good purchased by consumers within the market area by changing the price of the jth good relative to outside goods.
3. It changes the quantity of the good purchased by consumers in the market because of the traditional kind of income effect, unless there is compensation for the price change.

4. It changes quantity through a special kind of effect, the specification effect, unless there is compensation for specification.

The first three effects can be identified as the inside substitution effect, the outside substitution effect, and the income effect, respectively, and they call for no special comment. The fourth, the specification effect, requires some discussion. As the market width increases as a result of a fall in P_j, the additional consumers are buying goods which are even more distant from their most preferred specification than the existing consumers. If money incomes were uniform over the market, the real incomes of these consumers would be less than the average real incomes of the existing buyers because of this specification distance. Thus, a change in the market width will change the average real incomes of consumers in the market even if all receive the same money income and even if that money income is adjusted to compensate for price in the usual way. In addition, the specification effect involves a special kind of price effect because the marginal customers are paying a price $P_{jh(u)}$ for a unit of most-preferred-good equivalent and thus a higher price for this equivalent than intramarginal customers. The 'average price' per most-preferred-good equivalent rises as the width of the market increases, partly offsetting the fall in P_j which causes the increase in width. Note that the specification effect works in the opposite direction to the two substitution effects and the income effect (assuming all goods are normal), tending to reduce demand when price falls. It cannot, however, be greater than the inside substitution effect, so that the sum of the inside substitution and specification effects has the regular sign. If consumers are compensated for specification in the same way as under the full optimum analysis, the specification effect vanishes.

Aggregate demand over the market depends, of course, on the distribution of individuals over the spectrum and on the distribution of incomes over the individuals within the market. It will be assumed for the analysis here that individuals are distributed uniformly over the preference spectrum, and demand will be considered for two different distributions of income over a market area – (a) a uniform distribution of money income and (b) a distribution of money incomes that represents compensation for specification. In distribution b, individuals near the market fringes receive higher incomes than those near the centre and all consumers reach the same welfare after optimal expenditure of their money incomes.

By taking the derivative with respect to u in the individual demand equation (11.5a), the variation of q with u can be shown to be given by

$$\frac{\partial \log q}{\partial u} = -1 (1 - m)(\sigma - 1) \frac{d\log h(u)}{du} \qquad (11.7)$$

when income is not compensated for specification, and

$$\frac{\partial \log\ q}{\partial u} = [1 - (1 - m)\sigma]\frac{d\log\ h(u)}{du} \tag{11.8}$$

when there is compensation for specification.[14]

In all the succeeding discussion, $Q(u)$ will denote the integral of q from 0 to u and $e_Q(u)$ the elasticity of Q with respect to u. The properties of $q(u)$ and thus $Q(u)$ and $e_Q(u)$ will be determined by (11.8) or (11.7) above, according to whether there is compensation for specification or not. Note that when the elasticity of substitution, σ, is less than unity for demand uncompensated for specification, or less than the value $1/(1 - m)$ for demand which is compensated for specification, q is an increasing function of u, Q is a convex function of u, and e_Q is greater than unity. When the elasticity of substitution is greater than unity or $1/(1 - m)$, whichever is the relevant value, q is a decreasing function of u, Q is concave, and e_Q is less than unity. At the crossover value (unity or $1/(1 - m)$) q is a constant, Q is linear in u, and e_Q is constant and equal to unity.

The market demand function for the jth good depends on the properties of the compensating function, the elasticity of substitution with respect to outside goods, the relative importance of group goods in total expenditure, and the prices and specifications of the $(j - 1)$th and $(j + 1)$th goods,[15] as well as its own price, the existence or otherwise of compensation for specification and/or compensation for price, and the level of income. For the particular case in which the difference in specification between the jth good and each of the adjacent goods is the same, and when the prices of the jth good and adjacent goods are equal, the own-price elasticity of demand is given by

$$E(P,\Delta;\sigma,m) = s^*e_Q(\Delta) + (1 - m)\sigma + (1 - \gamma)m \tag{11.9}$$

where the spacing between pairs of adjacent goods is 2Δ and the degree of price compensation by γ, $\gamma = 0$ meaning no price compensation and $\gamma = 1$ meaning full compensation. In the above formulation, the compensating function is assumed given and the elasticity depends on two market variables, P and Δ (since firms can vary both price and specification), and on the system parameters which are varied for comparative static analysis, σ and m.

The first term in (11.9) represents the combined inside substitution and specification effects, e_Q being chosen for the quantity function $Q(u)$ appropriate to the case with compensation for specification or without, whichever is relevant in the context. The factor s^* needs explanation, since this is its first appearance. For a half-market in which the marginal customer is at distance u from the market centre and the next good in that direction is at a distance 2Δ, $s(\Delta,u)$ is the elasticity of u with respect to P multiplied by the ratio u/Δ, the elasticity being taken with the positive sign. In the case in which adjacent prices are equal, $u = \Delta$ and $s^*(\Delta)$ is the elasticity of the market width with respect to price. From the dividing condition (11.6) it can be shown that

$$s^*(\Delta) = \frac{1}{2}e_h(\Delta)$$

(11.10)

where $e_h(\Delta)$ is the elasticity of the compensating function $h(u)$ with respect to u, at the value $u = \Delta$.[16]

The second term in (11.9) corresponds to the outside substitution effect and the third term to the income effect. If income is fully compensated for price, $\gamma = 1$ and the third term vanishes. All three terms are non-negative.

It can be shown that, in general:

1. The quantity E varies inversely with the spacing between adjacent goods, becoming infinite when that spacing approaches zero. It is, however, bounded below by the sum of the outside substitution and income effects as the spacing becomes very large.
2. The quantity E varies with price through second-order effects even though price does not appear explicitly in (11.9). For values of the elasticity of substitution at least equal to unity when there is no compensation for specification, or at least equal to $1/(1 - m)$ when there is such compensation, the elasticity of demand increases with price.[17]
3. The quantity E increases when the elasticity of substitution increases, provided $m \neq 1$, that is, provided outside goods are actually purchased.

For the analysis which follows, it is convenient to make use of the market parameter R, defined as the ratio of price to marginal revenue in the market and referred to as the marginal revenue ratio. Since $R = [1 - (1/E)^{-1}]^{-1} = E/(E - 1)$, it is a function of E only. Changes in R and E are inversely related, so that

1. the quantity R increases with the spacing between goods, is equal to unity when the spacing becomes zero, and is bounded above for large spacings;
2. the quantity R decreases as price increases, if $\sigma \geq 1$ or $1/(1 - m)$, whichever is relevant to the compensation pattern; and

3.   the quantity R decreases as the elasticity of substitution increases.

MARKET STRUCTURES

Within the general context of the model set out above, the following market structures are investigated:

1.   Single-product firms
Perfect monopolistic competition. This is the structure defined by perfect information on the part of both consumers and firms, full flexibility in choosing and varying specifications of goods by firms, and free and willing entry into the group when profits are positive.
Imperfect monopolistic competition. These structures are determined by non-collusive single-product firms when one or more of the conditions for perfect monopolistic competition are not met. The resulting structures will differ according to which of the 'perfect' conditions are not attained – information less than perfect, costly specification changes, or the existence of barriers to entry.

2.   Multi-product firms
Full group monopoly. A single firm possesses monopoly power over the whole group.
Island monopoly. A single firm possesses a monopoly over some part of the spectrum covered by the group but not the whole group. It is assumed that the remainder of the spectrum is covered by single-product firms.
Multi-firm, multi-product structures. These structures arise when there are interproduct economies, so that there is a two-part fixed cost, one arising from operating in the group at all, the other associated with each product.

The term 'perfect' monopolistic competition is used for the first structure, since this arises from non-collusive behaviour among firms under conditions of perfect information and perfect flexibility in a context in which there are economies of scale, variable product specifications, and diversity in consumer preferences. It cannot be regarded as imperfect competition because no more perfect form of competition is possible within the same context.

The equilibrium under perfect monopolistic competition satisfies conditions of the same form as those for the traditional Chamberlin model, except that here the demand properties are fully derived from preferences[18] and the consumption technology and, in particular, the demand for any product is given as a function of its specification relative to the specifications of other goods as well as of prices. The equilibrium conditions can be written in the form

$$P = RF' \tag{11.11a}$$
$$R = \theta \tag{11.11b}$$

where R is the marginal revenue ratio (defined earlier) and θ the degree of economies of scale (ratio of average to marginal cost). The first condition is the equality of marginal revenue to marginal cost; the second is the combination of this and the equality of price to average cost. All firms will charge the same prices and will produce goods which are evenly distributed along the spectrum,[19] the spacing being determined from (11.11b) since both R and θ (through the quantity produced) are functions of this, given the price relationship of (11.11a) (see Lancaster 1979, Chapter 4).

If consumers are ignorant about specifications of the goods available, it is assumed they choose at random among the goods. The specifications and distribution of the goods along the spectrum do not appear in the demand functions, but the elasticity of demand (with respect to price) can be considered to be an increasing function of the number of goods. An equilibrium can be shown to exist, giving the same formal conditions as in (11.11a) and (11.11b) but with a different value of R because of the different demand conditions. In general, it can be argued that the value of R will be lower under conditions of ignorance (E higher) and that this implies fewer goods than under perfect monopolistic competition. The specifications of the goods are not determined, and may be chosen in any way by the firms.

If some consumers are informed, firms will distribute themselves evenly over the spectrum (assuming informed consumers to be evenly distributed over the population) and reach an equilibrium which again has the same form as (11.11a) and (11.11b), except that the value of R is now between that for perfect monopolistic competition and that for the complete ignorance case.

It can be shown that if consumers are ignorant about the specifications of the goods actually produced but know their own preferences concerning specifications, it will be in the interest of firms to provide the information concerning specification, so ignorance of this kind will be temporary.

The other forms of imperfection–entry barriers and costs of specification change – will lead to fairly obvious effects. Entry barriers will result in fewer firms, and thus goods, than in their absence, while specification-change costs will result in some degree of irregularity in the spacing of firms on the spectrum and, generally, some reduction in the number of goods produced (see Lancaster 1979, Chapter 8).

Full group monopoly exists when a single firm has no actual or potential competition with respect to goods produced within the group. It is obvious that it will be optimal for the firm to distribute whatever number of goods it chooses to produce within the group evenly over the spectrum and to charge the same prices for all. The elasticity of demand for the group as a whole, which is the monopolist's elasticity of demand, depends only on the substitution properties for the group with respect to outside goods and on income effects and has no intragroup component. The profit-maximizing condition with respect to price has the form of (11.11a), but the value of R is greater (because E is smaller) than under monopolistic competition. Solution for the most profitable number of goods in the monopoly case is somewhat complex, but the appropriate condition is given in equation (11.12) (see also Lancaster 1979 Chapter 9):

$$e_Q = (R - \theta)/(R - 1) \tag{11.12}$$

The right-hand side of (11.12) is constant except in so far as the degree of economies of scale varies with the output because R does not depend on the spacing between goods in this case. The quantity elasticity e_Q does, however, depend on this spacing and thus the relationship determines the most profitable spacing and, thus, the number of goods.

An island monopoly exists when there is a portion of the spectrum into which other firms cannot intrude (because of patent or other protection, presumably), but firms outside this area can certainly compete for the potential customers near the edge of the monopoly segment. The island monopolist can isolate his segment from outside competition by setting up 'boundary stakes'–goods at or near the edge of his monopoly area which are sold at the monopolistic competition equilibrium price and which are preferred to all goods beyond the monopoly area by all consumers whose most preferred goods lie within the area, since they are closer in specification and no more expensive. If the monopoly segment is large enough, the monopolist can treat most of the interior as though it were a group monopoly. There will be some edge effects involving goods near the fringes of the area and, if the segment is small, there may be no interior portion free of these, but the island monopolist will sell fewer goods at higher prices over his segment than would be the case if the segment were occupied by monopolistic competitors.

Finally, multi-product firms may exist without explicit entry barriers if there exist interproduct economies so that part of the fixed cost of producing within the group can be spread over several products within the group. Suppose that the economies are such as to be effectively used up over M products, then the group can be expected to consist of firms each producing at least M different products when an equilibrium is reached. There exists, in effect, an entry cost for any new firm which cannot find a space for M of its products, but there also exists a limit price for the products in the group above which it will pay a new firm to enter with even a single product. The structure developed under these conditions depends on how the products of the firms come to be distributed over the spectrum. At one extreme, each firm might produce M products which are adjacent on the spectrum, putting it somewhat in the same position as an island monopoly except for the upper-limit price. At the other extreme, every pair of products produced by the same firm might be separated by the products of several other firms, in which case the equilibrium will resemble that of monopolistic competition.

Each of these possible structures will lead to a different degree of product variety, and the next section will consider the relationships between the degree of product differentiation under the various competitive configurations with each other and with the optimum.

COMPETITION AND PRODUCT VARIETY

Before discussing the effect of different types of competition on the degree of product variety, there are some features common to all configurations which should be noted.

1. There can be no equilibrium market solution of any kind unless (a) there are outside goods, and (b) the elasticity of substitution between the group goods and outside goods, σ, is greater than some lower limit which is always at least unity (otherwise second-order conditions are not satisfied) and less than some upper limit which is related to the degree of economies of scale (otherwise even a monopolist cannot break even). The existence of variable product specifications narrows the viability possibilities for the market, as compared with a finite number of goods of given specifications.
2. The equilibrium degree of product variety (and the optimum degree) is a function of the parameters of the system and varies with the parameters, which include:

   (a) the degree of economies of scale;
   (b) the preference relations over the group (compensation function properties), the elasticity of substitution between group goods and outside goods, the relative importance of group goods in total budgets, and whether goods are divisible or indivisible; and
   (c) the width of the spectrum and the size of the total market.

Only the degree of economies of scale and width of the spectrum (difference between the most preferred specifications of the extreme consumers) have the same effect on the optimum and all market configurations, variety being increased by a decrease in the degree of economies of scale or an increase in the width of the spectrum. An increase in the elasticity of substitution sometimes leads to an increase in product differentiation, sometimes to a decrease, depending on the configuration and the parameter values, for example see Lancaster 1979, Chapters 5,6, and 9.

The greatest degree of product variety in the market will be reached under perfect monopolistic competition if there are no interproduct economies. Contrary to the received wisdom and to my earlier results (Lancaster 1975b), perfect monopolistic competition may, however, lead to a less than optimal degree of product variety if the elasticity of substitution with respect to outside goods is high. All forms of imperfection in the monopolistic competition setting–imperfect information, entry costs, and costs of specification change–will decrease the degree of product variety as compared with perfect monopolistic competition. In the long run, imperfect monopolistic competition will converge to perfect monopolistic equilibrium since entry and specification-change costs wash out eventually, and it will be in the interests of firms ultimately to supply missing information.

Under a full group monopoly, the monopolist will normally provide a variety of products within the group. This variety will always be less than under perfect monopolistic competition and will be less than the full optimum (with compensation for specification) except at $\sigma = 1$, which is the lower limit for equilibrium.[20] The monopolist will, however, produce more variety than appropriate for a second-best optimum (with no compensation for specification) if the elasticity of substitution is relatively small and the group a relatively large sector of the economy.

The island monopolist, whose monopoly power covers only some segment of the spectrum, will produce fewer goods over that segment than would be produced if the segment were under perfect monopolistic competition. As the segment size increases relative to the spectrum, the number of goods per unit segment length will approach that of the full group monopolist, so that the typical island monopolist will provide a degree of variety per unit segment length in between that of monopolistic competition and full group monopoly–it could, in fact, be the optimal variety, but only by coincidence.

Perhaps the most interesting market structure is that which will result from the existence of interproduct economies, in which the economies of scale for a product are reduced if the firm already produces a product in the group. It is eminently reasonable to suppose that some of the components of the fixed cost associated with production within the group (such as technical and market information) can be used over several products, so that the degree of economies of scale (per product) is a decreasing function of the number of products produced by the same firm. Denote by θ_k the degree-of-economies-of-scale function for each product when the firm produces K products within the group, so that it can be assumed that $\theta_J > \theta_K$ if $J < K$, at least up to some limiting value M, where all θ's refer to the same levels of output.

Such interproduct economies will obviously lead to the emergence of multi-product firms, even though no monopoly elements are present and entry remains free. If M, the number of products which exhausts the interproduct economies, is small relative to the total number of goods that would be produced under perfect monopolistic competition, then the industry will be characterized by the existence of several firms, each producing several products.

The possible equilibrium states for such an industry depend on how the products of an individual firm are spread over the spectrum. If the industry has grown randomly, as a mixture of new entries and acquisitions within the group, it can be assumed that the products of each firm are scattered over the spectrum and each such product typically has products of other firms as neighbours on the spectrum. However, if each firm produces M products which form a segment of the spectrum, with no other firm's product in that segment, the outcome may be different.

Consider first the scattered case, and suppose that if all firms produced a single product there would be N such firms and products, the economies of multi-product operation remaining unused. Compare this with a situation in which the N products are produced by N/M firms, each of which produces M products and exhausts all interproduct economies. If the products of each firm are scattered, and if the economies affect only fixed costs and not variable costs, the elasticity of demand (and hence R, the marginal revenue ratio) will be the same in both cases, as will marginal costs. Thus the profit-maximizing condition $P = RF'$ will be the same in substance as well as form for both cases, and so will the price. But the firms will make positive profits in the multi-product case, since they break even on a single product without taking any economies, and new multi-product firms will be attracted into the group. Ignoring the problem of integer solutions, the equilibrium will have the form

$$R(\Delta_m) = \theta_M \qquad (11.13)$$

where Δ_M is the goods spacing with multi-product firms, as compared with

$$R(\Delta_1) = \theta_1 \tag{11.14}$$

Since $\theta_M < \theta_1$ and R is an increasing function of Δ, the product spacing will be closer and thus the number of products greater with multi-product firms than with single-product firms. (Price will certainly be higher with multi-product firms if the marginal cost curve is falling since $P = RF'$, R is higher, output is smaller, and thus F' is higher. If marginal cost is rising, the price relationship may go either way.)

In the scattered-product case, the multi-product firms end up behaving rather like monopolistic competition firms, providing the number is not too small. But if the firms can assemble blocs of products which are contiguous on the spectrum, they possess some additional market power. Products in the interior of the spectrum have potential competition from products of other forms only if these enter the bloc, and the retaliatory power of the firm is considerable with respect to such entry, which it can attack not only by varying the price of the good which is closest in specification to the intruder but by varying specifications and prices of other goods close in specification. A new entrant would, in order to gain the economies from multi-product operation, have either to try to enter a bloc with M products or enter several blocs at the same time. Thus, each multi-product firm would have some implicit monopoly power within its segment. Contacts with the other firms are essentially limited to the products at the boundary of each segment, minimizing the oligopolistic elements. The overall result of bloc operation in terms of product variety would be to give less product differentiation than with scattered products, certainly more than with true island monopolies, probably more than with single-product firms since the single-product case provides a kind of limit behaviour. If the firm's spacing and pricing policy were such as to attract M single-product firms into its segment, it would find this relatively hard to combat.

NOTES

1. Originally published in *Journal of Business* **53** (1980), S79–S103.
2. But Spence has shown that monopolistic competition (in a rather different version from that here) leads to less-than-optimal differentiation when goods are complements: see Spence (1976a).
3. See Hanoch (1975) for an extended discussion of relationships of this kind. He uses the term 'elasticity of scale' in much the same way as the degree of economies of scale is used here.

4. It is not surprising that economies of scale which themselves increase with scale will cause destabilizing problems.

5. Note that the properties of the compensating function depend on the combined properties of the indifference curves and the product-differentiation curve, as well as the choice of distance measure.

6. Uniformity requires a special relationship between the preferences of consumers as one moves across the spectrum and the shape of the product-differentiation curve, as well as a suitable choice of distance measure.

7. If $q(u), y(u)$ are the quantities of group and outside goods required for a consumer at distance u from the available good, the optimal compensation mix is defined by the differential equations $d[\log q(u)]/du = [1 - (1 - m)\sigma] \, d[\log h(u)]/du$, $d[\log y(u)]du = m\sigma \, d[\log h(u)]/du$.

8. This is obvious from the differential equations given in note 7 above.

9. θ is constant if the production function is homogeneous, in which case it is equal to the degree of homogeneity.

10. $e_Y = 1$ at $\sigma = 0$ and increases with σ, while e_q varies inversely with σ and is equal to unity at $\sigma = 1/(1 - m)$, being less than unity for higher values. Nevertheless, the weighted average is always greater than unity.

11. By 'equal distribution of welfare' is meant the distribution obtained by giving every individual the same quantity of both outside good and most preferred good or most-preferred-good equivalent. Nothing is implied concerning interpersonal comparisons of actual welfare indexes.

12. That is, unless the price of a more distant good on the spectrum is so low relative to the closer good that the latter is passed over. In such a case the passed-over good will not be purchased by anyone and will drop out of the market.

13. $A = (a/1 - a)^{-\sigma}$. Note that P and I are assumed given in terms of the outside good.

14. Note that the equation (11.8) for $q(u)$ is the same as in the optimum mix for the non-market analysis: see note 7 above.

15. With more than two characteristics there will be more than two adjacent goods.

16. The factor 2 appears because both $h(u)$ and $h(2\Delta - u)$ change, equally but in opposite directions, in response to a change in u.

17. For lower values of the elasticity of substitution, the effect of price on the demand elasticity depends on the degree of price compensation.

18. There are no 'perceived' demand curves in this analysis–the demand conditions are true conditions.

19. Note that although this model has many features in common with neo-Hotelling spatial models, it differs in that the compensating function is strictly convex as compared with linear transport costs and that there is smooth substitutability with respect to outside goods. These differences are crucial. See Salop (1979) for a survey of neo-Hotelling models.

20. This is contrary to my earlier assertion (Lancaster 1975b) that the full group monopolist will produce an optimal degree of product differentiation. This is true if there are no outside goods, but then there is no stable monopoly equilibrium because the monopolist's elasticity of demand is less than unity.

12 Sustainable defensive monopoly[1]

This chapter seeks to answer a simple question: Can a sole incumbent in an industry make positive profits without attracting entry, by choice of an appropriate strategy in prices and the degree of product variety, when there is complete symmetry as to information, access to resources and consumers, and speeds of action and reaction, between the incumbent and potential entrants?

The 'sustainable monopoly' in the title refers to the existence of a long-run equilibrium configuration in which the industry consists of a single firm which makes no losses and attracts no entrants, and conforms to the general meaning of the term as used elsewhere.[2] The qualifier 'defensive' is added to make it clear that the firm does not have the freedom of action it would have from a guaranteed monopoly and, in general, must be content with less than full monopoly profits.

In spite of the considerable work on barriers to entry and limit pricing, there is not a precise answer to the question when posed exactly as above, even for the much analysed single-product industry, and certainly not for the product-differentiated one. This lack is due to emphasis on entry in asymmetric situations where either the incumbent or the entrant has some advantage in cost, information, consumer loyalty, or manoeuvrability over the other party, and to trying to answer the question from cost functions only, when it cannot be answered fully except in terms of the relationships between cost and demand.

Only strictly symmetric non-stochastic cases are considered here, in which the incumbent and the potential entrant have access to the same information, technology, and consumers, and both can act and react with equal rapidity. This rules out both hit-and-run by the entrant [3] and many of the traditional barriers to entry set by the incumbent. In the classic study of barriers to entry by Bain (1956), only economies of scale are potentially symmetric, and his analysis emphasises asymmetric features associated with these, such as the difficulty of entering except on a very small scale at first. Asymmetric cases make poor generalizations. For every asymmetric case that favours the entrant and leads to the conclusion that the monopolist has little freedom of action (as in the contestable market case), one can find an opposite asymmetry that gives the incumbent an edge over potential entrants.

The one asymmetric element is the essential structure of the situation –

that one firm is the incumbent and the other is an outsider looking in. In some game-theoretic approaches there is no 'incumbent' since the market is viewed as a game that is replayed from scratch every market period with synchronous moves, but the notion of incumbency is essential here.

The appropriate interpretation of the present model is that of continuous time (no discrete market periods), so the incumbent has the ability to signal, by maintaining a certain pattern of behaviour for a finite time period, in a way that is not possible in a finite number of discrete periods. In particular, steady behaviour over a finite time interval signals willingness to maintain that behaviour indefinitely, and additional credibility is provided by sustained defensive behaviour which is suboptimal in the short run.[4] because of the symmetry of information, the potential entrant will immediately recognize a sustained defensive strategy for what it is, and for what it signifies.

The analysis is divided into two parts. Although the ultimate interest is in multi-product industries, it is necessary to establish first the events for the single-product industry in which product differentiation is ruled out altogether for technical or other reasons. This is examined in the first section. It is shown that a sustainable defensive monopoly may exist, but only if the market is in just the right size range relative to the scale economies in production, neither too small nor too large. There is an optimal market size which gives the largest sustainable defensive monopoly rent. An interesting corollary is that the successful defensive monopolist may wish to avoid doing anything that increases the demand for its product-we should not expect to find such a product widely advertised!

As shown in the second section, however, the picture is changed dramatically for multi-product industries where it is possible to vary the characteristics of the goods to give infinite product differentiability, provided there is a wide range of variation in preferences over the consumer population. An incumbent can become a successful defensive monopolist under a very wide range of circumstances by choosing the appropriate combination of product differentiation and product price. In effect, the firm can almost always choose the degree of product differentiation to ensure the optimal size of market for each individual variety.

Except in cases of what will be called 'inherent monopoly', the market structures analysed here might be called 'semi-contestable' because entry would be possible and profitable if it were not for the defensive action taken by the incumbent. In addition, the pricing behaviour of the incumbent will be somewhere between monopoly and contestability.

THE SINGLE-PRODUCT INDUSTRY

To set the stage for discussion of the defensive multi-product incumbent, consider first the situation in an industry technically confined to a single homogeneous product. A potential entrant has no choice of product specification to make. If he enters, he must produce and sell a product identical to that of the incumbent. Although there is asymmetry in the pre-entry situation, because the incumbent is free to establish the going price while the potential entrant is free to choose the price at which he will sell the product upon entry, the situation is completely symmetrical after entry and any post-entry equilibrium must reflect this, as must pre-entry strategy choices.

One possible kind of entry is the 'body-snatchers' gambit[5] in which the entrant attempts to bankrupt or otherwise remove the original firm through a price war or other process, in order to take its place and continue its policies, including any elements of monopoly. Such attempts can occur in any market structure and, although more disastrous to the incumbent (if successful) than sharing a market, there is no sure defence in the kind of policies being examined here. It is assumed that potential entrants are not body-snatchers, a role inconsistent with post-entry symmetry, but contemplate becoming a second firm in the industry.

The incumbent is taken to have been selling the product at price p_i for some length of time prior to the point at which the story takes place. Given this context, consider rational entry strategies and their outcomes, viewed from the perspective of the potential entrant. By 'rational' strategies is simply meant strategies that take into account the symmetry of the post-entry situation. The potential entrant can be expected to reason as follows:

If I charge more than the incumbent I will sell nothing. If I charge the same price, I can expect, at best, to obtain half the buyers on the basis of random choice (less if there is any loyalty effect). If I lower the price, I can gain all the customers so long as the incumbent does not follow suit. But he *will* follow suit, because his costs are the same as mine and any price that is profitable to me is profitable to him also. He is just as likely to be the survivor of a price war as I am, so it would be dangerous to start one–at best we would end up splitting the market at a price lower than that at which we started. If I enter at the existing price and can make a profit on half the market share I can probably keep this position, since the monopolist can also make a profit on his half. My acceptance of his price leadership would allow us to collude implicitly and share the market. This strategy dominates all other entry strategies, so if I cannot make a profit with it, I certainly will not enter.

Thus the best attainable symmetric outcome for the potential entrant is implicit collusion at the going price, p_i, provided this is not above the monopoly price p_m. The best of all symmetric outcomes for the entrant would, of course, be implicit collusion at the monopoly price, but he has no way of achieving this if $p_i < p_m$. Among the possible implicit collusion solutions is one with the Cournot equilibrium values, should the price p_i have been set at exactly the appropriate level.

Deterring Potential Entry
In order to deter entry, the incumbent need only take note of the *best* strategy available to the potential entrant. If this can be made unprofitable, no other entry strategy can be profitable and no firm will enter. It will be assumed that the world is well populated with eager potential entrants who would indeed enter if their best rational strategy had positive expected profits. A sustainable single-product defensive monopoly is possible if there is a strategy for the incumbent which gives positive profits while the best available outcome for a potential entrant gives non-positive profits. It is obvious that no such strategy can exist without some economies of scale, which may need to be considerable in the single homogeneous product case. The precise requirements are set out in the proposition which follows.

Proposition 1
In an industry in which it is impossible to vary the product, an incumbent firm can inhibit entry and draw positive profits indefinitely if and only if there is a non-empty range of prices S such that the average cost and demand functions, $AC(x)$ and $Q(p)$ are related as follows:

(i) $AC[Q(p)/2] \geq p > AC[Q(p)]$ for all $p \in S$
(ii) $AC[Q(p)/2] \geq p^L$ for all $p < p^L$

where p^L is the lowest price in S.
If the conditions are satisfied, then the appropriate strategy for the incumbent is to establish the going price as the defensive price p_d given by:

$$p_d = \min [p_m, \max(p \in S)]$$

Such a price will generate positive profits for the incumbent but inhibit entry.

Proof Provided S is non-empty, the incumbent can always make a positive profit while deterring entry by charging a defensive price p_d equal to any p in S. A potential entrant cannot make a profit even with implicit collusion at any price in S (by virtue of condition (i)) nor at any price less than the lowest price in S (by virtue of condition (ii)), and cannot sell anything at any price higher than p_d. Thus there is no entry strategy giving a positive profit and entry is deterred successfully. But since $p_d >$ $AC[Q(p_d)]$, from condition (i), the incumbent, being in sole possession, would make a positive profit at this price and thus would have a sustainable strategy. Although the largest p in S is such a strategy, it is not always the optimal one. If $p_m \notin S$, then it must be that $p_m > p$ for all $p \in S$ and profit is increasing in p. Then $p_d = max(p \in S)$ will indeed be the optimal defensive price. If $p_m \in S$, however, profit declines as p increases beyond p_m so that $p_d = p_m$ is optimal and the firm can sustain behaviour as a full monopolist even though there are no institutional barriers to entry or asymmetries.

If no set S exists, then one of the following must be true:

(a) $p \leq AC[Q(p)]$ for all p.
(b) $AC[Q(p)] \geq AC[Q(p)/2]$ for all p.
(c) $p > AC[Q(p)/2]$ for all p.
(d) $p > AC[Q(p)/2]$ for some $p \leq p^L$.

In none of the four cases is it possible for the incumbent to find a price which generates positive profit and inhibits entry–in case (a) because there is no price at which a positive profit could be made even by a full monopolist, in (b) because production by a single firm gives no cost advantage over splitting production between two firms over the relevant output range, in (c) because two firms can make positive profits at all prices and thus entry cannot be deterred, and in (d) because the entrant can push the implicit collusion price down to a level at which two firms make profits.

Proposition 1 is illustrated in Figure 12.1(a)–(c), in which three different relationships between the demand curve and the two average cost curves, one for average cost when the whole output is produced by a single firm, $AC(Q)$, the other when output is split evenly between two firms, $AC(Q/2)$. In Figure 12.1(a), the portion of the demand curve which lies below $AC(Q/2)$ but above $AC(Q)$ defines the sustainable defensive price range S. Since the demand curve lies below $AC(Q/2)$ everywhere below the S range, condition (ii) is satisfied as well as condition (i). This is not true of the situation shown in Figure 12.1(b), where condition (ii) is not satisfied and there is no sustainable defensive price. In Figure 12.1(c), the demand curve

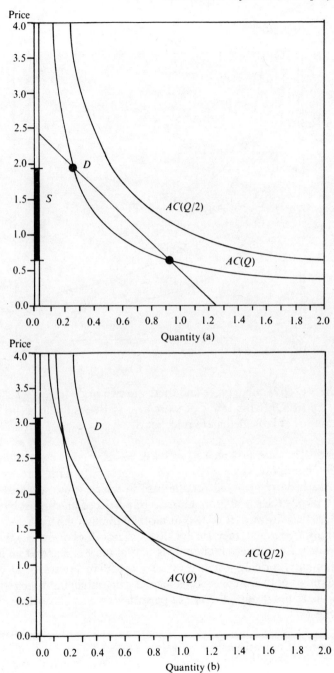

Figure 12.1

Figure 12.1 continued

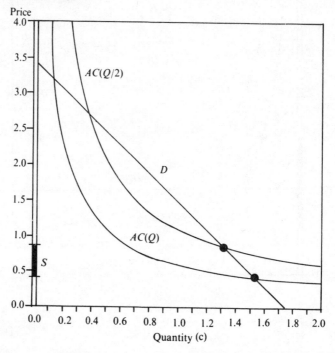

cuts the $AC(Q/2)$ curve twice and there are two price ranges which satisfy condition (i). Only the lower of these also satisfies condition (ii), so this gives the sustainable defensive price set S.

Remark   The case in which $p_m \in S$ will be referred to as a situation of *inherent* monopoly, since the otherwise appropriate term 'natural monopoly' has been pre-empted for the case in which some specified output level (typically the social optimum) can be produced at less cost by a single producer than by any set of two or more. Although inherent and natural monopoly are related, they are not the same nor does one imply the other. The context for inherent monopoly is that of market demand under non-discriminatory pricing when revenue more than covers cost, whereas natural monopoly is a concept associated with public utility regulation in which the optimal output may not be sustainable as an ordinary market outcome.

The Cournot Comparison
Since the Cournot equilibrium is so closely associated with the duopoly market structure it seems desirable to compare the post-entry equilibrium

under a defensive strategy (implicit collusion at the defensive price) with the potential post-entry Cournot solution. The relationship is expressed in Proposition 2.

Proposition 2
If there is a defensive price having the properties given in Proposition 1, then this is less than the Cournot equilibrium price. Thus the potential entrant cannot induce a Cournot equilibrium.

Proof Denote by $\phi(Q)$ the inverse demand function for the market being considered. Then the profit for either of the firms under Cournot duopoly assumptions is given by

$$\pi = \phi(\bar{q} + q)q - C(q)$$

and the effect of a quantity change by

$$\frac{d\pi}{dq} = \phi(\bar{q} + q) + \phi'(\bar{q})q - C'(q)$$

where $\bar{q}$ is the output of the other firm.

Only symmetric situations are of interest, so put $q = \bar{q}$, giving

$$\frac{d\pi}{dq} = \phi(2q) + \phi'(2q) - C'(q)$$

Consider this derivative at the value of $2q$ corresponding to the defensive price $p_d = AC(q)$, so that q satisfies the relationship $\phi(2q) = AC(q)$. Then

$$\frac{d\pi}{dq} = AC(q) - C'(q) + \phi'(2q)q$$

$$= - \left[\frac{d}{dq} AC(q) - \phi'(2q) \right]$$

From Proposition 1, a defensive price only exists if the demand curve cuts the $AC(Q/2)$ curve from above. Thus $d\pi/dq < 0$ at the values corresponding to the defensive price, so that the Cournot equilibrium is at a lower quantity than that corresponding to this price.

The Cournot equilibrium price must therefore be higher than the defensive price, and the Cournot equilibrium cannot be induced by the entrant because he can push the price down but not up.

The Cournot duopoly equilibrium, it might be noted, may well be more profitable than the monopolist's defensive configuration. In such a case, however, it can be shown that there will be incentives for additional firms to enter, so that the eventual configuration will not be duopoly. It is possible to conceive of a defensive duopoly, with a price set so as to make it unprofitable for a third firm to enter. This would require explicit collusion, however, and is not therefore considered in this chapter.

The Firm's Optimal Market Size

Proposition 1 has set out the conditions that must be satisfied for a profitable entry-deterring strategy to exist in any given case, conditions that depend on the properties of the cost function and the relationship between the cost function and the demand function. The only case in which existence can be determined without reference to the demand function is when there is no range of output for which average cost declines (constant or rising marginal cost and no fixed cost), in which case no such strategy exists.

If average cost declines over some range of output, a profitable entry-deterring strategy may exist, provided demand is neither too small nor too large. In order for the firm to be profitable even without a rival, the demand must be large enough for the firm to sell some output at a price above average cost. At the other extreme, if demand is so large relative to cost conditions that two or more firms can operate profitably at minimum cost output, there is no way the incumbent can keep others out.

For important classes of cost functions, therefore, an incumbent firm would make no profit even without potential rivals if the market demand for the product were sufficiently small, and could make no profits without attracting entrants if the market demand were sufficiently large, yet for some intermediate range of market demand the firm could maintain a profitable defensive posture, drawing some positive rents indefinitely without attracting rivals. In such a case, there must be some market demand (or range) which gives the largest possible level of permanently sustainable rents for the defensive monopolist, this being the firm's *optimal market size*.

To examine this idea in more detail, note first that there are two potentially profitable ranges of market demand for a given firm which call for quite different approaches by the firm. The lowest profitable range is that for which the firm possesses an inherent monopoly, and in which its behaviour is determined by the ordinary principles of profit maximization under full monopoly. The firm's profit in this range is determined by the elasticity of demand as well as the size of the market (defined appropriately) together with the properties of the cost function. For any family of demand curves of the form $Q = f(p,\alpha)$ where α is a size parameter such that $\partial f(p,\alpha)/\partial \alpha > 0$ for all p, the profit in the inherent monopoly range increases monotonically with α because average cost is necessarily falling in that range.

Next to the inherent monopoly range is the range in which there is potential entry. From Proposition 1, the incumbent firm will charge a price p_d and sell a quantity $Q(p_d)$ given by the equation

$$p_d = AC[Q(p_d)/2)]$$

The profit to the incumbent firm is then given by:

$$\pi_d = p_d Q(p_d - C[Q(p_d)]\}$$
$$= 2C(Q_d/2) - C(Q_d)$$

after substituting for p_d.

Note that the properties of π_d above depend only on the properties of the cost function and the level of Q_d, the latter being obviously correlated directly with the size of the market. The effect of market size on profitability in this range depends only on the cost function and, in particular, its convexity-concavity properties. Write $C(Q)$ in the form $C(Q) = V(Q) + F$, where $V(Q)$ is variable cost $[V(0) = 0]$ and F is fixed cost. Then

$$\pi_d(Q_d) = F + [2V(Q_d/2) - V(Q_d)]$$

and

$$\frac{d\pi_d}{dQ_d} = V'[Q_d/2 - V'(Q_d)]$$

where $V'(q) = dV/dq$ (marginal cost).

The bracketed expression in the first relationship and the sign of $\partial \pi_d/\partial (Q_d)$ are both zero if $V(Q)$ is linear, negative if $V(Q)$ is strictly convex (increasing marginal cost, the most commonly assumed property), and positive if $V(Q)$ is concave (decreasing marginal cost, a possible but unusual case).

For a linear cost function the maximum sustainable profit level is independent of the market size and equal to the fixed cost. This is because, with average variable cost constant, payment of the fixed cost (a flow) is the membership fee for the industry so that, if the incumbent firm sets a price which generates a profit greater than this amount after covering its own fixed cost, it is profitable for a second firm to enter.

If the variable cost function is convex (increasing marginal cost), the incumbent firm's profit, in the range in which there is potentially room for a second firm, is always strictly less than the fixed cost and is decreasing with output and thus market size. In this case the optimal size of the market from the incumbent's point of view is never greater than the largest for which an inherent monopoly exists. As the market grows, not only does it become sub-optimal in size from the firm's point of view, but eventually the profits from defensive monopoly become zero and then turn into losses as the average cost at the large single-firm output exceeds average cost when output is split.[6]

For a strictly concave variable cost function (ever decreasing marginal cost), the incumbent's profit continues to increase beyond the market size for which the firm has an inherent monopoly and thus the defensive monopolist gains without limit from increased market size. Such a case would surely be extremely rare. Decreasing marginal cost, if it occurred at all, could be expected to occur early and be succeeded by constant or rising marginal cost, as in the common textbook diagram of a U-shaped average variable cost curve. If minimum average variable cost occurred at an output beyond the inherent monopoly range, the market size for which the defensive price corresponded to sales at that minimum level would give the firm its maximum profit.

Thus, leaving out the possibility of ever-decreasing marginal cost, the incumbent firm's profit under defensive conditions will be at a maximum for a market of a certain size (or size range) and will decrease or, at best, remain constant if the market grows beyond this.

MULTI-PRODUCT FIRMS

In contrast to the assumptions of the previous section, it is now assumed that it is technically feasible for product design to be varied so that firms can produce more than one good within the same product group. To deal with product variation in combination with a well-defined product group, it is assumed that all goods in the group share a set of common characteristics. The relative proportions of these characteristics can be varied over some range, each variant (defined by its specification, or characteristics content) corresponding to a different model within that product group, and the group itself to a continuous spectrum of potential product variants. The terms 'models', 'variants', 'differentiates', 'products' and 'goods' will be used more or less interchangeably, to avoid some monotony. The general context is that of the kind of neo-Hotelling product differentiation modelling that has been treated extensively by the author and others.[7]

There are no inter-product economies or diseconomies and no economies or diseconomies of management or pure organizational size, so that a multi-product firm's costs of production are the same as the sum of the costs of single-product firms producing the same output bundle.[8] Fixed costs and economies (or diseconomies) of scale apply separately and independently to each product. Finally, it is assumed that the cost functions and quantity units are so related that the quantity Q of any product variant has the same costs as the quantity Q of any other good in the product group.

Demand

The analysis will be carried out in terms of a two characteristics model in which the characteristics proportions can be represented on a one-dimensional line spectrum, as for a food group with different sour–sweet ratios or sports cars with different speed–comfort ratios. It can also be applied more or less directly to pure locational variation. In any case, it will be assumed that each individual consumer has a given location or a most preferred characteristics combination represented by a definite point on the spectrum, and that his/her interest in other products diminishes with their distance away from the most preferred choice. In spatial models, this diminution of desirability with distance is treated as a transport cost. In the characteristics model it can, if one wishes, be regarded as a 'psychic transport cost'.

The individual's demand function for a good which is the only good available in the group, which is located on the spectrum at distance v from his most preferred good, and which sells at price p, is taken to have the form

$$q = q(p,v); q_p < 0; q_v \leq 0$$

The sensitivity of $q(p,v)$ to v, the distance between the specifications (or actual locations) of the available good and the consumer's most preferred good (the consumer himself in spatial models), is very important in the analysis. It is determined by two things:

1. The importance to the individual of differences in location on the spectrum. If transport costs are zero, or variations in these characteristics do not enter the consumer's preferences, all goods in the group are perfect substitutes and q_v is zero, irrespective of other factors.
2. The substitutability of outside goods for goods in the group. If there is zero outside substitutability, then q_v may be zero even though spectral distance counts. This is true for the original Hotelling spatial model in which there are transport costs but an inelastic demand for the good. A common assumption in recent locational models is inelastic demand up to a reservation cost (= price plus transport), which gives a step function for q.

When distance counts and there is some degree of substitutability between group goods and outside goods, q will be a smooth function with q_v strictly negative. This will be taken to be the normal case.

When two goods in the group are both available, an individual will choose the one that gives him best value per £1, buying the closer if both have the same price, the cheaper if both are at the same distance (in opposite directions of course, or they would not be different), otherwise weighing distance from his most preferred specification against price. An individual will be indifferent between buying a certain good at price p and buying the adjacent good on the spectrum which is at distance s from the first good and sells at price P, if his most preferred specification is located between the two goods and at some distance V from the first good, where V is assumed to have the form

$$V = V[(p/P),s]; V(1,s) = s/2; V_{p/P} < 0; V_s > 0$$

When both goods have the same price, the indifferent consumer is the one equidistant between them. As the price ratio changes, the indifference position moves closer to the higher-priced product.

Two very heroic assumptions are made at this point. First, that all consumers have individual demand functions of the same form so that the demand by a particular individual for a particular product depends only on the position of that good *relative* to the individual's most preferred specification, and not on the absolute positions of either. The second is that the distribution of the most preferred specifications of individuals is uniform along the spectrum. Thus the functions $q(p,v)$ and $V[(p/P),s]$ do not change along the spectrum. These are the two main assumptions of what will be referred to as the *uniform* market.

Consider the market for a particular good at price p, when there are other goods available in the product group, in particular the two neighbouring or adjacent goods along the spectrum, one in each direction. The individuals to the left of the good will choose between it and the adjacent good to the left, while the consumers to the right will choose between it and the right adjacent good. Thus the market for the good is made up of two separate *half-markets*, which can be treated separately. Take either half-market and denote the distance of the furthest purchaser of that good by V. Then the sales in that half-market will be given by:

$$Q(p, V) = k \int_0^V q(p,v) \, dv$$

where k is the density of consumers along the spectrum. Without loss of generality, this will be taken to be unity henceforth. Note that $Q(p,V)$ is strictly concave in V except in special cases, since q_v is strictly negative in general. This property plays an important role in the analysis.

The edge of the firm's half-market will be where the marginal customer is indifferent between the firm's good and the adjacent good, that is, where $V = V((p/P),s)$, so that the half-market quantity can be written as $Q(p,P,s)$, where:

$$Q(p,V) = k \int_0^{V(p/P),s)} q(p,v) \, dv$$

The following properties of Q(p,P,s) can easily be derived:

$$Q_p < 0, Q_P > 0, Q_s > 0$$

For a good selling at price p in a market with neighbours at distances s_R, s_L to the right and left selling at prices P_R, P_L, the demand function is:

$$Q^T(p,P_R,P_L,s_R,s_L) = Q^R(p,P_R,s_R) + Q^L(p,P_L,s_L)$$

Much of the analysis will be concerned with symmetrical situations in which $P_R = P_L = P$ and $s_R = s_L = s$, giving the demand function

$$Q^T(p,P,s) = 2Q(p,P,s)$$

For a single-product firm in a symmetrical context, the profit function can be written

$$\pi(p,P,s) = 2pQ(p,P,s) - C[2Q(p,P,s)]$$

where the first argument is the price of the firm's own good and the second the price of the adjacent goods.

The analysis here will be restricted to the uniform market, the special case discussed fully in Lancaster (1979), in which it is assumed that:

1. An individual's view of a particular good depends on the position of the good on the spectrum *relative* to the position of his most preferred good, and not on the absolute positions of either.
2. Individual demands are identical except as to their most preferred specifications, and individuals need to be identified only by their most preferred goods.
3. The population and income density of individuals having the same most preferred good is the same everywhere on the spectrum.

4.   End-of-spectrum effects can be ignored.[9]

The uniform market leads to symmetrical solutions, with equilibria described in the minimum number of parameters. The results which are derived can be used as a guide to events in non-uniform cases, the analysis of which becomes extraordinarily complex even with small departures from uniformity.

Benchmark Configurations

There are two market structures that provide reference data for comparison with defensive monopoly configurations. These are the traditional monopolistic competition or zero-profit, non-collusive Nash equilibrium of single-product firms with free entry, and 'full group monopoly', the equilibrium of a single multi-product firm having an institutionally guaranteed monopoly over all products within the group, actual or potential.

Since the cost functions for all products are identical and the demand functions depend only on prices and relative, not absolute, positions of goods on the spectrum, any non-collusive Nash equilibrium will be completely symmetrical with all firms charging the same price $\hat{p}(s)$ and products placed along the spectrum at a uniform spacing s inversely proportional to the number of firms. The value of $\hat{p}(s)$ will be given by

$$\pi[\hat{p}(s),\hat{p},s] = \max_p \pi[p,\hat{p}(s),s]$$

The profit $\pi(\hat{p}(s),\hat{p},s)$ at the Nash equilibrium for spacing s is a monotonically increasing function of s, provided average cost is non-increasing. Thus profit per firm is a monotonically decreasing function of the number of firms in the non-increasing average cost range and free entry will cause profits to fall as new firms enter until they reach zero and the incentive for entry ceases. Because the number of firms must be an integer, an exact 'zero-profit' equilibrium may not be possible and the term will be used in the expanded sense to mean the largest possible number of non-losing firms.

The monopolistic competition equilibrium will be given by the price-spacing pair (p^*,s^*) such that

$$\pi(p^*,p^*,s^*) = \max_p \pi(p,p^*,s^*) = 0$$

with the condition appropriately modified if the integer effect must be considered.

An important property of a monopolistic competition equilibrium, brought out in Chamberlin's original analysis, is that (p^*,s^*) will always be such that the average cost is falling at the equilibrium output $2Q(p^*,p^*,s^*)$.

By 'full' monopoly is meant a firm which is the only producer of goods within the group under consideration and which faces no potential entrant into the group, whatever its behaviour. Such a monopoly (or cartel) can co-ordinate the prices and locations of the individual goods to maximize overall profit. Since there are assumed to be no inter-product economies of any kind, the only advantage of the multi-product firm or the cartel over individual single-product firms is this power to co-ordinate.

It is obvious before proceeding further that the monopoly equilibrium in the uniform distribution case will be such that all products will be sold at the same price and will be spaced evenly along the spectrum, so the monopoly equilibrium can be described by a single price-spacing pair (p_m,s_m), just as for the monopolistic competition structure.

The maximand in the monopoly case must be considered carefully. Whereas the single-product firm will maximize profit from the production and sale of its one product, the monopolist will not choose the price and number of products so as to maximize profit per product, but to maximize overall profit. This may call for few products at a large profit per product, or more products at a smaller profit per product. Since the number of products is proportional to $1/s$, the inverse of the spacing, the total profit from the monopolist's complete range of products is proportional to $z(p,s)$, defined as

$$z(p,s) = \frac{\pi(p,p,s)}{s}$$

where $\pi(p,p,s)$ is the profit per product when every product is sold at price p and products are uniformly spaced at distance s. It is convenient to take as maximand $z(p,s)$, the 'profit density', since this is proportional to aggregate profit.

It has been shown elsewhere[10] that the full monopoly solution will give fewer products than would the monopolistic competition equilibrium, and that these will be sold at higher prices than would be the case for an equal number of products sold by non-collusive single-product firms. Since these established results are in conformity with expectations, it is not proposed to attempt to repeat the proofs here, even in simplified form.

Entry and the Multi-Product Firm

As in the first section the initial position will be one in which there is a single incumbent firm, now actually or potentially multi-product, which is acting as either a full monopolist or as some kind of defensive monopolist. The options open to a potential entrant who is contemplating entry with a single product are more varied than in the fixed-product industry since the entrant must choose both the product specification and the price in this case, not just the price.

It is obvious that the most desirable way to enter would be into an *empty region*. If there is some part of the market which is not covered by the incumbent, in the sense that his closest good is so far away that it can be all but ignored, then the entrant can choose to produce and sell a good in this segment of the market spectrum virtually as though it were a local monopoly. Since the market is assumed uniform throughout and thus potential demand is the same everywhere, such a sector must be as profitable as any other. But it is equally obvious that this market sector would be just as profitable for the incumbent, so the rational and fully-informed incumbent would already have it covered. Empty sector entry is obviously important in a dynamic and evolving industry in which new entrants can appear faster than the incumbent is able to cover the market, leading to a structure in which there are several firms, each the sole incumbent in a certain part of the market.

The main concern of this chapter is with the mature incumbent who has been able to move into his desired strategic configuration prior to being assailed by potential entrants, although it can be extended to cover a firm which has been able to do so only over its own market sector. Such a firm will have adopted either the full monopoly equilibrium configuration of goods uniformly spaced at distance s_m and sold at the same price p_m, or the configuration appropriate to some other defensive strategy.

In the uniform market case, it is obvious that any rational defensive configuration will be characterized by uniform prices and a uniform spacing between goods, since a potential entrant is free to choose the point (or points) of entry. The most profitable price-spacing combination which still inhibits entry will be the same in one portion of the spectrum as in another. Thus the mature multi-product incumbent will produce goods with specifications spaced at some uniform distance s_i and sell them all at price p_i.

With the incumbent so configured, the potential entrant has two basic choices to make concerning the type of entry:

1. *Face-to-face entry*. The entrant produces and sells a good which is identical to one of the goods being produced and sold by the incumbent.
2. *Interstitial entry*. The entrant produces and sells a new product which

is located at a point on the spectrum between two of the goods produced by the incumbent.

Face-to-face entry is basically similar to entry in the single-product case, and from the same arguments, as in that case, it follows that the best attainable outcome for the face-to-face entrant will be implicit collusion at the incumbent's going price, p_i, with the incumbent and entrant each having, on average, half the market for that product. Actually, the incumbent can force the entrant to do worse than this by varying the adjacent goods' specifications, something it is not necessary to explore further because of Proposition 3 below.

The mode that determines the entrant's entry strategy and the incumbent's defensive posture is interstitial entry, not face-to-face entry, because of the following result.

Proposition 3
In any market with a continuous spectrum of potential product variants and a uniformly-spaced, uniformly-priced initial configuration, interstitial entry dominates face-to-face entry in the sense that for the best available face-to-face entry strategy there is an interstitial entry strategy which is strictly superior in general (when $Q(p, V)$ is strictly concave in V) and is no worse in the limiting case (when $Q(p, V)$ is linear in V).

Proof Consider first an initial configuration in which the incumbent is producing products arranged uniformly over the spectrum at spacing s and selling tham all at price p. The quantity sold in either half-market for any of the goods will be $Q(p,s/2)$, since each half-market will end at the mid-point between adjacent goods. For face-to-face entry the best available outcome for the entrant is the implicit collusion solution at price p, with expected sales in each half-market (for both the entrant and the incumbent) of $Q(p,s/2)/2$, or total sales for each firm of $Q(p,s/2)$.

Now consider interstitial entry at a point on the spectrum at a distance $\alpha \leq s/2$ from the location of the incumbent's good, and at the same price p as the incumbent's good. The entering firm's total sales will be made up of sales in each of two half-markets, one of width $\alpha/2$ and the other of width $(s - \alpha)/2$.

For any strictly concave function $f(x)$ such that $f(0) = 0$, it can easily be shown that

$$f(x_1) + f(x_2) > f(x_1 + x_2)$$

provided $x_1, x_2 > 0$.

In this case, since $Q(p,V)$ is, in general, strictly concave in V and $Q(p,0) = 0$:

$$Q(p,\alpha/2) + Q(p,(s - \alpha)/2) > Q(p,s/2)$$

Thus the sales from interstitial entry at the price of the incumbent's good exceed those from the entering firm's share from implicit collusion for all $\alpha > 0$. Since average cost must be non-increasing at the relevant output level, interstitial entry is more profitable than face-to-face entry when the entrant's price matches the incumbent's in both cases. But the interstitial entrant is able to vary the price of his product (which the face-to-face entrant is not), giving an additional edge in potential profitability.

It is easily shown that interstitial entry is most advantageous at $\alpha = s/2$, halfway between the existing goods, when the market is uniform and the initial configuration has uniform prices and spacings, except when $Q(p,V)$ is linear in V, in which case all entry points are equally profitable.

If the initial spacing is non-uniform (but the underlying market distribution is uniform), the superiority of interstitial entry still holds. Suppose that all prices are the same but spacings vary. Then the optimal face-to-face entry will be at the good with the largest average space from its two neighbours $(s_R + s_L)/2$. Suppose that $s_R > s_L$ for this good. Then it is easy to show that interstitial entry to the right strictly dominates face-to-face, since

$$Q(p,\alpha/2) + Q(p,(s_R - \alpha)/2 > Q(p,s_R/2) > \left[[Q(p,s_R/2)\right] + Q(p,s_L/2)]/2$$

In the limiting case in which distance along the spectrum is irrelevant to choice or in which there are no outside substitutes available for goods in the group, so that $q_v(p,v) = 0$ and $Q(p,V)$ is linear in V, location has no effect on sales and interstitial entry is no better (and no worse) than face-to-face entry. Thus the proposition is established.

The results for entry by a single-product firm hold without change for entry by a multi-product firm which is planning to produce goods at the same spacings as the incumbent. In that case, the spectral positions of all products of the entrant are either in phase with those of the incumbent, giving simultaneous face-to-face entry everywhere, or out of phase, giving interstitial entry everywhere. By the same arguments as above, interstitial entry will dominate.

Defensive Strategy for the Multi-Product Firm
The incumbent firm in the single-product industry has only one variable at its disposal with which to devise a defensive strategy. As a consequence, a

sustainable defensive monopoly strategy is possible only when the size of the market stands in a special relationship to the scale properties of the production function, as shown in the first section. Such a strategy will not be possible, in general, when the market is either too small or too large, and within the appropriate range there is an optimal market size for which the profitability of defensive monopoly is at its greatest. A multi-product firm, on the other hand, can vary the spacing of its products on the spectrum as well as their price, making the market for each product as large or as small as policy requires. In effect, the multi-product firm can choose the degree of product variety so as to make the market size for each product optimal relative to the firm's strategic objectives.

It has been shown above that it is always optimal for the entrant to adopt an interstitial entry strategy rather than enter face-to-face. Thus the face-to-face defensive strategy – essentially the same as the single-product defence – is irrelevant. The successful defensive incumbent must be in such a posture that he can make a positive profit while ensuring that all interstitial entry is unprofitable. With variable product differentiation, a defensive monopoly configuration is possible under a wide range of circumstances.

Proposition 4

In any uniform market in which it is possible to have a zero-profit (expanded sense) non-collusive Nash equilibrium of two or more single-product firms, a multi-product defensive monopoly strategy is possible. In particular, a sustainable defensive monopoly strategy is possible if a monopolistic competition equilibrium is possible.

If the zero-profit Nash equilibrium is described by the price-spacing pair (p^*, s^*), both the price and spacing being the same across all goods because of the uniformity of the market, then there is some $\alpha \geq 0$ such that the price-spacing pair $(p^*, s^* + \alpha)$ is a sustainable defensive strategy, although not necessarily the best of such strategies.

Proof Consider interstitial entry when the price of the incumbent's goods is p^* and the spacing is s^*. Since 'zero-profit' is being used in the expanded sense, the spacing s^* is inversely proportional to some integer N^* which is the largest number of non-losing firms possible in the industry without collusion, so $s^* = k/N^*$.

Interstitial entry would result in the entrant facing adjacent competitive goods at an average distance of $s^*/2 = k/2N^*$. Since firms make losses at spacing $s \leq k/(N^* + 1)$ and $2N^* > N^* + 1$, the entrant would make a loss.

The incumbent could make a positive profit, however. If (p^*, s^*) is a true zero-profit (monopolistic competition) equilibrium then the average cost is falling for each of the goods, so there is certainly some α such that for s in the range $s^* < s \leq s^* + \alpha$, $\pi(p^*,p^*,s) > 0$. If (p^*,s^*) is 'zero-profit' in the expanded sense, then $\pi(p^*,p^*,s^*) > 0$ and $\alpha = 0$ is a profitable defensive strategy.

Thus $(p^*,s^* + \alpha)$ is a profitable defensive strategy for some $\alpha \geq 0$, although it is not necessarily the optimal strategy since p^* has been held at the monopolistic competition value and not optimized for the firm.

To construct an optimal strategy, the incumbent must first determine those combinations of price and product variety for which the entrant can make no profit even with interstitial entry, the latter's best strategy. If the incumbent sets a uniform price-spacing configuration at (P,s), the interstitial entrant's sales will be determined by the price p of his own product when there are adjacent products at distances $s/2$ and selling at prices P. The entrant's profit function will have the form $\pi(p,P,s/2)$, where p is the only variable under his control. Thus the set of sustainable P,s combinations for the incumbent are those that satisfy the inequality $\max_p \pi(p,P,s/2) \leq 0$. From this set, the incumbent chooses the combination that maximizes his own profit density $z(P,P,s)$. This establishes the next proposition.

Proposition 5

In a uniform multi-product market in which a sustainable defensive strategy exists, the optimal defensive strategy is the price-spacing pair (P,s) which is the solution to the problem:

$$\max_{P,s} z(P,s) = \frac{1}{s}\pi(P,P,s)$$

Subject to

$$\max_{p} \pi(p,P,s/2) \leq 0$$

For functional forms with appropriate properties, the problem does not lend itself to easy analytical results, but numerical solutions can be generated for simple but acceptable numerical examples. Some properties can be established for the regular case in which the full monopoly solution is at a higher price and larger spacing than the monopolistic competition equilibrium and the integer problem is neglected.

1. For any entry price p, the entrant's potential profit $\pi(p,P,s/2)$ is an increasing function of both P and s, so that the boundary of the feasible set in P,s space will be downward sloping.
2. The point (p^*,s^*) will be strictly in the interior of the feasible set for the reasons outlined in establishing Proposition 4.
3. The point $(p^*,2s^*)$ will be on the boundary, since $\max_p \pi(p,p^*,s) = \pi(p^*,p^*,s^*) = 0$.
4. It does not appear that the full monopoly point (p_m,s_m) is necessarily exterior to the feasible set, although this would be the expectation in most cases.

Figure 12.1(c) illustrates the structure of the optimizing problem by showing the feasible set and contours of the function $z(P,s)$ for a model described by the demand function

$$Q(p,P,s) = \bar{p}^{2.5}P^{.5}s^{.5}$$

and the cost function $C(Q) = 1 + Q$, which represent acceptable properties.[11]

The optimal defensive solution (1.84,31), labelled D, is intermediate between the monopolistic competition solution MC at (1.67,17) and the full monopoly solution FM at (2,64). Although this is the generally expected result, it may not hold for all cases.

DEFENCE VERSUS PREDATION AND OTHER MATTERS

The results given in this chapter suggest that it may be easier for an incumbent firm to retain continued dominance over a market, without using any overt trade-restraining tactics, than has usually been thought to be the case, at least in industries in which the degree of product differentiation can be varied in a more or less continuous way. In one-product industries, dominance by a single firm may depend on the market remaining sufficiently small to give the optimal market size and the firm may become worse off as its product becomes more popular. The multi-product firm can avoid this problem by choosing the appropriate degree of product variety to ensure that the market for each individual variant is within the desired range.

At first glance the chapter may seem to prove too much, making it appear so easy for a firm to retain a monopoly in a product-differentiated industry that one would expect such a structure to be the norm, which is surely not the case. But there is fine print in the analysis, not to be neglected. In particular, the full defensive posture requires the incumbent to have covered the whole product spectrum with suitably arrayed variants *before* any other firm makes serious entry decisions.

Modified versions of the model are possible, such as a defensive monopoly covering an extended segment of the product spectrum but not all of it, like Boeing in the mainline commercial aircraft segment of the aircraft market, for example. Asymmetries may lead to less clear-cut structures than are implied by the symmetrical model, and a firm with cost or other advantages might impose an *ex-post* defensive monopoly structure even though it initially covers only part of the market. If no single incumbent has been able to cover the market early enough, a kind of defensive oligopoly structure may emerge, as in the 20-year golden age period of the United States car industry following World War II.

In general, the sustainable defensive strategy for the incumbent will be to set a price less than the full monopoly price and also, in the multi-product case, to produce a greater variety of products than under full monopoly. Almost certainly, these are moves which bring the price-variety combination closer to the optimum than is the full monopoly point, and thus sustainable defensive monopoly can be regarded as socially more desirable than full monopoly, subject to the usual caveats on second-best solutions. In the single-product case, the defensive monopolist's limit price will be brought part of the way to the minimum average cost level by threat of potential entry, but never the whole way as in the theory of contestable markets. Thus defensive markets might be called 'semi-contestable', as suggested earlier.

On the other hand, since the incumbent's price/variety combinations are specifically designed to inhibit they might also be regarded as predatory practices[12] that prevent a more competitive market structure being achieved and thus as undesirable. These strategies have been termed defensive here because that is the correct description from the point of view of the firm devising them.

In any case, the final outcome of free entry in the differentiated products case would be a monopolistic competition equilibrium which would itself be suboptimal and almost always produce too many products.[13]

It will almost always be true that neither the defensive monopoly nor the free entry monopolistic competition equilibrium is the optimum, and a comparison of the two is a comparison of suboptimal situations. The intuition that the monopolistic competition solution will be superior to the defensive monopoly is given some support by computing a crude welfare measure (consumer surplus per unit of the spectrum) for the numerical example given above. Compared to an index of 1 for full monopoly, this gives 1.56 for the defensive configuration and 2.32 for monopolistic competition, but does not take account of the differences in resource use by the industry (considerably lower for the defensive solution) or consider producer surplus. Only a full welfare analysis can give a definitive answer, however.

NOTES

1. Previously unpublished conference paper, presented in 1984.
2. As, for example, in Baumol, Bailey and Willig (1977).
3. Important in the idea of contestable markets. See Baumol, Panzar and Willig (1982).
4. The incumbent can be considered to be signalling his intention to act as a Stackelberg leader, as in Dasgupta and Stiglitz (1980).
5. After the well-known science-fiction film in which alien beings take over the bodies of humans without causing visible change.
6. This assumes that there are diseconomies of scale which inhere in the firm *per se* (management, for example), since plant diseconomies can be eliminated by multiple plants.
7. Lancaster (1979), Salop (1979), Economides (1981, 1983), for example.
8. This is a major difference from the multi-product firms studied by Baumol, Bailey and Willig (1977), Baumol, Panzar and Willig (1982), and Bailey and Friedlaender (1982), in which inter-product economies are a predominant feature.
9. Goods at the end of the spectrum have a neighbour on only one side, so the symmetry assumed in the analysis does not hold for these. Adjustment for asymmetries at the ends causes asymmetries through the whole spectrum. The technique often used to avoid this problem in the pure spatial model – a circular spectrum with no ends, as in Salop (1979) – does not make sense in characteristics. It is assumed here that the effects can simply be neglected, as in an infinite spectrum.
10. Lancaster 1979, Chapter 9.
11. The one special property is that, because of the separable nature of the demand function, the optimal price for a single-product firm is always $5/3$ ($=p^*$), whatever the price P of the adjacent good. In general, we would expect p to be increasing in P.
12. See Schmalensee 1978 for a discussion of increased product variety as a predatory practice, also Salop et. al. 1981. Ordover and Willig 1981 discuss the economic theory of predation, with primary emphasis on price.
13. See Spense 1976a. Dixit and Stiglitz 1977, Lancaster 1979, for cases in which monopolistic competition gives too little product variety.

References

Adelman, I. and Z. Griliches, (1961), 'On an Index of Quality Change', *Journal of the American Statistical Association,* **56**, 535–48.

Arrow, K. J. and F.H. Hahn, (1971), *General Competitive Analysis,* Holden-Day.

Bailey, E. E. and A. F. Friedlaender, (1982), 'Market Structure and Multiproduct Industries', *Journal of Economic Literature,* **20**, 1024–1148.

Bain, Joe S. (1956), *Barriers to New Competition,* Cambridge, Mass: Harvard University Press.

Baumol, W. J. (1977), 'On the Proper Tests for Natural Monopoly in a 'Multiproduct Industry', *American Economic Review,* **67**, 809–22.

Baumol, W. J., E. E. Bailey, and R. D. Willig, (1977), 'Weak Invisible Hand Theorems on the Sustainability of Prices in a Multiproduct Monopoly', *American Economic Review,* **67**, 350–65.

Baumol, W. J., J. C. Panzar, and R. D. Willig, (1982), *Contestable Markets and the Theory of Industry Structure,* San Diego: Harcourt Brace Jovanovich.

Becker, G. S. (1965), 'A Theory of the Allocation of Time', *Economic Journal,* **75**, 493–516.

Bernardo, J. J. and J. M. Blin, (1977), 'A Programming Model of Choice among Multi-Attributed Brands', *Journal of Consumer Research,* **4**, 111–18.

Blackorby, C., G.Lady, D. Nissen, and R. Russell, (1970), 'Homothetic Separability and Consumer Budgeting', *Econometrica,* **38**, 468–72.

Blaug, Mark (1980), *The Methodology of Economics,* Cambridge: Cambridge University Press.

Brown, J. and A. Deaton, (1972), 'Surveys in Applied Economics: Models of Consumer Behaviour', *Economic Journal,* **82**, 1145–236.

Brumat, C. M. and L. M. Tomasini, (1979), 'A Probabilistic Extension of Lancaster's Approach to Consumer Theory', *Zeitschrift Für Nationalökonomie,* **39**, 381–3.

Buchanan, J. M. (1965), 'An Economic Theory of Clubs', *Econometrica,* **32**, 1–14.

Burstein, M. (1961), 'Measurement of Quality Change in Consumer Durables', *Manchester School of Economic and Social Studies,* **29**, 267–79.

Cagan, P. (1965), 'Measuring Quality Change and the Purchasing Power of Money', *National Banking Review,* **3**, 217–36.

Capozza, D. (1982), 'Product Differentiation and the Consistency of Monopolistic Competition: A Spatial Perspective', *Journal of Industrial Economics*, **31**, 27–40.

Capozza, D. and R. van Order, (1978), 'A Generalized Model of Spatial Competition', *American Economic Review*, **68**, 896–908.

Chamberlin, E. H. (1933), *The Theory of Monopolistic Competition*, Harvard University Press.

Court, A. T. (1939), 'Hedonic Price Indexes with Automotive Examples', in *Dynamics of Automobile Demand*, New York: General Motors Corporation.

Dasgupta, P. and J. Stiglitz, (1980), 'Uncertainty Industrial Structure, and the Speed of R&D', *Bell Journal of Economics*, **11**, 1–28.

D'Aspremont, C., J. Gabszewicz, and J.-F. Thisse, (1979), 'On Hotelling's "Stability in Competition" ', *Econometrica*, **47**, 1145–50.

Debreu, G. (1959), *Theory of Value: An Axiomatic Analysis of Economic Equilibrium*, Cowles Foundation, monograph 17.

Debreu, G. (1960), 'Topological Methods in Cardinal Utility Theory', in K. J. Arrow, S. Karlin, and P. Suppes, (eds), *Mathematical Methods in the Social Sciences, 1959*, Palo Alto: Stanfield University Press.

Debreu, G. (1974), 'Excess Demand Functions', *Journal of Mathematical Economics*, **1**, 15–21.

Dixit, A. K. and J. E. Stiglitz, (1977), 'Monopolistic Competition and Optmum Product Diversity', *American Economic Review*, **67**, 297–308.

Dorward, N. (1982), 'Recent Developments in the Analysis of Spatial Competition and Their Implications for Industrial Economics', *Journal of Industrial Economics*, **31**, 133–52.

Downs, A. (1957), *An Economic Theory of Democracy*, New York: Harper and Row.

Eaton, B. C. and R. G. Lipsey, (1975), 'The Principle of Minimum Differentiation Reconsidered: Some New Developments in the Theory of Spatial Competition', *Review of Economic Studies*, **42**, 27–49.

Eaton, B. C. and R. G. Lipsey, (1976), 'The Non-Uniqueness of Equilibrium in the Löschian Location Model', *American Economic Review*, **66**, 132–57.

Eaton, B. C. and R. G. Lipsey, (1979) 'The Theory of Market Pre-emption: Barriers to Entry in a Growing Spatial Market', *Economica*, **46**, 149–58.

Economides, N. (1984), 'The Principle of Minimum Differentiation Revisited', *European Economic Review*, **24**, 345–68.

Ellickson, B. (1973), 'A Generalization of the Pure Theory of Public Goods', *American Economic Review*, **83**, 417–32.

Faulhaber, G. R. (1975), 'Cross-Subsidization: Pricing in a Public Enterprise', *American Economic Review*, **65**, 966–77.

Ferber, R. and F. Nicosia, (1973), *Human Behaviour and Economic Affairs*, Amsterdam: North-Holland.

Fishbein, M. (1970), 'Some Comments on the Use of "Models" in Advertising Research', in European Society of Market Research, *Proceedings: Seminar on Translating Advertising Theories into Research Reality*,297–318.

Fisher, F. M. and K. Shell, (1968), 'Taste and Quality Change in the Pure Theory of the True-Cost-of-Living Index', in J. N. Wolfe, (ed.), *Value, Capital, and Growth: Essays in Honour of Sir John Hicks*, Edinburgh: Edinburgh University press.

Friedman, James (1983), *Oligopoly Theory*, Cambridge: Cambridge University Press.

Friedman, M. and L. J. Savage, (1952), 'The Expected-Utility Hypothesis and the Measurement of Utility', *Journal of Political Economy*, **60**, 463–74.

Gabszewicz, J. J. and J. F. Thisse, (1979), 'Price Competition, Quality and Income Disparities', *Journal of Economic Theory*, **22**, 340–59.

Geistfeld, L. V. (1977), 'Consumer Decision Making: The Technical Efficiency Approach', *Journal of Consumer Research*, **4**, 48–56.

Georgescu-Roegen, N. (1966), *Analytical Economics, Issues and Problems*, Cambridge Mass: Harvard University Press.

Gorman, W. M. (1959), 'Separable Utility and Aggregation', *Econometrica*,**27**, 469–81.

Graitson, D. (1982), 'Spatial Competition à la Hotelling: A Selective Survey', *Journal of Industrial Economics* **31**, 13–26.

Greeno, D. W., M. S. Sommers, and R. N. Wolff, (1977), 'An Empirical Evaluation of Investigating Mode Attributes for Commodities', *Operational Research Quarterly*, **28**, 829–38.

Griliches, Z. (1961), 'Hedonic Price Indexes for Automobiles: An Econometric Analysis of Quality Change', in *Price Statistics of the Federal Government*, New York: National Bureau of Economic Research.

Griliches, Z. (ed.)(1971), *Price Indexes and Quality Change: Studies in New Methods of Measurement*, Cambridge Mass: Harvard University Press.

Hall, R. E. (1971), 'The Measurement of Quality Change from Vintage Price Data', in Z. Griliches (ed.).

Hanoch, G. (1975), 'The Elasticity of Scale and the Shape of Average Costs', *American Economic Review*, **65**, 492–7.

Hay, D. A. (1976), 'Sequential Entry and Entry-Deterring Strategies in Spatial Competition', *Oxford Economic Papers*, **28**, 240–57.

Hicks, J. R. (1956), *A Revision of Demand Theory*, Oxford: Oxford University Press.

Hotelling, H. (1929), 'Stability in Competition', *Economic Journal*, **39**, 41.

Houthakker, H. S. (1952), 'Compensated Changes in Quantities and Qualities Consumed', *Review of Economic Studies*, 19, 155–64.

Houthakker, H. S. and L. D. Taylor, (1970), *Consumer Demand in the United States*, 2nd edition, Cambridge, Mass: Harvard University Press.

Howard, J. and J. Sheth, (1969), *The Theory of Buyer Behaviour*, New York: Wiley.

Ironmonger, D. (1972), *New Commodities and Consumer Behaviour*, Cambridge: Cambridge University Press.

Itoh, Motoshige (1983), 'Monopoly, Product Differentiation and Economic Welfare', *Journal of Economic Theory*, 31, 88–104.

Jevons, W. S. (1957), *The Theory of Political Economy*, 5th ed, London: Macmillan. Reprinted – New York: Augustus M. Kelley (1965).

Johnson, H. G. (1958), 'Demand Theory Further Revised or Goods Are Goods', *Economica* N. S., 25, 149.

Karlin, S. (1959), *Mathematical Methods and Theory in Games, Programming and Economics*, New York: Pergamon Press.

Klevmarken, N. A. (1973), 'A Note on New Goods and Quality Changes in the True Cost-of-Living Index in View of Lancaster's Model of Consumer Behaviour', Stockholm: Institute of Statistics, University of Stockholm.

Koopmans, T. C. (1960), 'Stationary Ordinal Utility and Impatience', *Econometrica*, 23, 287–309.

Koopmans, T. C., P. A. Diamond, and R. E. Williamson, (1964), 'Stationary Utility and Time Perspective', *Econometrica*, 32, 82–100.

Krumm, R. J. (1980), 'Neighborhood Amenities: An Economic Analysis', *Journal of Urban Economics*, 7, 208–24.

Ladd, G. W. and M. Zober, (1977), 'Model of Consumer Reaction to Product Characteristics', *Journal of Consumer Research*, 4, 89–101.

Lancaster, K. J. (1957), 'Revising Demand Theory', *Economica*, 24, 354–60.

Lancaster, K. J. (1959), 'Welfare and Expanded Choice: Proof of the General Case', *Economic Journal*, 69, 805–7.

Lancaster, K. J. (1966a), 'A New Approach to Consumer Theory', *Journal of Political Economy*, 74, 132–57. (Included here as Chapter 2.)

Lancaster, K. J. (1966b), 'Change and Innovation in the Technology of Consumption', *American Economic Review* (papers and proceedings), 56, 14–25. (Included here as Chapter 3.)

Lancaster, K. J. (1971), *Consumer Demand: A New Approach*, New York: Columbia University Press.

Lancaster, K. J. (1975a), 'The Theory of Household Behaviour: Some

Foundations', *Annals of Economic and Social Measurement*, **4**, 5–21. (Included here as Chapter 7.)

Lancaster, K. J. (1975b), 'Socially Optimal Product Differentiation', *American Economic Review* **65**, 567–85, (Included here as Chapter 10.)

Lancaster, K. J. (1976), 'The Pure Theory of Impure Public Goods', in R. Grieson (ed.), *Public Finance and Urban Economics; Essays in Honor of William S. Vickrey*, Boston: D. C. Heath-Lexington, (Included here as Chapter 8.)

Lancaster, K. J. (1979), *Variety, Equity, and Efficiency*, New York: Columbia University Press.

Lancaster, K. J. (1980), 'Competition and Product Variety', *Journal of Business*, **53** (1980), S79–S104. (Included here as Chapter 11.)

Lancaster, K. J. (1982), 'Innovative Entry: Profit Hidden beneath the Zero', *Journal of Industrial Economics*, **31**, 41–56.

Lancaster, K. J. (1984), 'Protection and Product Differentiation', in H. Kierzkowski (ed.), *Monopolistic Competition and International Trade*, Oxford: Oxford University Press.

Leland, H. E. (1977), 'Quality Choice and Compeition', *American Economic Review*, **67**, 127–37.

Leontief, W. W. (1947), 'Introduction to a Theory of the Internal Structure of Functional Relationships', *Econometrica*, **15**, 361–73.

Lerner, A. P. and H. Singer, (1937), 'Some Notes on Duopoly and Spatial Competition', *Journal of Political Economy*, **45**, 145–86.

Mantel, R. (1974), 'On the Characterization of Aggregate Excess Demand', *Journal of Economic Theory*, **7**.

Marshak, J. and R. Radner, (1972), *Economic Theory of Teams*, New Haven: Yale University Press.

Matthews, S. A. and L. J. Mirman, (1983), 'Equilibrium Limit Pricing: The Effects of Private Information and Stochastic Demand', *Econometrica*, **51**, 981–96.

Meade, J. E. (1974), 'The Optimal Balance between Economies of Scale and Variety of Products', *Economica*, **41**, 359–67.

Menger, C. (1871, 1981), *Principles of Economics*, New York and London: New York University Press.

Milgrom, P. and J. Roberts, (1982), 'Limit Pricing and Entry under Incomplete Information', *Econometrica*, **50**, 443–60.

Miller, G. (1956), 'The Magical Number Seven, Plus or Minus Two', *Psychological Review*, **63**, 81–97.

Morishima, M. (1959), 'The Problem of Intrinsic Complementarity and Separability of Goods', *Metroeconomica*, **11**, 188–202.

Muellbauer, J. (1974), 'Household Production Theory, Quality, and the 'Hedonic Technique'' ', *American Economic Review*, **64**, 977–94.

Muellbauer, J. (1975), 'The Cost of Living and Taste and Quality Change', *Journal of Economic Theory*, **10**.

Musgrave, R. (1959), *The Theory of Public Finance*, New York: McGraw-Hill.

Mussa, M. and S. Rosen, (1978), 'Monopoly and Product Quality', *Journal of Economic Theory*, **18**, 301–17.

Muth, R. F. (1966), 'Household Production and Consumer Demand Functions', *Econometrica*, **34**, 699–708.

Ordover, J. A. and R. D. Willig, (1981), 'An Economic Definition of Predation', *Yale Law Journal*, **91**, 8–53.

Panzar, J. C. and R. D. Willig, (1975), 'Free Entry and the Sustainability of Natural Monopoly', *Bell Journal of Economics*, **6**, 346–56.

Panzar, J. C. and R. D. Willig, (1981), 'Economies of Scope', *American Economic Review*, **72**, 268–72.

Paroush, J. (1965), 'The Order of Aquisition of Consumer Durables', *Econometrica*, **33**, 225–35.

Pearce, I. F. (1964), *A Contribution to Demand Analysis*, Oxford: Oxford University Press.

Phlips, L. (1974), *Applied Consumption Analysis*, Amsterdam: North-Holland.

Prescott, E. C. and M. Visscher, (1977), 'Sequential Location Among Firms with Foresight', *Bell Journal of Economics*, **8**, 378–93.

Quandt, R. E. (1956), 'A Probabilistic Theory of Consumer Behavior', *Quarterly Journal of Economics*, **70**, 507–36.

Ratchford, B. T. (1975), 'The New Economic Theory of Consumer Behavior: An Interpretive Essay', *Journal of Consumer Research*, **2**, 65–75.

Ratchford, B. T. (1979), 'Operationalizing Economic Models of Demand for Product Characteristics', *Journal of Consumer Research*, **6**, 76–85.

Rosen, S. (1974), 'Hedonic Prices and Implicit Markets: Product Differentiation in Pure Competition', *Journal of Political Economy*, **82**, 34–5.

Rothenberg, J. (1976), ' "Inadvertent" Distributional Impacts in the Provision of Public Services to Individuals', in R. Grieson (ed.), *Public Finance and Urban Economics; Essays in Honor of William S. Vickrey*, Boston: D. C. Heath-Lexington.

Salop, S. C. (1979), 'Monopolistic Competition with Outside Goods', *Bell Journal of Economics*, **10**, 141-56.

Samuelson, P. A. (1948a), *Foundations of Economic Analysis*, Cambridge Mass: Harvard University Press.

Samuelson, P. A. (1948b), 'Consumption Theory in Terms of Revealed Preference', *Economica* N. S., **15**, 243–53.

Samuelson, P. A. (1953a), 'Consumption Theory in Terms of Over-Compensation Rather than Indifference Comparisons', *Economics* N. S., **20**, 1–9.

Samuelson, P. A. (1953b), 'Prices of Factors and Goods in General Equilibrium', *Review of Economic Studies*, **21**, 1–20.

Samuelson, P. A. (1956), 'Social Indifference Curves', *Quarterly Journal of Economics*, **70**, 1–22.

Samuelson, P. A. (1964), 'The Pure Theory of Public Expenditure', *Review of Economics and Statistics*, **36** 387–9.

Scherer, F. M. (1979), 'The Welfare Economics of Product Variety: An Application to the Ready-to-Eat Cereals Industry', *Journal of Industrial Economics*, **28**, 113–34.

Scherer, F. M. (1984), 'Measuring Surplus Attributable to Differentiated Products: Reply', *Journal of Industrial Economics*, **33**, 133.

Schmalensee, R. (1978), 'Entry Deterrence in the Ready-to-Eat Breakfast Cereal Industry', *Bell Journal of Economics*, **9**, 305–27.

Shaked, A. (1975), 'Non-Existence of Equilibrium for the Two-Dimensional Three Firms Location Problem', *Review of Economic Studies*, **42**, 51–6.

Shaw, R. W. (1982), 'Product Proliferation in Characteristics Space: The UK Fertilizer Industry', *Journal of Industrial Economics*, **31**, 97–114.

Shoup, C. (1969), *Public Finance*, Chicago: Aldine Press.

Sonnenschein, H. (1972), 'Market Excess Demand Functions', *Econometrica*, **40**, 549–63.

Sonnenschein, H. (1973), 'Do Walras' Identity and Continuity Characterize the Class of Community Excess Demand Functions?', *Journal of Economic Theory*,**6**, 345–54.

Spence, A. M. (1976a), 'Product Differentiation and Welfare', *American Economic Review*, **66** (papers and proceedings), 407–14.

Spence, A. M. (1976b), 'Product Selection, Fixed Costs and Monopolistic Competition', *Review of Economic Studies*, **43**, 217–35.

Stigler, G. J. (1945), 'The Cost of Subsistence', *Journal of Farm Economics*, **27**, 303–14.

Stone, R. (1956), *Quality and Price Indexes in National Accounts*, Paris: OECD.

Strotz, R. (1957), 'The Empirical Implications of a Utility Tree', *Econometrica*, **25**, 269–80.

Swan, P. L. (1970), 'Market Structure and Technological Progress: The Influence of Monopoly on Product Innovation', *Quarterly Journal of Economics*, **84**, 627–38.

Swann, G. M. P. (1985), 'Product Competition in Microprocessors', *Journal of Industrial Economics*, **34**, 33–54.

Tiebout, C. (1956), 'A Pure Theory of Local Expenditures', *Journal of Political Economy*, **64**, 416–24.

Uzawa, H. (1960), 'Preference and Rational Choice in the Theory of Consumption', in K. J. Arrow, and S. Karlin, and P. Suppes (eds.) *Mathematical Methods in the Social Sciences, 1959,* Palo Alto: Stanford University Press.

White L. J. (1977), 'Market Structure and Product Varieties', *American Economic Review*, **67**, 179–182.

Wilkie, W. and E. Pessemier, (1973), 'Issues in Marketing's Use of Multi-Attribute Attitude Models', *Journal of Marketing Research*, **10**, 428–41.

von Neumann, J. and O. Morgenstern, (1944), *Theory of Games and Economic Behavior*, Princeton: Princeton University Press.

Winter, S. (1969), 'A Simple Remark on the Second Optimality Theorem of Welfare Economics', *Journal of Economic Theory* **1**.

Index